# Max and Will

# Max and Will

MAX BEERBOHM AND WILLIAM ROTHENSTEIN
THEIR FRIENDSHIP AND LETTERS
1893–1945

Edited, with Introductions and Notes
by Mary M. Lago
and Karl Beckson

JOHN MURRAY

Printed in Great Britain by
W & J Mackay Limited, Chatham
0 7195 3185 3

# Contents

Preface     ix

Acknowledgements     xi

Abbreviations     xiv

PART ONE   DANDIES AND ARTISTS     1

Introduction     3

Letters 1–52     17

PART TWO   THE EX-ARCADIANS     65

Introduction     67

Letters 53–130     81

Epilogue     174

Bibliography     177

Index     185

# Illustrations

*Between pages 42 and 43*

Will and Max in 1893. *Mrs Ensor Holiday*

'Will R. in Faubourg & in Quartier.' Caricature by Max Beerbohm, *c. 1893. Sir John Rothenstein**

Self-caricature of Max in top hat, 1894. *The Houghton Library, Harvard University**

Oscar Wilde. Caricature by William Rothenstein, *c. 1893. William Andrews Clark Memorial Library, UCLA†*

Aubrey Beardsley. Drawing by William Rothenstein, 1894. *The Collection of Robert H. Taylor, Princeton, New Jersey†*

'Will Rothenstein Laying Down the Law.' Caricature by Max Beerbohm, *c. 1895. Mrs Christopher Powell**

William Rothenstein. Drawing by G. P. Jacomb-Hood, 1896. *Owner: Sir John Rothenstein. © Mr John Jacomb-Hood*

Max Beerbohm. Portrait by William Rothenstein, *c. 1900. Owner: Sir John Rothenstein, on loan to the University Art Collection, Hull. Photo: Brymor Jones Library†*

'Mr W. Rothenstein and Mankind.' Caricature by Max Beerbohm, 1916. *Manuscript Department, Lilly Library, Indiana University, Bloomington**

'Landed Gentry. No. 1. Mr. Albert Rothenstein.' Caricature by Max Beerbohm, 1913. *Mr David Rutherston**

Florence Beerbohm. Drawing by William Rothenstein, 1915. *Merton College, Oxford†*

Max Beerbohm. Drawing by William Rothenstein, 1915. *City Art Gallery, Manchester†*

Will and Alice Rothenstein with Gerhart Hauptmann at Rapallo, *c.* 1928. *Sir John Rothenstein*

Caricature of Will Rothenstein's hat. Max Beerbohm, undated. *Mrs Eva Reichmann\**

Max and Florence Beerbohm at Rapallo, 1921. *Mrs George Bagshawe*

*Between pages 122 and 123*

Max at Rapallo, 1921. *Mrs George Bagshawe*

William Rothenstein at the Royal College of Art, *c.* 1930. *Sir John Rothenstein*

Henry Tonks and William Rothenstein. Caricature by Max Beerbohm, 1926. *Mrs Eva Reichmann\**

The 'Edwardyssey' sequence of 9 caricatures. Max Beerbohm, 1903. *Mr and Mrs Benjamin Sonnenberg, New York, N.Y.\**

William Rothenstein in uniform, *c.* 1940. *Dr Ensor Holiday. Photo: Ensor Holiday*

Max and Florence Beerbohm at Abinger Common, *c.* 1941. *Mrs Noel Blakiston*

*In Text*
Facsimile of letter No. 96 on page 135†

*\* indicates that the picture is the copyright of Mrs Eva Reichmann and † that it is the copyright of Sir John and Mr Michael Rothenstein.*

# Preface

THE 130 LETTERS in the numbered sequence have been selected from a total of 221 extant letters exchanged by William Rothenstein and Max Beerbohm. Of Rothenstein letters to Beerbohm, Letters 22, 47, 57, 59, 60, 82, 84, and 102 are from the collection of Mrs Eva Reichmann. Letters 17, 110, and 128 are from the Beerbohm Papers at Merton College, Oxford. Letter 112 is from the collection of Alfred H. Perrin. All other Rothenstein letters in this sequence are in the William Andrews Clark Memorial Library of the University of California at Los Angeles.

Of the Max Beerbohm letters to Rothenstein, Letter 38 is from the collection of Sir John Rothenstein. Letters 41 and 94 are taken from transcripts at Merton College. The remaining letters are from the Rothenstein Papers in The Houghton Library at Harvard University.

Letters in the numbered sequence have been selected for their interest and for continuity. Those omitted deal, for the most part, with peripheral news of family and friends and with social and business matters such as invitations, appointments, introductions, and travel arrangements. A number of the more interesting and pertinent passages from the letters omitted will be found in the two introductory essays and in the annotations.

An important source of supplementary materials is the extensive collection of transcripts of Max Beerbohm's correspondence, now at Merton College. Wherever these or other transcribed materials are quoted, they are identified as transcripts; they have been used only when the original sources were not found in other collections.

All letter and manuscript materials, except as otherwise identified, have been copied from original materials, from microfilms, or from photocopies. With the exception of Letters 114 and 116, from which extended passages dealing with proof corrections have been deleted, the letters in the numbered sequence are published uncut. Throughout the book, unspaced ellipsis points, as ... , indicate a writer's ellipsis; editorial ellipses are indicated in the usual manner, by spaced ellipsis points. Obvious slips of the pen, where they do not affect meaning, have been silently corrected. Punctuation is, with a few exceptions, the writers' own. Some difficulty is occasioned by what appears as a hybrid punctuation mark—half dash and half comma—that Max used liberally, sometimes in constructions for which normal punctuation would prescribe a period. On at least one occasion he reprimanded an editor who substituted commas for his dashes, or 'strokes', but one must hope for posthumous indulgence on the plea that Max is not at hand to rule in cases in which his 'strokes' could be variously interpreted as comma, dash, or period. They have been transcribed, therefore, according to sense, as commas or as dashes when followed by a lower-case letter, and as periods when followed by a capital letter.

A number of unitalicised French words not in common English usage appear in the early letters, together with some Anglo-French hybrids: 'ridiculousment,' for example, in Letter 12. These have been transcribed as written; they are the product neither of faulty knowledge of French nor of editorial carelessness; they are merely the etymological fooling of high-spirited young men more than a little in love with France.

Since complete series of relatively rare periodicals such as *The Saturday Review* and *The Savoy* are increasingly available on film or as facsimile reprints, priority of space in the introductory essays and in the annotations has been given to unpublished letter and manuscript materials. The notes provide full references for all periodical publications. Books and all signed and identified works appear in the bibliography. Reference to all unsigned works and to collected Rothenstein and Beerbohm publications will be found in the index.

# Acknowledgements

I OWE debts of gratitude for the unflagging patience and support of Sir John and Mr Michael Rothenstein, who in 1967 gave me their permission for publication of letters by William and Alice Rothenstein; and of Mrs Eva Reichmann, who gave me permission for publication of letters by Max and Florence Beerbohm.

I am deeply indebted also for the sustained assistance and kindness of other members of the Rothenstein and Beerbohm family circles: Lady Rothenstein, Mr and Mrs Alan Ward, Dr and Mrs Ensor Holiday, Mrs Michael Rothenstein, Mr and Mrs David Rutherston, Mrs Christopher Powell; Mr and Mrs James Starr, Mr and Mrs George Bagshawe, and the late Miss Marion Bagshawe.

The Research Council of the University of Missouri at Columbia gave me three separate grants, in 1971, 1972, and 1973, for research and travel related to this project; for all of these I am most grateful. The Department of English at that University arranged for me to have a semester's leave of absence in 1974, without which the completion of this book would have been difficult, if not impossible.

Sir John Rothenstein and Sir Rupert Hart-Davis read an early draft of the manuscript, and at all stages of the work they have smoothed my way with advice, encouragement, helpful information, and corrections. I am grateful to the many other colleagues and friends who took time from their own labours to answer questions about mine, and I wish to mention, in particular, Dr Wendy Baron, Mrs Mary Bennett, Mr Lovat Dickson, Professor John Felstiner, Mr P. N. Furbank, Mr Michael Holroyd, Mrs Katherine Mix, Professor James Nelson, Miss Mary Thatcher, and Mr John Vickers.

It is impossible in this space to mention by name all of the many libraries, art galleries, and research institutions that have similarly assisted me: I hope that they will accept publication of this book as evidence of my appreciation for their services. I must mention, however, Miss Carolyn Jakeman and her staff at The Houghton Library, Harvard University; Mrs Edna C. Davis, of the William Andrews Clark

Memorial Library of the University of California at Los Angeles; Mr Thomas V. Lange, of The Collection of Robert H. Taylor, Princeton, New Jersey; Mr Peyton Skipwith, of The Fine Art Society Ltd, London; Dr Roger Highfield and Mr John Burgass of the Merton College Library, and Mr D. S. Porter of the Bodleian Library, Oxford; Miss Joan Gibbs of the Palaeography Room, University of London Library; and Mrs Ann Todd Rubey, of the Ellis Library at the University of Missouri, who performed miracles in obtaining materials that I had no way of seeing except through Inter-Library Loan.

All quotations from copyright materials in The Houghton Library are used by permission of the Harvard College Library. Those from the Beerbohm Collection at Merton College are used by permission of the Warden and Fellows of Merton College, Oxford.

Permission to quote from various letters and notes of William Rothenstein in their collections has been given by The William Andrews Clark Memorial Library; the Beinecke Rare Book and Manuscript Library, Yale University; Bibliothèque Nationale, Paris; Mrs Pamela Diamand; Faber and Faber Ltd; Sir Rupert Hart-Davis; The Library of the University of Illinois at Champaign-Urbana; The New-York Historical Society; Mr Alfred H. Perrin; Mr J-P. B. Ross; and Mrs Eva Reichmann.

Permission to quote from various letters and notes of Max Beerbohm in their collections has been given by The Houghton Library; Mrs George Bagshawe; the Beinecke Rare Book and Manuscript Library; Henry W. and Albert A. Berg Collection, The New York Public Library, Astor, Lenox and Tilden Foundations; The British Library (British Museum); Mr Douglas Cleverdon; Sir Rupert Hart-Davis; University of Leeds; Mr Stanley Marcus; Mr George Sassoon; Mrs James Starr; Sir John Rothenstein; and The Collection of Robert H. Taylor.

In addition, the following individuals and institutions have given permission for use of copyright materials: Mrs George Bagshawe; Mr Richard de la Mare; Mr Alan Dent; Mrs Mary Bennett (H. A. L. Fisher); Miss Jennifer Gosse (Edmund Gosse); Hauptmann Archive, Staatsbibliothek Preussischer Kulturbesitz, Berlin (Gerhart Hauptmann); Jonathan Cape Ltd (T. E. Lawrence); Mrs Prudence Rowe-Evans (David Low); Mrs René MacColl (D. S. MacColl); Sir Geoffrey Harmsworth (Lord Northcliffe); Mr Emile Norman (Ellis Roberts); J-P. B. Ross (Robert Ross); Mrs Noel Blakiston (Flora Russell); Mr David Rutherston (Albert Rutherston); Mr George Sassoon (Siegfried

Sassoon); Mrs Alix Strachey (Lytton Strachey); Dr Alice Leigh-Smith (Eugénie Sellers Strong); Brigadier H. G. Woods (Margaret L. Woods); the Society of Authors, on behalf of the Bernard Shaw Estate, for © Bernard Shaw Texts 1975 The Trustees of the British Museum, the Governors and Guardians of the National Gallery of Ireland and the Royal Academy of Dramatic Art. I am indebted to all of these individuals and institutions, to those who have allowed me to quote from letters and commentaries addressed to myself, and to all those who have been generous in providing the illustrations.

Finally, I wish to acknowledge with thanks the manifold kindnesses of my colleagues in the Department of English at the University of Missouri at Columbia, at times of editorial and clerical emergency; the work of Mrs Judy Holland, who typed a portion of the manuscript; and, by no means least, the support of my husband and my children.

*London, October 1974*                                                    M.M.L.

I AM especially grateful to Mr A. H. Perrin, of Berea, Kentucky, for sending me a photocopy of a letter from his collection written by Rothenstein to Beerbohm and for his approval for publication. I am also grateful to Mr Stanley Marcus, of Dallas, Texas, for lending me his copy of Rothenstein's *Twenty-Four Portraits*, with Beerbohm's pencilled comments and drawings.

To the following I am greatly indebted for their helpful responses to my queries: Professor Norman Alford, Professor J. O. Bailey, Mr J. Terry Bender (Curator of Rare Books, Syracuse University Library), Mrs Edna C. Davis (of the William Andrews Clark Memorial Library, University of California, Los Angeles), Professor Bruce Laughton, Professor Louis Marder, Mr Ernest Mehew, Professor Michael Millgate, and Mr Robert H. Taylor.

Finally, I am grateful to the Research Foundation of the City University of New York for a grant in assistance of this project.

*New York, July 1974*                                                    K.B.

# Abbreviations

BP:HL    Beerbohm Papers: The Houghton Library, Harvard University
BP:MC    Beerbohm Papers: Merton College, Oxford University
*Catalogue*    *A Catalogue of the Caricatures of Max Beerbohm*, comp. Rupert
       Hart-Davis
*IE*    *Imperfect Encounter: Letters of William Rothenstein and*
       *Rabindranath Tagore, 1911–1941*, ed. Mary M. Lago
*Letters*    Max Beerbohm, *Letters to Reggie Turner*, ed. Rupert Hart-Davis
*Max*    David Cecil, *Max: A Biography*
MCT    Merton College Transcripts
*MM* I    William Rothenstein, *Men and Memories: Recollections of*
       *William Rothenstein, 1872–1900*
*MM* II    William Rothenstein, *Men and Memories: Recollections of*
       *William Rothenstein, 1900–1922*
RP:HL    Rothenstein Papers: The Houghton Library
*SF*    William Rothenstein, *Since Fifty: Men and Memories, 1922–1938*
*SR*    *The Saturday Review* (London)
*WR*    Robert Speaight, *William Rothenstein: The Portrait of an Artist in*
       *His Time*

# Dandies and Artists

I have often thought that this selfish concentration, which is a part of dandyism, is also a symbol of that *einsamkeit* felt in greater or less degree by the practitioners of every art. But, curiously enough, the very unity of his mind with the ground he works on exposes the dandy to the influence of the world. In one way dandyism is the least selfish of all the arts.

> Max Beerbohm,
> 'Dandies and Dandies' (1896)

# INTRODUCTION

'IN THE SUMMER TERM of '93 a bolt from the blue flashed down on Oxford.' Thus begins the retrospective narrative in Max Beerbohm's story, 'Enoch Soames'. The bolt from the blue was Will Rothenstein, twenty-one years of age, come by way of the Slade School in London and Julian's Academy in Paris to do twenty-four lithographic portrait drawings of Oxford dignitaries, these to be published by John Lane from the Bodley Head. This Rothenstein, son of a respected Yorkshire wool merchant, was a phenomenon: 'He was a wit. He was brimful of ideas. He knew Whistler. He knew Edmond de Goncourt. He knew everyone in Paris. He knew them all by heart. He was Paris in Oxford.'[1]

In Paris, as well, Rothenstein had been something of a phenomenon. He did indeed know Whistler, who dubbed him 'the Parson', and Edmond de Goncourt, whose portrait he drew for an English edition of the de Goncourts' journals.[2] If Rothenstein did not know everyone worth knowing in Paris, he knew enough persons of note to make him the envy of at least one visiting Englishman. Grant Richards, then secretary to the crusading journalist W. T. Stead, recalled Rothenstein as an established figure in Parisian art-student circles, and himself as a wistful outsider on the fringes of Bohemia. Rothenstein gave him a letter to Roger Fry, who was becoming established in English art circles, and asked Fry to 'be kind to my friend Grant Richards, who likes to know painters'.[3]

Rothenstein's twenty-four lithographic drawings were to comprise his *Oxford Characters*. From Oxford he wrote to Richards: 'Just a few words to tell you that I am having an exceedingly good time. . . . I am going to do a series of character sketches for which York-Powell will write the text. Nothing has yet been arranged, but I hope to come to terms with the bookseller. Or do you think a London one would be as good. York-Powell suggests that it should come out every month, one by one. It will be, I believe, a very good thing for me.'[4]

It was indeed a good thing; through *Oxford Characters*, he met Max Beerbohm, whose air of composure, of being, even as an undergraduate, a finished personality, secured him a place in Rothenstein's series. In the note to accompany his portrait of Max, Rothenstein wrote: 'A dandy. His use of curious and obsolete words, as of boot-buttons in his

3

cuffs, has earned him a place in a larger circle than that of Mr Street's "elect". His brilliant caricatures which were the joy of his friends at Oxford, where they were eagerly passed from hand to hand, have since given him the well-deserved reputation of our only caricaturist. Suave, smiling, polished, and cynical, we can but wish him the successful career which should accompany talents of so precious an order.'[5]

Max observed Rothenstein with amused affection and a lively sense of the absurd. Commanding and confident, Rothenstein flashes through 'Enoch Soames', inveigling 'dignified and doddering old men, who had never consented to sit to anyone', to sit to him.[6] The pleasant absurdity of the situation was more apparent, however, from the vantage point of 1914–15, when Max wrote 'Enoch Soames', than during the sittings for *Oxford Characters* in 1893 and early 1894. Manifold complications arose. Several of the dignitaries *had* sat to other artists. Sir Henry Acland pointed out his portrait by George Richmond of the Royal Academy and bade Rothenstein go and do likewise; Rothenstein tried again, with results more pleasing to his subject.[7] Robinson Ellis urged Rothenstein to study a portrait of him by G. P. Jacomb-Hood.[8] 'I did a lithograph of dear Robinson Ellis,' Rothenstein wrote to his Oxford friend, Margaret L. Woods, 'and he quite seriously told me that on no account must I publish it as it might spoil his chances of election to the Latin professorship! He thought he looked like a Kalmuck Tartar—I think that was his expression. So I had to do another one, and paint and powder the face of my drawing and make his ears smaller; and now he is satisfied and has asked me to dine with him to-morrow. But he is really a dear, kind gentleman, and I have become very much attached to him. But the vanity of men is a strange thing—I suppose the professor of Greek will want a waist and a patch near his eye.'[9]

There was friction also between Rothenstein and his publisher. He found Lane hopelessly Philistine, and, when they visited the Louvre together in September 1893, Rothenstein told Lane that he had no taste in art.[10] Rothenstein subsequently wrote to Mrs Woods: 'John Lane, my publisher, has again been here [Oxford] with a pack full of new geniuses. He must have the flaire for the right thing, though in Paris a few weeks ago, he mistook St Sulpice for Notre Dame and went to sleep over some music of Brahms.'[11]

In October Rothenstein was settled in Oxford, and in December there was a renewed clash with Lane, this one over the price and whereabouts of a drawing proposed as frontispiece for Richard Le Gallienne's *Prose Fancies*. Rothenstein told Lane:

4

I distinctly wrote some 10 days ago that I required a definite answer about it, saying if it were not to be used for publication, I desired to have it *instantly* myself. How is it then, that Mr Le Gallienne now has it in his possession? Must I presume that he has bought it himself? If the drawing is not to be published, no one except myself has any right to it. I confess that I do *not* understand your position. Will you kindly let me know in *writing* how this is, and to whom the drawing belongs. . . . I am sorry that the publication is not doing well here [at Oxford], but do not see why *all* the blame should be put down to my portrait of Sir Henry Acland. It seems to me, the more portraits the public see, the more chance of success it has.[12]

Five days later, from Bradford, Rothenstein wrote more equably. His father, he admitted, had given him 'sane and sound advice. . . . If you have not given Le G's portrait to anyone else, I am willing to eat humble pie and show my good will by undertaking to do another one. . . . I quite admit that I have not been grateful enough to you of late, but my dear Lane, we are all human and youth, as the saying goes, hot-blooded, and I am sure you will admit that you can understand a person like myself being occasionally a little quick tempered.'[13]

Also in December 1893, Rothenstein moved to London. After a few weeks in a Chelsea studio loaned by Jacomb-Hood, he engaged rooms in Glebe Place, just off the King's Road. He renewed friendships begun in Paris, became a familiar figure among John Lane's new geniuses and in the New English Art Club, and set about finding new models and patrons. The Yorkshireman and sometime Parisian was now a Londoner.

Max Beerbohm was a Londoner born and bred. His father, like Rothenstein's, was an immigrant and a merchant, a dealer in corn.[14] Max had spent his childhood in late-Victorian London and his school years at Charterhouse. He entered Oxford in 1890, but his scholarly commitment there was never whole-hearted. Early in 1893 he had extricated himself from one set of examinations by professing a wish to read for Honours, but Honours was not at all what he desired. He confessed to his friend Reggie Turner: 'Now that I have been so very very near a pass and freedom after the third year I cannot help regretting rather that I did not seize these good things once and for all. But I am young and strong and Europe is before me.'[15]

He knew himself very well. Max in a professorial study, Max in a law office, Max at a merchants' exchange: all such projections were incongruous. Politicians and statesmen, as characters in the drama of current events, had always fascinated him, but although he essayed a speech at the Oxford Union on Irish Home Rule, he did not fancy himself as 'irregular Unionman' and certainly not as embryonic statesman. While still an undergraduate he had begun to find publishers for his essays and reviews. Now, gradually, and contrary to impressions conveyed by his air of insouciance, he began in all earnestness to work his way into London's literary and artistic circles. Reggie Turner remained his closest friend; Max now saw less of other Oxford acquaintances and more of the group gathered around John Lane, to whom Rothenstein introduced him in the autumn of 1893. He was already widely acquainted in theatrical circles, for the actor-manager Herbert Beerbohm Tree was his elder half-brother, and plays and players had figured in Beerbohm family affairs for as long as Max could remember. In the winter of 1894–95 Herbert's company toured in the United States; Max went with them as secretary, and his by-line appeared with increasing frequency thereafter on both sides of the Atlantic.[16]

In April 1898, George Bernard Shaw chose Max to succeed him, at the close of the current season, as drama critic of *The Saturday Review*. Max received the accolade with misgivings. He dreaded deadlines. He disliked having to be disagreeable on occasion, and he actually disliked the theatre. He and Herbert might compromise each other's positions. Above all, it would be difficult to follow Shaw. Max would wait and see what Frank Harris thought.[17]

Not Harris, but Shaw's left foot forced the issue in mid-April. He developed a necrosis of the bone and was ordered off his feet, out of the theatre, and into the country. He wanted Max to take over with minimum delay and maximum fanfare, and, when this decision met with resistance from Harris, Shaw wrote to Henry Blanchamp, manager of *The Saturday Review*:

In God's name look at this foolish telegram. These two men are drunk. Write to them, and impress on them that there is no question or possibility of hanging on, and that my place must be filled instantly. Damn them! I nearly killed myself last week to keep things going the day after the operation; and this week I have sent in a short article of leavetaking, leading up to Max. What else is there to be done? I have a big cleft in my instep, into which I lose sixpences and fountain pens and all manner of things. The moment I can move I must get away to the country. It is utterly, absolutely, unchangeably, stark raving impossible that I should go to the

6

theatre, or keep up my work. There is nobody but Max to take up the running, at least nobody that I know of; and I presume when I proposed him some time ago Runciman would have told me if there was anyone else in view. Harris got some asinine notion that I was only coquetting; but I thought I had knocked that brilliant idea endways.

Beerbohm says he wants to write an article on becoming a dramatic critic; and you can't do better than let him, and tack it on to the screed I have just sent Strangeways. It is of great importance that the continuity of the theatrical articles should be kept up, and that Max's succession should be duly boomed as an important event. All that will be lost if there is an unexplained break and a lame cobbling up of the breach later on.

Take the matter into your own hands, and tell the two roysterers at St Jean de Luz either to come back and look after the paper themselves or else stick to their holiday business of drinking and gambling, and let you alone.

It makes me perfectly mad to get an idiotic wire like that in such an emergency. 'Hang on' be damned! Idiots![18]

Shaw asked Max to begin by attending a play across the river in Camberwell, but Max was determined to accept the new role on his own terms:

I am quite ready to try to succeed you. But to Camberwell I cannot go, as I am irretrievably engaged every night this week—except Thursday, the night of the new piece at the Gaiety. In any case, George Bancroft's play would be a rather dreary occasion for my début. A début within a début would be awful. So Mulholland and maiden-efforts be blowed! Besides, in the next 'Saturday' my second article about you will appear—(I did go to a Vestry, only the other day, on some absurd deputation of residents in this street, anxious for a wood-pavement; but I don't yet believe in Vivisection) and I do think that you ought to have some kind of farewell to your . readers in the next issue. You must not turn your back on them without a word. If you are well enough to write me such a charming letter, you could surely do a column or so for the public.[19]

Max did not go to Camberwell, and Shaw did write a column or so for the public: his 'Valedictory', which concludes, 'The younger generation is knocking at the door, and as I open it there steps sprightly in the incomparable Max'.[20]

Despite his misgivings, Max faithfully discharged this new responsibility for twelve years, all the while perfecting his skills as a caricaturist. Throughout the 1890s his style evolved from a rather crude, heavy line to the intricately elegant understatement that became his hallmark, and his conception of caricature as his true vocation became as precise as his drawings. In 1903, in response to a review by the critic E. F. Spence, Max wrote:

> But I don't agree with you that I get at the soul of a man without getting at his physical aspect. That would be an impossible feat, I think. When I draw a man, I am concerned simply and solely with the physical aspect of him. I don't bother for one moment about his soul. I just draw him as I see him. And (this is how I come to be a caricaturist) I see him in a peculiar way: I see all his salient points exaggerated (points of face, figure, port, gesture and vesture), and all his insignificant points proportionately diminished. *Insignificant:* literally, signifying nothing. The salient points do signify something. In the salient points a man's soul does reveal itself, more or less faintly. At any rate, if it does not always reveal itself through them, it is always latent in them. Thus if one underline these points, and let the others vanish, one is bound to lay bare the soul. But that is not sacrificing physical resemblance. It is simply an intensifying of physical resemblance. If, instead of intensifying it, one misses it, then one misses the soul also. It is because (and only because), or, let us rather say, when (and only when) my own caricatures hit exactly the exteriors of their subjects that they open the interiors, too. Do I make myself plain? (I don't mean, do I caricature myself? I never do: I am much too sensitive: the bully is always a coward.) When one can do a thing, it is so difficult to explain, even to oneself, *how* one does it; and I suppose really one ought not to try; not for fear of being thought self-important, but because creative power does play the deuce with critical power and put[s] its owner at a grave disadvantage to argument.[21]

Max never deviated from these fundamentals in his view of himself as caricaturist. Rothenstein, as a painter, was no less certain of his desired goal, but his method of working toward it was more complex. When Roger Fry commented on several of Rothenstein's works exhibited in 1901, Rothenstein replied, 'You praise and blame alike too much. . . . But don't worry over my truthfulness, for it doesn't worry me. I am painting quite respectably, and will some day paint well—but my well isn't necessarily yours. . . . One thing I will say in self-defence—when I do paint a bad picture, I leave it bad, and don't try to make it *look* good.'[22]

In 1909 Rothenstein responded to another of Fry's inquiries with a review of his own career and an assessment of his present position:

> I believe at the time [1898–99] I was perhaps more under the influence of Rembrandt than of Goya—you remember there was a great exhibition of his work at Amsterdam a little time before, but I expect Spain was still fresh in my mind. I worked under Legros for a year and a half, from the spring of '88 to the autumn of '89, when I went to Paris, and worked at Julian's, virtually under no one, as none of the Professors there appealed to my undisciplined imagination. There people like Degas, Whistler, Puvis, Fantin Latour, Rodin and old Alfred Stevens were very kind to me, and I should really have got something in the nature of discipline from their work. From immediate contemporaries I got more pleasure than instruction, as their work was of the more personal order— Conder of course was my great friend, and later Ricketts and Shannon, Steer and Sickert, but you remember in those days we both thought the first two on a different plane from the rest. What I care for most now is architectural construction of figure and mass, and precision and impressiveness of statement of elemental fact. I have no faith whatsoever in my work unless I get some inspiration of the kind, nature having endowed me with none of the qualities of charm which make up for this in others.[23]

Rothenstein underestimated his own qualities of charm. When combined with his energy and his talent for organisation, they enabled him to exert extraordinary influence upon the arts. Persistently he reminded the community of its obligations toward practitioners of all the arts, and he spent time and money, sometimes with serious consequences for himself, to help other artists to achieve positions of strength. In 1910, for example, when Post-Impressionism, with Fry as its impresario, burst upon the London scene, Rothenstein, who had been one of French Impressionism's early advocates in England, was on the opposite side of the world enquiring into the welfare of Indian artists. This was not altogether an aberration; his interest in Indian art had begun in Paris, and he was increasingly concerned over widespread English ignorance of the artistic heritage of so important a part of the Empire. In 1910, his concern led to the organisation of the India Society in London; his work

9

for this Society led him to India in the winter of 1910–11.[24] Ordinary Englishmen usually went there on business; ordinary English artists went only if they had commissions to paint maharajas. But Rothenstein in India was transfixed by 'architectural construction of figures and mass' in the temple sculptures, and by the cave-paintings that presented such fascinating and frustrating problems of aesthetic theory and artistic practice. He wrote to Eric Gill:

> I believe both you and Epstein desire immortality. Let me recommend you to go to Heaven by one route only, and that, via the caves of Elephanta, Ellora and Ajanta. I doubt whether you have ever conceived what rock sculpture is; that it should have existed in India centuries ago in order to inspire you both was quite obviously preordained and foreseen, and this is a fortunate fact for others who, like myself, are allowed the privilege of gazing at these wonders. You would both I think go quite mad if you could see these places— I don't believe you can conceive them. Even if you see photographs, you only look at the bits of rock which have been carved by men, you don't see the marriage between nature and man's handiwork which is solemnised perpetually, with the birds as choir and the bats as pew holders, and an occasional tourist looking in at the door as witness.[25]

Between such exhilarating flights of inspiration he had sharp attacks of homesickness, for home was now much more than a Chelsea studio. In 1899 he had married Alice Mary Knewstub, an actress who used the stage name Alice Kingsley. They had met in 1895, and Rothenstein's concern for his own 'qualities of charm' became more pronounced during a courtship that was, for him, by turns anxious and idyllic. The anxious note was sounded often, as in a letter written from Bradford: 'I shall be glad to see you again, because I love you. But your own affection for me is not so entirely clear to me, as I might, in my vanity, wish. At least, there have been moments when you have loved me, and if they were only moments, still, the love was sure. I shall always treasure them, and keep them close, within my mind. And if I have not that power, of keeping a woman's affection, that is my fault and none of hers.'[26]

They were married on June 11, 1899, and after a honeymoon in France they settled in Edwardes Square, Kensington. Alice soon perceived that Will's moods were much affected by objects and by their qualities of beauty—or their lack of it. She wrote to his parents: 'Will, poor fellow, is rather upset at hearing from you that his uncle is getting some ugly silver or something—he would have loved to have bought himself something. He has such very exquisite taste that he cannot exist with ugly things—it is a positive pain to him. I wish the uncle knew this. Will was quite depressed about it today . . . it is *so* nice being married to Will.'[27]

Max was neither married nor engaged. In 1897 he had been engaged to Grace Conover, an actress in Herbert Tree's company, whom Max had met during the 1895 American tour. According to Max, she was known at the Garrick Theatre as 'Kill-Scene Conover'; also according to him, she wept when he told her this.[28] They overcame this inauspicious beginning, but Max's friends wondered whether he would ever marry. 'Max, Kilseen, and Mrs Beerbohm had supper here yesterday', Robert Ross reported on one occasion. 'Max looks more unmarried than ever and poor Kilseen does not look particularly engaged. I feel so deeply for her. I think the Beerbohms are kinder to her now. She was dressed very prettily. Max might end up one of his fairy stories with "So they were *engaged* and lived happily ever afterwards".'[29]

This engagement drifted until June 1903, when it was broken off. In July the English actress Constance Collier was seen regularly with Max; by December they were engaged; by April 1904 it was all over.[30] Constance made the break, and although Max knew that this was both inevitable and wise, he had a sad sense of aftermath and failure. His engagements had been, perhaps, an escape from the kind of loneliness that he described, lightly but with an undercurrent of sober truth, when he found himself solitary among strangers at Dieppe:

> I am on the verge of departure. It is just 11 o'clock, and I go by the day-boat. My things are packed, but I dread the bill and the tips and the 'à l'année prochaine' and the registering of luggage and all the other horrors. But they are as nothing to the horror of staying another moment in Dieppe, cursing the sunshine that would have made my August so lovely, mooning around talking to myself because there is no one else to talk to (though the place is still as full as it was in race-week). It is odd, but the departure of Constance and you and the others has quite pricked the bubble of my self-importance. I really did feel as if the place belonged to me, so long as my 'set' was here: *now* I am a pariah—uniform with the man who was turned out of the diplomatic service.[31]

In June 1904, Florence Kahn, a young American actress, arrived in London with a letter of introduction to Max. She was from a well known and highly respected family in Memphis, Tennessee. Her father, like Moritz Rothenstein and Julius Beerbohm, had emigrated from Germany; he had become a naturalised citizen and co-owner of Memphis' largest department store. He was an amateur Shakespeare scholar, and Florence had grown up in a home filled with books and music. She had studied at the American Academy of Dramatic Art in New York and had a promising reputation as an interpreter of Ibsen roles, but her diffident manner frequently caused observers to overlook the strength of her character and the quality of her wit, which was often pointed but never malicious.[32]

Her first meeting with Max almost failed to take place because a message went astray. He wrote to her: 'I *am* so sorry. But it isn't my fault. I wrote to you last night, and entrusted the letter to a man who had been dining at the house and was returning to town by a late train. Evidently he forgot to post the letter. No Englishman would be guilty of such a dastardly sin of omission. But this was not an Englishman. It was—prepare yourself for a blow!—an AMERICAN. He seemed to be, like all other American men, a fine, chivalrous, justice-loving, lion-hearted, freedom-breathing, self-sacrificing, grand, money-making, good and great man. But evidently I was deceived. Well, but for him, you would have heard that I was going to call on you at 3.30, but that if you were not in at that hour I would wait till you came. And to that plan I adhere.'[33]

On June 22 Max wrote to say that he had had 'a *lovely* day with you' and hoped to see her on the twenty-third, since he was leaving London for the week, and she 'for aught I know [may] be going to sail early next week; in which case I should hardly see my dear little friend again'.[34] She stayed in England until November. Max wrote:

I should like you to see me always on my very best behaviour, and to be very highly respected by you—the European at his best. I should like you to be wondering 'Are *all* Europeans like *him*?' Perhaps that is just what you *do* wonder. But then you hope that they *aren't*. And it is only fair to assure you that they aren't indeed. Archer is a type of them. They are a fine race. Every prospect pleases, and only I am vile. But mine is an amiable sort of vileness, after all, and I don't think you need really have nothing to do with me. I mean well—and I will try to behave well. I should hate not to see the dear little dignified friend again, and I hope she won't want me not to see her again. Little though she is, she is very like the

12

Landseer mastiff, sometimes; and I feel very like the pendant. Only, the Landseer mastiff's is an ugly dignity, and yours is a pretty one, and an unconventional one, but not the less impressive for that. And may I come and call on you on Monday and show you how well I can behave when I give my mind to it?[35]

After Florence had returned to the United States, Max confessed to a feeling that his letters to her

always seem to me so very egoistic; and yet you say you don't know enough. Am I well? Am I happy? Quite well, thank you, dear. And nothing to complain of on the score of happiness. I don't think I ever am or shall be happy in the full sense, as some people are. As I think I told you, I can only stand life when it is made pleasant for me. Usually, it *is* made pleasant for me. I have really been rather pampered than otherwise. So I have been all right, on the whole. But I do not like life when it does not offer me something nice every day. And if it ever offered me something *not* nice I should feel myself very much aggrieved. A *happy* person, it seems to me, is the sort of person who requires no aids to happiness—who can grapple with life on any terms. And I never shall be that sort of person. That is all I have to complain of. And it is little enough in comparison with average grounds of complaint—so *there*, dear, I have told you as fully as I could—at tedious length, I am afraid. But you did ask me to tell you.[36]

Early in 1905, Florence wrote of feeling lonely in Boston, and Max replied: 'But it is your own little fault, and your own little choice. You are the sort of person whom everybody would want to see a very great deal of, if you would only let them—if you weren't so fastidious. You, perhaps call it shyness. But it is just fastidiousness. It is a wonder to me how *I* ever got to know you. For I am decidedly not a pushing person, as a rule. I should be quite rich, by now, if I were. But in your case, somehow, I *was* pushing (*insisted* that you should go to a theatre with me, and that you should come and see my people, and so on—and thus I did acquire my friendship with you—riches, certainly.'[37]

Throughout six years of a friendship so quiet that many wondered whether to call it a courtship, Max's letters to her maintained this gentle, wistful tone. Then, in 1910, with characteristic neatness and despatch, he made three decisive moves: in April he resigned from *The Saturday Review*; in May he and Florence Kahn were married; and in

13

June they departed for Italy, to live there, except for two wartime periods and occasional visits abroad, for the remainder of their lives. Thus Will Rothenstein and Max managed, in the same year and for very different reasons, to astonish those who could not imagine them anywhere but at the centre of things. That Rothenstein should suddenly disappear to India struck many as quixotic in the extreme. That Max, paradigm of cosmopolitanism, should renounce the life of London and retire to the Italian provinces, seemed to signal the end of an era. It *was* the end of an era, in their friendship, as in the Edwardian ambience. Geographical distance would begin to give their letters a mellowed tone, and new occasions would summon them to duties that were new but not altogether unpredictable.

M.M.L.

¹ Beerbohm, 'Enoch Soames: A Memory of the Eighteen-Nineties', *The Cornhill Magazine*, n. s. 40 (1916), 717–742; reprinted as 'Enoch Soames', in his *Seven Men*, pp. 3–48. See ibid., pp. 4–5.

John Lane (1854–1925), publisher and bookseller; with Elkin Mathews (1851–1921), founder, 1887, of the Bodley Head. William's father, Moritz Rothenstein (1836–1914), emigrated from Germany to Bradford in 1859; Bertha Dux (1844–1913) followed as his bride in 1868. J. M. Whistler (1834–1903), American painter, a Londoner after 1859. Edmond (1822–1896) and Jules de Goncourt (1830–1870), aristocratic Parisian brothers, art critics, historians, novelists, who kept journals from 1851 to 1896.

² On Rothenstein as 'the Parson', see *MM* I, 58. For Rothenstein's drawing, see *Edmond and Jules de Goncourt, . . . Journals*, comp. and trans. M. A. Belloc and M. Shedlock, II, facing p. 234.

³ Rothenstein to Fry, March 18 [1893]. Grant Richards Papers: Library of the University of Illinois at Urbana-Champaign.

Grant Richards (1872–1948), author and publisher. W. T. Stead (1849–1912), staff member, *Pall Mall Gazette*, 1880–1883, and its editor, 1883–1889; founder, 1890, *The Review of Reviews*. Roger Fry (1866–1934), painter and critic. See Richards, *Memories of a Misspent Youth, 1872–1896*, pp. 182–192. See also *MM* I, 124–125, 131–132.

⁴ Rothenstein to Richards, May 4 [1893]. Richards: University of Illinois. Rothenstein, *Oxford Characters: Twenty-Four Lithographs*, first issued in five parts, June 1893–June 1894. Frederick York Powell (1850–1904), barrister, historian; Lecturer in Law, Christ Church, Oxford, 1874–1894; Regius Professor of Modern History, 1894–1900.

⁵ Ibid. [plate 14]. G. S. Street (1867–1936), author of *The Autobiography of a Boy*, a satire on the 1890's; 'elect': the allegedly effete and unmanly English decadents.

⁶ Beerbohm, 'Enoch Soames', in his *Seven Men*, p. 4.

⁷ George Richmond (1809–1896), English painter. Sir Henry Acland, of Oxford, 1st Baronet (1815–1900), Regius Professor of Medicine, Oxford, 1857–1894. See Rothenstein, *Oxford Characters* [plate 1]; *MM* I, 141–142.

8 Robinson Ellis (1834–1913), University Reader of Latin Literature, Oxford, 1883–1893; Corpus Professor of Latin Literature, 1893–1913. G. P. Jacomb-Hood (1857–1929), painter, etcher, illustrator.

9 Rothenstein to Margaret Woods, October 28 [1893]. RP:HL. Cf. *MM* I, 139–143.

Margaret Bradley Woods (1856–1945), poet and novelist; wife of the Reverend Henry Woods (1842–1915), President, Trinity College, Oxford, 1887–1897; from 1904, Master of the Temple, London. Ingram Bywater (1840–1914), Regius Professor of Greek, 1893–1908. On Ellis and Bywater, see Rothenstein, *Oxford Characters* [plates 3, 15].

Mrs Woods wrote: 'I am not at all surprised to hear that dear old Robby Ellis wanted to be made beautiful for ever. When Mr Jacomb Hood painted his portrait he was most particular about the tone of his complexion and also his expression. He complained one day that he was being made too pale and the next that his smile had not been caught. However I daresay he smiles more naturally now than then, because at that time he often felt so anxious. He had some money left him and said it was nice of course to have money, but he could not help fearing it might lead to his being "entrapped into an imprudent marriage".' (Margaret Woods to Rothenstein, November 1, 1893. RP:HL.)

10 See Beerbohm, *Letters*, pp. 69–70.

11 Rothenstein to Margaret Woods, October 28 [1893]. RP:HL.

Lane and Mathews had a 'flaire' also for artistic book production. See James G. Nelson, *The Early Nineties: A View from the Bodley Head*, pp. 36–76. For a Beardsley caricature of Rothenstein and Lane in Paris, see J. Lewis May, *John Lane and the Nineties*, p. 53.

12 Rothenstein to Mathews and Lane, December 6 [1893]. Rothenstein Family Papers. Cf. *Letters*, p. 90.

Richard Le Gallienne (1866–1947), poet and critic; a principal Bodley Head adviser. Frontispiece of Le Gallienne's *Prose Fancies* is a lithographic portrait by P. Wilson Steer (1860–1942). On the Le Gallienne portrait by Rothenstein, present owner unknown, see *The Portrait Drawings of William Rothenstein, 1889–1925*, comp. John Rothenstein, p. 4, item 24.

13 Rothenstein to Lane, December 11, 1893. Rothenstein.

14 See David Cecil, *Max: A Biography*, pp. 3–28. Julius Beerbohm (1810–1892) came to London from Germany about 1830. Max's mother, Eliza Draper Beerbohm (1831–1918) was Julius' second wife.

15 Beerbohm to Turner [1893?]. Beerbohm Papers: Houghton Library.

Reginald Turner (1869–1938), journalist and novelist; at Merton College, 1888–1892; after 1900, a resident of the Continent.

16 Herbert Beerbohm Tree (1852–1917), proprietor-manager, Haymarket Theatre, 1887–1897, and Her Majesty's Theatre, 1897–1917. On the American tour, see Hesketh Pearson, *Beerbohm Tree*, pp. 79–83. See also *Letters*, pp. 97–102.

17 Frank Harris (1856–1931), novelist, biographer; editor, *The Fortnightly Review*, 1887–1894; proprietor, *The Saturday Review*, 1894–1898. G. B. Shaw (1856–1950), drama critic, *The Saturday Review*, 1895–1898; see his *Collected Letters, 1898–1910*, ed. Dan H. Laurence, pp. 25–26.

18 Shaw to Blanchamp, March 18, 1898. The Collection of Robert H. Taylor, Princeton, N.J. The 'foolish telegram' was probably from Harris and J. F. Runciman (1866–1916); on Runciman, see Shaw, *Collected Letters, 1874–1897*, ed. Dan H. Laurence, p. 221. Strangeways and Sons, Cambridge Circus, printed volumes 84–85 of *The Saturday Review*. Shaw had submitted his 'Valedictory', see *SR*, 85 (1898), 682–683.

¹⁹ Beerbohm to Shaw [May 17? 1898]. G. B. Shaw Papers: British Museum. On the Bancroft play and Mulholland, see Shaw, *Collected Letters, 1898–1910*, pp. 42–43.

Shaw had been feuding with the St Pancras Vestry; see ibid., p. 41. See also Shaw, 'G.B.S. Vivisected,' *SR*, 85 (1898), 657–658. For Max's début, see Beerbohm, 'Why I Ought Not to Have Become a Dramatic Critic', ibid., pp. 709–710; reprinted in his *Around Theatres, 1898–1903*, pp. 1–4. For Shaw's 'charming letter', see his *Collected Letters, 1898–1910*, pp. 42–43.

²⁰ Shaw, 'Valedictory': see above, note 18.

²¹ Beerbohm to Spence, May 31, 1903. The Beinecke Rare Book and Manuscript Library, Yale University.

E. F. Spence (1860–1932), barrister and drama critic, commented on a Beerbohm caricature of Claude Lowther (1872–1929), politician, playwright, and actor. See E. F. S[pence], 'The Stage from the Stalls', *The Sketch* (London), 42 (May 27, 1903), 198. For Max's caricature, see ibid. (May 20, 1903), p. 149.

²² Rothenstein to Fry, November 25, 1901. Mrs Pamela Diamand.

²³ Rothenstein to Fry, September 30, 1909. Diamand.

Rembrandt works were shown in an exhibition at Amsterdam in 1898. In 1895 Rothenstein had visited Spain and North Africa with R. B. Cunninghame Graham (1852–1936), a founder of the Scottish Labour Party, author, sometime rancher in Argentina. Alphonse Legros (1837–1911), French-born artist and art teacher; Slade Professor of Fine Art, University of London, 1876–1892. Charles Conder (1868–1909), English painter in the style of Watteau. Charles Ricketts (1866–1931) and Charles Shannon (1863–1937), artists, book designers, connoisseurs, who lived together in The Vale, Chelsea. Walter Richard Sickert (1860–1942), German-born English painter.

²⁴ See *IE* pp. 2–8, 27–34.

²⁵ Rothenstein to Gill, November 26, 1910. Rothenstein.

Eric Gill (1882–1940), sculptor, stone-carver, designer. See Gill, *Letters of Eric Gill*, ed. Walter Shewring, pp. 32–34. Jacob Epstein (1880–1959), American sculptor who settled in England, with Rothenstein's help, in 1905.

²⁶ Rothenstein to Alice Kingsley [Knewstub] [1897?]. Rothenstein.

Alice Mary Knewstub (1870–1958), daughter of Walter Knewstub (1831–1906), pupil of John Ruskin; assistant and only pupil of D. G. Rossetti.

²⁷ Alice to Moritz and Bertha Rothenstein [August? 1899]. Rothenstein.

²⁸ Grace Conover (1872–1948).

²⁹ Ross to Rothenstein, September 11, 1899. RP: HL. See *Max*, pp. 219–220. Robert Ross (1869–1918), art dealer, author, literary executor for Oscar Wilde.

³⁰ Constance Collier (1880–1955), a member of Herbert Tree's company, 1902–1908.

³¹ Beerbohm to Turner [August 1903]. *Letters*, p. 154.

³² Florence Kahn (1876–1951). Louis Kahn (d. 1902).

³³ Beerbohm to Florence Kahn [June 1904]. Mrs Eva Reichmann. The delinquent American is unidentified.

³⁴ Beerbohm to Florence Kahn, June 22, 1904. Reichmann.

³⁵ Beerbohm to Florence Kahn, June 24, 1904. Reichmann.

William Archer (1856–1924), dramatic critic and avowed Ibsenite. The Landseer mastiff appears in the painting, 'Dignity and Impudence', by Sir Edwin Landseer.

³⁶ Beerbohm to Florence Kahn [December? 1904]. Reichmann.

³⁷ Beerbohm to Florence Kahn [September? 1905]. Reichmann.

16

Wednesday [Summer 1893]

Dear Will

I waited a long time for you by the breakfast table: why did you not come? I had accepted your invitation—what kept you? Tell me.

By the way, I should have told you before—John Lane has consented to publish a series of caricatures of Oxford Celebrities by me: they are to appear concurrently with yours, in order to make the running. In case any ill-feeling should arise between us on this account, I am sending you the proofs of the first number. Very satisfactory, I think. Do not think harshly of John Lane for publishing these things without consulting you. There is a taint of treachery in the veins of every publisher in the Row and, after all, though our two styles may have something in common and we have chosen the same subjects, I am sure there is room for both of us. Yours Max

P.S. I have sent a copy of Sir Henry's picture to Miss Acland: she has just acknowledged it: such a nice graceful note of thanks. She says it will be one of her chief treasures.[1]

[1] Max is joking; there was no 'Oxford Celebrities', and he did not send a drawing to Sarah Acland (1849–1930), Sir Henry's daughter. See *MM* I, 145.

❖2      The Bodley Head, Vigo Street, London      August 24, 1893

My dear Will

Whilst I write I am coming of age: I was born twenty one years ago today and am ever so sorry that I cannot possibly come & live with you in Scarborough as you so charmingly ask me. I have to go into the country tomorrow for a week to stay with relations & cannot possibly put them off.[1] Why do I write on this odd paper? Because it was wrapped up with two very lovely drawings by Aubrey Beardsley which J. Lane has just given me. They lie before me as I write: I am enamoured of them. So is John Lane: he said "How lucky I am to have got hold of this young Beardsley: look at the technique of his drawings! What workmanship! *He never goes over the edges!*" He never said anything of the kind but the criticism is suggestive for you, dear Will? And characteristic of Art's middleman, the Publisher—for of such is the Chamber of

Horrors. How brilliant I am! I forget whether you like Salomé or not—Salomé is the play of which the drawings are illustrative? I have just been reading it again—and like it immensely—there is much, I think, in it that is beautiful, much lovely writing—I almost wonder Oscar doesn't dramatise it.[2]

But brilliancy to the winds! I am in love—in love with Cissie Loftus and, oh my dear Will, though it may not seem paradoxical to say so, it is very very charming to be in love: you may not believe me—I could not have foretold it two weeks ago but now my whole being is changed: I have become good and am really happy at last.[3]

My moral sense has awakened. The other night I 'interviewed' her for an imaginary newspaper: she is not fifteen yet and wears a pink ribbon in her hair. I am utterly changed. Do write and be sympathetic with me. She let me hold her hands, telling them by palmistry, for a long time and the whole thing was quite a little idyll in its way.

I must see you to rave about her; you would hardly know me. But you must not see her: a caricature might dissillusionise me. Oh my dear Will I am so happy and good. Yours Max

She has a small oval face and long eyes and full lips: her hair is quite straight as it falls over her shoulders and she has been in a convent for four years. As yet, in spite of her great success in art, she is utterly unspoiled. My love for her is utterly reverent: you, I know, regard woman simply as the accusative after the second auxiliary verb: or do I wrong you? I could not ever wrong *her*, but I should love to marry her. I am so good and changed. Yours again Max

All love to you in Scarborough: how I wish I could have come.

---

[1] Rothenstein was at the Grand Hotel, Scarborough, Yorkshire. He returned to London on August 28. Max was to join Herbert Tree's family at Totteridge; see Letter 3.

[2] In 1894 Aubrey Beardsley (1872–1898) became art editor of *The Yellow Book*, published, 1894–1897, by Lane and Mathews. Beardsley had illustrated Oscar Wilde's play, *Salome: A Tragedy in One Act*, and his name became inextricably linked with that of its author. During the Wilde trials in 1895, Lane yielded to pressure from other contributors and fired Beardsley.

[3] Marie Cecilia (Cissie) Loftus (1876–1943), music-hall mime and actress, made her London début in July 1893, at the Oxford Music Hall. In other letters Max refers to her as Mistress Mere and as The White Girl.

◇3        77 Sloane Street [London]
          or rather Fair Lawn, Totteridge, Herts.
          [late August 1893]

Tomorrow, dear Will, I shall be in dear London though only I believe till Saturday. How I wish I could stay there and never leave it again: I simply cannot bear to be so far away from the Lady Cecilia—(that is what I think of Cissie Loftus as). Have you seen her, Will, at the Tivoli? It is very, very hot here and I am so tired and affected. Oh for the Lady Cecilia to sit by my sofa and bathe my hands in eau-de-Cologne and tell me she does not love anybody else a little bit. The heat is awful and the provinces are quite yellow with wasps. I have two lovely portraits of the White Girl and a lovely little portrait of her in a tiny green case. I look at them all day and long for the Tivoli. Here with my brother and his wife there is little sympathy for my love. Will you be sympathetic when I see you? Yours Max
PS In London my love was simple & pure & rather pastoral: but here, in the pale provinces, passion has overtaken me and I long to sacrifice something, to make a fool of myself for her sake. She is sweet and she is a great artist. Go to the Tivoli tonight; I shall look you up tomorrow.


◇4        4 Chandos Square, Broadstairs    [early September 1893]

My dear Will

I made my entry into Broadstairs quite quietly last Sunday. I find it a most extraordinary place—a few yards in circumference and with a population of several hundred thousands. In front of our house there is a huge stretch of greenish stagnant water which makes everything damp and must, I am sure, be very bad for those who live near to it. Everybody refers to it with mysterious brevity as the C. I am rather afraid of the C. And oh the population. You, dear Will, with your love of Beauty that is second only to your love of Vulgarity would revel in the female part of it.[1] Such lots of pretty, common girls walking up & down—all brown with the sun and dressed like sailors—casting vulgar glances from heavenly eyes & bubbling out Cockney jargon from perfect lips. You would revel in them but I confess they do not attract me: apart from the fact that I have an ideal, I don't think the lower orders ought to be attractive—it brings Beauty into disrepute. Never have I seen such a shady looking set of men in any place at any season: most of them look

19

like thieves & the rest like receivers of stolen goods & altogether I do not think Broadstairs is a nice place. Are you in Paris? How charming. I am sending this to your publishers who know probably your address. By the way did you remember when you saw that poor fly in the amber of modernity, John Lane, to speak of my caricatures? Do write to me and tell me of anything that you are doing or of anyone you have seen. By the papers I see that Mistress Mere is still at the Tivoli: it is terrible not to be able to see her—for all practical purposes I might as well be blind. But I have her photographs & they are a very great comfort indeed. Photography—what a safeguard it is against infidelity. If Ulysses had had a photograph of Penelope by Elliot & Fry in his portmanteau, the cave of Calypso might have lost an habitué. But good God, what a ghastly place Broadstairs is & how miserable—after a fashion—am I! Mind you write to me if you ever receive this letter. Yours ever Max

Have you entered any Studio yet? I would recommend you to draw from the life: nothing like it.

[1] David Cecil altered both the text and the implications for Rothenstein's tastes by transcribing this sentence, 'You, dear Will, with your love of Vulgarity would revel . . .' (*Max*, p. 85).

◇5        19 Hyde Park Place [London]        [late September 1893]

Never mind, my dear Will, the long letter of which you tell me is none the less delightful for not reaching my hands or for that matter, it may be, for not being written by yours. The short one is very enjoyable. Fancy you in the country: your description is very rural indeed: what a funny coincidence that there should be such places both in England & France! And the model! Great heaven, is she really 1830?[1] The Lady Cecilia is only 15 and yet I love her: I think 15 a charming age but however...to each his own. She must be very entertaining, your model. I have seen Cissie again to speak to—at the Tivoli again as she watched the performance: very sweet she was & very frank in her guileless brown frock and she has written her name on three of my photographs of her. Such a good hand too she writes for a child—and it is a great solace to see her name as she wrote it herself with the simple unaffected admission that she is mine—mine sincerely.

Such a brilliant first night at the Haymarket on Wednesday.[2] The stalls were simply infested with politicians, whilst peeresses-in-their-own-right were hustled into tiny boxes over the chandelier. Zola was to have come but, being travel-worn, did not & went instead to the Alhambra. Oscar was also at the Alhambra, dancing attendance upon Zola's attendants.[3] Àpropos of him, did I tell you that I saw a good deal of his brother Willie at Broadstairs? Quel monstre! Dark, oily, suspecte yet awfully like Oscar: he has Oscar's coy, carnal smile & fatuous giggle & not a little of Oscar's esprit. But he is awful—a veritable tragedy of family-likeness.[4]

It has just struck me that this note may not ever reach you at the address you give: so I will write no more.  [Max]

[1] Rothenstein's letter, if written, is not extant. He was painting in Gloucestershire. '1830': a phase (unidentified) in Rothenstein models.

[2] *The Tempter*, by Henry Arthur Jones (1859–1929), produced by Herbert Tree, ran September 20–December 2, 1893.

[3] The Alhambra Theatre was noted for its corps de ballet. Emile Zola, invited by the Institute of Journalists, came to London on September 20, 1893.

[4] William Wilde (1852–1899), London journalist. Oscar Wilde and Zola had met in Paris in 1883. See *Letters*, p. 63; Wilde, *The Letters of Oscar Wilde*, ed. Rupert Hart-Davis, p. 135.

᧖6  19 Hyde Park Place  Sunday [October 22, 1893]

Dear Will

If I were not afraid my people might keep it out of the newspapers, I should commit suicide tomorrow. Really I am rather miserable. I know what disappointment is.

In my unregenerate days, I was far too much of an egoist to seek for any pleasure save in the contemplation of myself: taking myself as the standard of perfection, I always found myself quite perfect and never was disappointed. But now I have become a tuist and all is changed.

Yesterday I woke dimly in the morning, murmuring to myself "Tonight 'Don Juan' is produced and from my stall I shall see my love in the white kirtle of Haidée." I breakfast and open the paper and find a dastardly postponement till Saturday next "owing to an accident to one of the principal performers." Heigho. I suppose there is such a thing as Saturday next—do you think so, Will?

What was the accident? To whom had it happened? I went down to the Gaiety to ask and found that it was not, as I had almost hoped, the Lady Cecilia who had broken her heart for me—but only Mr Robert Pateman who had sprained his ankle.[1]

To Solferino's I went in solitary wretchedness and tried to forget the fates under a crown of vine-leaves—but they only deepened the shadow upon my brow.[2]

By the way, Harry Cust was clandestinely married, a day or two after we saw him at Solferino's, to Miss Welby, an exotic girl who has spent her life hitherto in making pencil-drawings of Lady Granby. The match seems in every way a most desirable one and was effected against the wishes of all the parents concerned.[3]

My dear Will, do pity me a little about Cissie Loftus even if you have to take your pen-knife and cut a heart-line across your hand. Last night my people saw her at "Sowing the Wind"—the 1830 piece—and of course I was not with them.[4] (By the way, before I forget it, have you tried Arthur Sidgwick of Corpus for the series? Certainly he *must* come in—the very man of men.[5] Also I have written an impression of you for the "Sketch"—but enough of other people's interests—let me return to myself.)[6] I had gone instead to your beloved Trocadero which is rather a swindling place I think. Outside they advertise R G Knowles & Marie Lloyd and Albert Chevalier "and all the stars" and when you go in you find the entertainment consists of Miss Maggie Mayhew and Mr Hugo Robbins and—for the rest—of extra-turns.[7]

No stars but any number of asterisks. However one of the asterisks was very jolly—I wish I knew her name. A tall girl of about twenty-three with short brown curls and a very poignant, tomboyish face. She had the rare charm of really *round* eyes and did clever imitations of schoolboys and street-urchins. You would rave about her. She has an air of chastened devilry that is hard to resist. But oh what a vast difference between the admiration that goes forth from the eye and that which goes from the heart. Heaven grant you the latter some day!

Arthur Roberts was sitting there drinking a great deal of champagne and looking altogether splendid: what a distinguished cad he is.[8]

Do come and see me again soon: I am so sorry your last visit was a wild goose-chase but have not seen my brother since. In the meanwhile write and keep me in the current: also tell the Macfies that I am regaining my strength.[9] Yours Max Beerbohm

Postscript

Do you know, I have quite solved the problem of your personality? Your whole secret lies in the way you call attention to and imbue with the deepest artistic significance all the little trivial actions and most commonplace circumstances which form your existence.

Do you remember when you stopped to have your boots blacked the other day? Surely it was a fairly ordinary thing to do: thousands do it every day. I stood by and began to think of myself: suddenly looking up I found you beaming at me with a smile of the most intense meaning. "Yes?" I said vaguely. "How very, very few men," you said triumphantly, "who would stop like this and have these boots blacked in open street. Really it is very *precieux*. C'est l'audace d'artiste! My dear Max, admit that it is very unrastaqueurish of me!" "Very" I echoed feebly and since then have told everyone how that *extraordinary* man Will Rothenstein actually stopped in *the middle* of Regent Street &c &c.

And that is how personalities are made.

¹ Cissie Loftus was Haidée and Robert Pateman (1841–1924) was Lambro in a burlesque version of *Don Juan*, at the Gaiety Theatre, October 28, 1893–June 16, 1894. George Mudie was promoted from a minor role as replacement.

² Solferino's: Rupert Street restaurant favoured by artists and journalists.

³ Henry Cust (1861–1917), politician and journalist; editor, *Pall Mall Gazette*, 1892–1896. Emmeline (Nina) Welby Cust (1867–1955), daughter of Lady Victoria Welby-Gregory (1851–1912). Lady Granby, later Duchess of Rutland (d. 1937).

⁴ *Sowing the Wind*, by Sydney Grundy (1848–1914), a play set in the 1830's, at the Comedy Theatre, September 30, 1893–January 31, 1894. Rothenstein had seen this play: 'I took him last week to "Sowing the Wind" which was rather silly of me, for his temperature immediately went up to 1830.' (Beerbohm to Robert Ross [October 27, 1893]. BP:MC).

⁵ Arthur Sidgwick (1840–1920), Fellow, Corpus Christi College, Oxford; author of books on reading and writing Greek; in Rothenstein, *Oxford Characters* [plate 22].

⁶ No 'impression' appeared in *The Sketch* in 1893 or 1894.

⁷ Richard Knowles (1858–1919), Marie Lloyd (1870–1922), Albert Chevalier (1861–1923): well-known music-hall entertainers. Hugo Robbins and Maggie Mayhew: minor performers.

⁸ Arthur Roberts (1852–1933), music-hall performer, was Don Pedrillo in *Don Juan*.

⁹ Rothenstein hoped to do a portrait drawing of Herbert Tree. W. S. and M. A. Macfie let rooms at 19 Merton Street (see Letter 8), now the site of a new residence of the Warden of Merton College.

❖7          19 Hyde Park Place    Sunday [October 29, 1893]

My dear Will

And how is Oxford and how go your victims? I have begun reading already and have made some progress with my subject which—for Greats—means *all* history & *all* philosophy: however I am not afraid: a giant may wear other people's shoes upon his little toes. Apropos of philosophies, I saw Bosie Douglas today and am dining with him tonight: aren't you, dear straightlaced timid wonderful Will, very shocked?[1] But oh last night—the first night—at the Gaiety: all my profecies are verified: Mistress Mere was very *very* bad: though to my super-subtle heart there was an intense charm in the very stiffness and staginess of her performance: and she was a success indeed and the audience liked her amazingly—not knowing, they, that she acted so ill but admitting the loveliness of her looks: she was indeed sweet to look at—quite her old primitive début-ridden self.

The piece itself rather heavy and full of a thickened plot: also overburdened by the constant appearance of Edmund Payne—who is a kind of Little Tich—all Little Tich's lack of humour & none of his deformity. We must go and see the play together.[2]

Yesterday I went down to Maidenhead & saw Parker at his school: I quite envied him his nice, primitive life after four years of complicated dissipation—wine and tobacco and my friendship—at Oxford.[3]

Write and give me all news. Yours Max

I dined at Solferino's last night for this reason: that having dressed like a very fop and gone to Limmer's Hôtel—there to dine with the Odd Volumes—some other man in evening dress, a waiter I suppose, came forward smiling to say that the Odd Volumes were going to dine there on the Friday following. At Solferino's I met Whibley and we talked with more or less brilliancy—I more—he less.[4]

[1] 'Bosie': Lord Alfred Douglas (1870–1945), son of the Marquess of Queensberry. Rothenstein reported: 'Young Lord Alfred Douglas, who was at Oxford, if you remember, last term, has been going in for the wildest folly in London, and, I imagine, will shortly have to take a tour round the world, or something of the kind.' (Rothenstein to Margaret Woods, October 28 [1893]. RP:HL.)

[2] Edmund Payne (1865–1914), comedian, played Lambro's lieutenant. 'Little Tich': stage name of Harry Relph (1868–1928), music-hall comedian, acquired when he shared the bill with huge Arthur Orton, the Tichborne Claimant.

[3] Eric Parker (1870–1955), author of books on sport, the English countryside, and natural history; editor, *Field*, 1930–1937. He was an usher at a boys' school at Bray, near Maidenhead.

[4] Ye Sette of Odd Volumes, founded 1878 and still in existence, comprises twenty-one Odd Volumes (members), men prominent in science, art, and literature, to match the number of volumes of the 1821 Variorum Shakespeare. Supplemental Volumes may be added.

Charles Whibley (1859–1930), journalist, critic, biographer; member of 'the Henley Regatta', as Max dubbed the staff of *The National Observer*, formerly *The Scots Observer*, edited, 1888–1893, by W. E. Henley (1849–1903). See *MM* I, 285.

Max wrote to John Lane: 'When the waiter at Limmer's Hotel broke it to me that the dinner was not for another seven days I went off to console myself at

Solferino's where was a perfect nestful of the young vipers of the National Observer and much discussion about Will Rothenstein—his past and future.' (Beerbohm to Lane [October 29? 1893]. Taylor.)

◇8          19 Merton St. [Oxford]     December 3 [1893]

My dear Max, not a word have I heard either of or from you since I left Town. With any one else, this would but little disturb me, but I am in constant dread, when you are concerned, lest you be dropping back into your old lethargic state of ultra refinement. Would that I could send you off a sirloin of vulgarity packed in ice—but alas, vulgarity, unlike beef, will not keep, but is as ephemeral as unselfishness, or even success.

So Robinson Ellis & St Cyres have at [last] appeared, multiplied into 450 copies, for the benefit of the eleven philanthropists who subscribe to my, shall I call it, pièce de résistance.[1] Walk up, gents & ladies, gents & ladies, walk up. Pay your three guineas & have your penny worth. Three shots at the artist for a halfpenny, the prize for whoever knocks his head off first—a golden book cover. Kindly presented by the publisher. There you are, sir, take your aim, three for a 'arfpenny.

And what has my gentle Max been doing. I hope he has been stopping at home, like a good boy, looking after his complexion in this cold weather. I hope he has been spending his nights at the nice warm music halls, where there are plenty of nice, pleasant ladies to look after him. I sincerely hope he has not been doing any of those horrid caricatures, or silly verses & absurd writing, which things no respectable idler ever does. And so, when I leave Oxford this week & come to live in Town, where I have got a commission to paint a portrait, I will bring him a nice present, well suited for my precious darling. And, in order that his artistic mind may not be spoiled by the moral & commonplace, I will bring him some nice story books. The Arabian Nights, by Burton, Apuleius' Golden Ass, the history of Suetonius, & the Kama Sutra.

But seriously, I am coming up to Town for good at the beginning of next week. Do you know of any digs where I can have a decent bed room & sitting room—furnished of course, until I can find a studio. I am to paint Miss Williams, whose brother I know, formerly of New Coll[ege] & now clerk at the House of Commons—do you by any chance know her?[2] I hope you will be in Town. Do write me before I come up. You have been neglecting me shamefully. Have you taken

Hartrick your drawings?[3] With very kindest regards to your mother & sisters—ton affectueux Will R

[1] Stafford Henry Northcote, Viscount St. Cyres (1869–1926), at Merton College, 1888–1892; don at Christ Church, Oxford, 1893. In his rooms, Rothenstein and Beerbohm first met. See *MM* I, 144; Rothenstein, *Oxford Characters* [plate 4].

[2] Edith Lockyer Williams (1868–1947) in 1894 married Dalhousie Young (1866–1921), composer, one of Oscar Wilde's last friends and benefactors. The portrait was Rothenstein's first London commission; present owner, Tate Gallery. Miss Williams' brother was A. F. Basil Williams (1867–1950), Clerk of the House of Commons, 1892–1901; journalist and historian.

[3] A. S. Hartrick (1864–1950), painter, photographer, illustrator for *The Daily Graphic* and the *Pall Mall Budget*. The drawings are unidentified: perhaps another instance of Rothenstein's 'puffing' Max in strategic quarters; see *Letters*, p. 63.

◇9                         19 Hyde Park Place     [early 1894?]

Dear Sir

I have great pleasure in sending you my autograph. I am dining at the Monico Restaurant tomorrow (Thursday) at 7.15—when you will, if it is really your wish, have an opportunity of seeing me in person. I shall pass in through the Piccadilly Circus entrance. Very faithfully yours

Max : Beerbohm

◇10            14 Quebec Street [London]     [March 15? 1894]

My dear Will

Remember, I pray you, tomorrow and have all things ready—all apparatus. A bell-shaped hat tilted back—pale gray trousers—the lights of the hat echoed in the boots—and a white carnation. All these things shall come to pass—times of jolliness & glad indulgence.[1] Yours Max

[1] On these sittings, cf. *Letters*, p. 93. 'All these things': quoted in advance of publication, from Beerbohm, 'A Defence of Cosmetics', *The Yellow Book*, 1 (1894), 65–82; revised as 'The Pervasion of Rouge', in his *Works*, pp. 85–106.

Before one such appointment, Max wrote: 'I am sitting to Will in the morning. I wish you could "drop in" to support me and prevent me from being bullied. You and he can be as metaphysical and ethical and aesthetic as you like.' (Beerbohm to Robert Ross, n.d. J-P. B. Ross.)

For the drawing included in this letter see illustration no. 3.

Dear Confrère[1]

The Town lies before me praying for slavery at my hands: young, exquisite, of the kind that dominates. I shall (absint jactatoris praemia[2]) go very far.

In the meanwhile please call upon me at 19 Hyde Park Place.

Yours Max B. (a concession)

P.S. Whistler once made London a half-way house between New York & Paris & wrote rude things in the visitor's book. Splendid.[3]

[1] A Whistlerism.

[2] 'May the rewards of a braggart be absent.'

[3] After a period of baiting Whistler with wry comments on the demands and postures of fame, Max repaid Whistler's rudeness with a sincere compliment. See Beerbohm, 'Whistler's Writing', *Pall Mall Magazine*, 33 (1904), 137–141; reprinted in his *Yet Again*, pp. 103–116. See also John Felstiner, *The Lies of Art: Max Beerbohm's Parody and Caricature*, pp. 34–36.

◇12                53 Glebe Place, Chelsea    Monday [late April 1894]

My dear Max, you are soon, it would seem, to have the melancholy pleasure of seeing me once more, for I come to Oxford on Saturday, to stay, until Monday, with Mrs Woods at Trinity. And I shall have a good excuse for calling upon you, O you dear great man, for I bring with me proofs of your portrait, which I think represents the most intimate one I have done of you. "Nay, but it is useless to protest," for it is the portrait of a caricaturist and not of a writer.[1] For did not my kingly pencil send your chin retrograde, nor did the glib tongue of the poser avail to turn the hair from its old course, the point over the collar. It is the artist that perfects you, not you the artist, so must you crossly acquiese. Like the other little Oxford characters, you must acquiese in the dance. And now that the appreciation for my most exquisite portraits (βλυδι: as Lucian told us they were) is becoming general, and most men, as time goes by, become younger than I painted them, it may be asked curiousment how such a prejudice against them ever came into being. For though man has so ridiculousment confounded body with soul by keeping his watch upon his body, & telling the time by his soul, and though his very lip salve savours of paint & even though his powder be fumeless, still there is much confounding of soul with body, and, just as the one, achetant at the price of its life that so wonderful & exquisite

27

unguent, which Herodotus tells us was ϛω βαδ νορ θε ϛκιν snuffed itself, as who should say, out, so the other, with that degraded determination which our own Elizabeth so strongly showed when she threw dust in the eyes of Crosse & Blackwell, of shameful memory, almost eliminates that other mixture of soul, which men have so rapidly mistaken for body. How fatal it is, this confusion, so illiterate, of body & surface![2]

No, but seriousmy, my own Max, I enjoyed your ridiculous literature immensely, more I must frankly admit, than anything else in the book. And my heart bled for you, sometimes, as I read the unsympathic (a good word for you) presse cuttings on your article.[3] It was like Don Quixote raging against the windmill, or Apuleius of golden memory, stabbing the bladders he so risibly took for burglars.

These last lines merely to keep up my reputation as a man of bitter speech. And now I may tell you how all my friends chuckled over your dear cosmetics as they read & reread them. Oscar [Wilde], solitary exception, was moved to a torrent of tears, so strong was his emotion.

I have done much new work, amongst other things a monumental portrait of the sisters of the Vale, your fervent admirers. Also Pinero, mine.[4] I fly to lunch. Your very affectionate—Will R
Write me a word avant Saturday.

---

[1] Throughout this letter Rothenstein borrows from Max's 'A Defence of Cosmetics', which had just appeared. The portrait of Max is the lithographic drawing for Rothenstein, *Oxford Characters*. For Max on *Oxford Characters*, see Beerbohm, 'Ex Cathedra III: Modern Statuary, Oxford a la Rothenstein,' *To-Morrow*, 2 (1896), 259–263.

[2] Lucian and Herodotus said nothing of the kind. 'θλυδι': transliteration of 'bloody.' 'ϛω . . . ϛκιν': transliteration, 'So bad for the skin.'

[3] An outraged press attacked 'A Defence of Cosmetics'. See, for example, Frederick Wedmore, '"The Yellow Book"', *The Academy*, 45 (1894), 349. For Max's retort, see Beerbohm, 'A Letter to the Editor', *The Yellow Book*, 2 (1894), 281–284.

Rothenstein wrote from Yarmouth: 'I had a case of books sent me from Town, amongst which I found the Yellow Book No. II. I have only just glanced at it, but it seemed as though all the writers had written autobiographical sketches of themselves with favourable criticisms of their own work, and facsimiles of their autographs appended—or should have been.' (Rothenstein to Margaret Woods, August 1 [1894]. RP:HL.)

[4] The 'sisters of the Vale': Ricketts and Shannon. There was little mutual admiration between Max and Arthur Wing Pinero (1855–1934), playwright and critic; see, for example, Beerbohm, 'Mr. Pinero's Literary Style', *SR*, 96 (1903), 511–512; reprinted in his *Around Theatres*, pp. 286–290.

◇13            19 Hyde Park Place      [early March 1896]

My dear Will

Perhaps—as they really do seem to think your caricature might be construed absurdly & indecently and if you think it would look well, if well engraved upon wood, your caricature had better be given to the wood-engraver. He could tone down the hip without spoiling the effect greatly. Critics, you see, would naturally be upon a keen scent over any quarry set loose by Smithers. For myself—I think the whole notion of the 'indecency' idiotic—as you know.

What do you think? Please communicate with me as soon as you can—for I have to let Smithers know.[1]

It was so nice seeing you again yesterday.

And till [Saturday?]. Yours Max

[1] Apparently a Rothenstein caricature, unidentified, for Beerbohm, *Caricatures of Twenty-Five Gentlemen*, to be published by Leonard Smithers (1861–1907), bookseller and publisher with a reputation as purveyor of pornography, but also publisher of *The Savoy* and of works by Beardsley, the poet Ernest Dowson (1867–1900), and the critic Arthur Symons (1865–1945), all of whom were rejected by 'respectable' publishers after the Wilde trial in 1895. James Nelson suggests that 'they' could be 'lawyers or advisers to whom Max had submitted any questionable items before proceeding to press'. (Nelson to Mary Lago, October 7, 1972.) Rothenstein withdrew the caricature; see Letter 14.


◇14        Haymarket Theatre     Thursday [early March 1896]

My dear Will

I am so sorry you are vexed about the caricature and quite understand your being so. Also I am sorry for my own sake it can't appear in my book—but I hope you will let me have it for my own upon the same terms. I should not like it to pass out of my possession. Of course, knowing me, you must know how idiotic I think the idea of it not being as innocent as the babe unborn—but people seem to have a mania for impropriety. I can't help their folly. Till Saturday. Yours Max

I have written to tell Smithers you withdraw the drawing—


◇15      West Cliff Hotel, Folkestone     Saturday [July 18, 1896]

My dear Will

We "waited dinner" for you the other day for some minutes & I think that as you were not coming you might have let me know: in which case our hunger could more quickly have been appeased and I might—however inadequately—have filled your place at the table. Here I am, as you see by the royal device under which I write, ensconced at Merry Folkestone. Firminger is with me by the way and I find him a very nice camarade de voyage—very sympathetic & so forth, though fearfully extravagant in the way of champagnes and flies to rather remote places of very remote interest.[1] However we get on amazingly well and the place itself I find quite passable: it is at present in the off-season and how charming in its contrast to London with her streets packed with faces and her pavements covered with feet! And how nice to be in a town where the season is just about to commence: charming in its expectant emptiness and not unreminiscent of Hardy's sweet distinction between the light—the twilight—of dawn & of sunset: "The degree of light is equal exactly, it may be, at both times; but at dawn the bright element is active and the shadow passive & quiescent":[2] so here in the middle of July there is none of the dreadful depression of spirits which falls as one watches the boats & the trains full of departing figures & the emptying streets & the houses as they grow blank. Good God, I write as tho' I have developed a sense of beauty or sentiment or something equally inappropriate to a modern (or "modd'n") letter. Are you working? Are you, in my charming phrase, staining the hair of a cammel in gaudy chemicals and wiping them off on a bit of coarse canvas?[3] Or have you given up that kind of thing? Talking of painters, by the way, I was taken to see a man—a nouveau riche named Crofter—the other day: he shewed me some chalk sketches by Whistler—nude women drawn in rough & short strokes—which I really found rather charming. I began to think that perhaps you were right in your idolatry & that the man really does possess a touch of genius.[4]

Firminger is clamouring for a country walk over the shingle & will not be comforted: so Adieu, petit. Yours Max

19 Hyde Park Place

P.S. This letter, as you will have seen, was written at Folkestone: however, I had left your address at home and so the despatch of it was delayed: enfin le voiçi: there is no news to add: by the way your own letter (or was it merely a rough copy?) pleased me very much: also the sketch of yourself—only why have you gone in for idealism: far better stick to caricature & though I cannot hate you as a rival do not let me brand you as a backslider.[5] Your pardon. I am not rude—merely brilliant!

[1] Walter Firminger (1870–1940), Max's Oxford contemporary, who took holy orders, served in Africa and India, and in 1926 became Chaplain to the King at Hampton Court Palace.

[2] Max quotes approximately; compare Thomas Hardy, *Tess of the D'Urbervilles: A Pure Woman* (1919 ed.), I, 173–174.

[3] See Beerbohm, 'Dandies and Dandies', in his *Works*, pp. 16–17.

[4] Both Crofter and the Whistler sketches remain unidentified.

[5] Rothenstein's letter and sketch of himself are untraced.

◇16                          Monday [postmark August 10, 1896]

Dear Max—Herbert Horne wants to review your book for Harris—send him a copy *at once* & he will do it immediately.[1] En attendant I have lent him mine. Et mes caricatures? I must have them soon.[2] In great haste: always Yours—Will R

Horne will do it for next week if he gets the book.

       H. H. 14 Cheyne Walk
          Chelsea

[1] Herbert Horne (1864–1916), architect, biographer, poet; a founder, 1886, of The Century Guild of Artists; editor, *The Century Guild Hobby Horse*, 1887–1891, and of its successor, *The Hobby Horse*, 1893–94. He reviewed Max's *Works*; see [Horne] 'The Precocious School of Humour', *SR*, 82 (1896), 221.

To Edmund Gosse (1849–1928), poet and literary historian, Max wrote: 'I send you a copy of my first book, and my excuse is that you, unconsciously, suggested the title of it. One afternoon of last summer, in the garden of a certain club, you were complaining of the folly of journalists, and you declared that, next time they asked you what works you had found most "helpful", you would say "The Works of Max Beerbohm." So I send you the little monster that has been born of your *mot*, hoping you will be one of its keepers.' (Beerbohm to Gosse, June 1896. Ashley Library: British Museum.)

[2] Rothenstein, whom Frank Harris had asked to edit the 1896 Christmas Supplement of *The Saturday Review*, invited Max to submit caricatures but rejected his first lot, suggested others, and eventually used only the Wilson Barrett caricature; see Letter 20, note 5; *MM* I, 288–289.

◇17          29 Argyll Road, Bognor, Sussex     [mid-August 1896]

My dear Will

Listen! I don't think I can do *all* statesmen—those that I have done I have emptied out and others have been overdone by Harry Furniss & Co. *But* what do you think of the following for the page of four?
*The Duke of Devonshire* (very good and amusing)
*Lord Rowton*—as being very prominent as a Courtier, "Social Butterfly" and so on—

31

*Carson E.C. M.P.* (I can do him more amusingly than Edward Clarke and he is quite as important just now)
*Barney Barnato*—financier.

All these are well known to the public, of course. Is there any objection to any of them? I can do a gem of each—Barnato I have by me now.

*Alec Yorke* is perhaps not well enough known outside his circles. Otherwise it would have been nice to have him.[1] Do let me have a line as soon as possible! All four could be reproduced with ½ tone blocks—but there is no doubt wood-engraving makes no end of difference to my things. I saw your beautiful and distinguished book at Lane's. It will live for ever, I think. And what a nice appreciation of yours.[2] Max

---

[1] These caricatures were proposed but not included in the 1896 Christmas Supplement, *SR*.

Harry Furniss (1854–1925), caricaturist, illustrator, author, actor, lecturer. Victor Cavendish (1868–1938), 9th Duke of Devonshire. Montagu Lowry-Corry, 1st Baron Rowton (1838–1903), Disraeli's Private Secretary, 1866–1868, 1874–1880. Edward Carson (1854–1935), barrister; defence counsel for the Marquess of Queensberry in the Wilde trial; later Ulster leader and Lord of Appeal. Sir Edward Clarke (1841–1931), former Law Officer of the Crown, represented Wilde in the Queensberry case and in two subsequent trials. Barnett Isaacs Barnato (1852–1897), head of the Barnato Mining Company, South Africa. Alexander Yorke (1847–1911), Groom-in-Waiting to Queen Victoria, 1884–1901; Extra Groom-in-Waiting to King Edward VII, 1901–1910.

[2] That is, Rothenstein's note on Max in *Oxford Characters*.

---

↜18            Berkeley Hotel, Bognor      [mid-August 1896]

My dear Will

I have had a fling at Bill Watson—though I remember him rather faintly.[1] I send you my Rowton also—you *must* have heard of Rowton—Disraeli's secretary & friend & executor & always all over the place. After all even if he weren't at all known outside the aristocracy—you, as an Editor, should remember that the aristocracy is a class to be catered for too. There are said to be 10,000 of them. However—just as you like. And I hope you will like the other caricatures. Also that F[rank] H[arris] won't think they will give offence. Do take a high hand with him.[2]

I am enjoying myself here fairly well. Early to bed and so forth. I drink an extraordinary amount of whiskey. Yours Max : Beerbohm

What about my writing something for the thing? You see, I don't know what sort of writing they want—essay, fairy story?

1 William Watson (1858–1935), poet in the heroic mode rejected aspirant to the Laureateship in 1913; see Beerbohm, *The Poet's Corner* [plate 8]. On the Rowton caricature, see *Catalogue*, p. 124.
2 As of September, Harris was unoffended; see *Letters*, pp. 111–112.

❖19                    Berkeley Hotel, Bognor, Sussex    August 1896

My dear Will

Don't be so foolish—of course I am not angry—why should I be? I know quite well the difficult quality of my caricatures and am rather proud of it than otherwise. Caviare to the general, tripe to the few—something to every body—que veux-tu? And having this clear notion of the law of supply & demand I will readily send you a couple more drawings— Forbes Robertson for one.[1] My brother I did too recently. I may be going to Wales in about a week—but I shall be passing through London for a day or so, at least.

Also I will do some kind of skit. Possibly parodies of various writers writing on the subject of Xmas—
"Seasonable Tributes
    levied by
Max Beerbohm" or something of the sort. What do you think? Mrs. Meynell on "Holly"—Arthur Symons on "Xmas Eve in Piccadilly"— Henry James never mentioning Xmas by name and so forth. Rather amusing if acceptable.[2] Yours Max

1 Johnston Forbes-Robertson (1853–1937), actor-manager and painter.
2 Max's parody of Alice Meynell (1847–1922), poet, essayist, and critic: 'Holly: Al*ce M**n*ll', in 'A Christmas Garland Woven by Max Beerbohm', Christmas Supplement, *SR*, 82 (1896), 8–11; reprinted in Beerbohm, *Leaves from the Garland Woven by Max Beerbohm*. The Symons parody was apparently never written. The James parody was written much later; see 'A Christmas Garland: The Mote in the Middle Distance by H*nry J*m*s', *SR*, 102 (1906), 702–703; reprinted in Beerbohm, *A Christmas Garland woven by Max Beerbohm*, pp. 1–10.

❖20                        19 Hyde Park Place    February 7, 1896

My dear Will

I wrote to Alfred Austin, under an assumed name, asking to let me interview him for the *English Illustrated*.

This morning came an exquisite letter saying that "The Poet Laureate greatly regretted that owing to his rule" &c.

Isn't it rather marvellous of him to call himself these names—to a stranger.[1]

I can't think of anyone else. Can you? Isn't Labby a draw?[2]

My article on Scott is to be in the next *Saturday*—I am awaiting a proof.[3] Yours Max

My sister, Constance, has heard from Mrs. Campbell. She says she is "afraid Mr. Rothenstein did not succeed in his drawing, *but perhaps when he has got it in his Studio he will be able to touch it up.*"[4]

My italics—

An idea!

Wilson Barrett in the Sign of the X—will go and see him in it and copy the drapery in the British Museum. He would really be a draw.[5]

---

[1] Alfred Austin (1835–1913), poet, critic, journalist; editor, *The National Review*, 1883–1895; Poet Laureate, 1896–1913.

[2] Henry Du Pré Labouchere (1831–1912), journalist, politician; Liberal Member of Parliament, 1880–1906; founder, 1877, *Truth*.

[3] Clement Scott (1841–1904), playwright, translator; drama critic, *The Daily Telegraph*, 1872–1898; editor, *The Theatre*, 1877–1897. Max's unsigned review of Scott's *Lays and Lyrics*, the first Beerbohm contribution to *The Saturday Review*, appeared in September and drove Scott to fury. See [Beerbohm] 'An Unhappy Poet', *SR*, 82 (1896), 315–316; Scott, 'Come Out of Your Hole, Rat!' *The Era*, October 3, 1896, p. 13; Beerbohm, 'Hold, Furious Scot!' *SR*, 82 (1896), 395–396. For Max's account of this feud, see *Letters*, pp. 83–127 *passim*.

[4] Mrs Patrick Campbell (1865–1940) first starred in 1893, in the title role of Pinero's *The Second Mrs Tanqueray*. Emotion may have hampered Rothenstein's art: he disliked his subject; see *MM* I, 258.

[5] Wilson Barrett (1846–1904), theatre manager, actor, playwright, best known for his play, *The Sign of the Cross* (1896). For Max's caricature, see his 'Mr. Wilson Barrett as "Marcus Superbus" ', Christmas Supplement, *SR.*, 82 (1896), facing p. 8.

---

◇21                    19 Hyde Park Place      September 25, 1896

My dear Will

Do you remember I told you, a year ago, that there was to be an Exhibition of Caricature at the Fine Arts? Often postponed, it is coming off, at length, next month.[1] I suppose it would take from my Wilson B[arrett] any value it may have if it were exhibited before the appearance of the Supplement? I don't understand such matters—and for all I know the value of Wilson [Barrett] might be increased. Do let me know—just which you like—and do let us meet again—you need but name your day. Yours Max

I cannot remember whether I saw you last *after* your second Goya had been printed. I enjoyed and admired it so very much.[2] Felicitations. But you mustn't neglect canvas entirely. The thing on Marie Corelli in tomorrow's Saturday is mine.[3] Today, for the first time in my life, I had a printer's devil waiting for genius to correct its proof. Very distinguished.

[1] 'A Century and a Half of English Humourous Art from Hogarth to the Present Day', at The Fine Art Society, New Bond Street, October 26–December 5, 1896. Max exhibited drawings of the Rt. Hon. Henry Chaplin, M.P.; Frank Harris, Richard Le Gallienne, George Meredith, George Moore, and Herbert Beerbohm Tree; see *Catalogue*, pp. 44, 75, 91, 100, 102, 149.

[2] Rothenstein wrote the first book in English on the Spanish painter; it appeared first in two installments. See his 'Goya', *SR*, 82 (1896), 252–254, 307–308; reprinted as *Goya*.

[3] Marie Corelli (1855–1924), novelist, responded angrily to a slighting remark about herself in a Beerbohm article on Alice Meynell. He replied with comment on Miss Corelli's knack for getting her books advertised in newspaper paragraphs. See Beerbohm, 'Ex Cathedra: Mrs. Meynell's Cowslip-wine', *To-Morrow*, 2 (1896), 161–162; Corelli, 'Miss Marie Corelli and "Sport"', *The Westminster Gazette*, September 17, 1896, p. 3; Beerbohm, 'Miss Marie Corelli and Mr. Max Beerbohm', *The Westminster Gazette*, September 18, 1896, p. 3; Beerbohm, 'Our Lady of "Pars"'. *SR*, 82 (1896), 337. See also Beerbohm, 'The Sorrows of Millicent, A Christmas Cameo. M*rie C*r*lli', Christmas Supplement, *SR*, 82 (1896), p. 8; reprinted in Beerbohm, *Leaves from the Garland*, pp. 11–16.

◇22                 Hotel de l'Écu, Vitteaux       [late July 1897]

My dear Max—I write you from this minion & planturous country firstly to send you greetings, to assure you of my perfect friendship, consideration, admiration, consommation (Burgundy is my drink) & separation, for & from you, & secondly, to send you the very perfect text you so gracefully presented me with to face my drawing of Arthur Wing [Pinero]. If, très cher, you can soften the drawing of the eye, show fewer wrinkles round the mouth, without taking away from that truth, & honesty of outline from which I trust you will never depart, do it: otherwise, send it in to Grant Richards ( & in any case without delay) as it is. I confess to slightly craven feelings, for any suspicion of malice might get *me* hanged.[1]

I hope you are well, & happy as any sensible person can be. As for me, I am restored to primaeval, indeed, somewhat savage health, subsisting chiefly on roots, fruit, meat & other things cooked in the French fashion.

Favour me, I beg you, with a letter of a couple of dozen words for which I will pay you, like the S-t-y, some day, on any subject you care to choose—I give you carte blanche.[2] With the habitual greetings to your family which are never, they tell me, delivered, believe me, my very dear Max, to be your very prudent, economical, lacking, I frankly admit, in any advanced knowledge of topography, but affectionate friend—Will

[1] A drawing for Rothenstein, *English Portraits*, published by Richards, whose partiality for prominent persons reasserted itself. He and Rothenstein quarrelled over portraits of Richards' cousin, the writer Grant Allen (1848–1899), whom Richards wanted included, and of Cunninghame Graham, whom Richards wished to exclude in favour of Admiral Lord Charles Beresford. (Richards to Rothenstein, March 31, 1898. RP:HL.) For Richards' account of this episode, see his *Author Hunting*, pp. 67–68. In *English Portraits*, Pinero is plate 9; Allen, plate 19; Cunninghame Graham, plate 23. Lord Charles Beresford did not make the running.

[2] 'S-t-y': *The Saturday Review.*


◇23                  Berkeley Hotel, Bognor    August 1897

My dear Will

Many thanks for your letters. I have already corrected the proofs of Henley's innocence—and despatched them to Grant Richards.[1] I hope you will think them conclusive. Also, I return your postal order. I presented it at the Bank here, but they told me you had no account with them and referred me to drawer. I protested feebly that you were a lithographic-painter and could not draw. *Enfin*, keep your absurd piece of paper.

I am much amused by your difficulty with Sebastian. I thought his lines had some witty things in them—"an open secret" is lovely—but they were rather too antithetical and unfriendly—and too obviously written by Oscar. I am glad it is all right. You will now have a further set of interesting letters for your collection.[2] "A few months later, he is in Burgundy, engaging in an animated controversy with the poet, Oscar Wilde, then but lately released from prison. It would seem that he considered one of his protégés, William Henley, to have been unfairly treated in one of those monographs which" &c &c. I always admire your feeling for posterity. A paragraph in the *Sketch* satisfies ME.

I have bought a charming sign-board—a portrait of Dick Tarlington the harlequin, dancing in an avenue, with a memorial urn behind him, and a mask and a tambourine at his feet. It was painted in about 1805— by one 'W Evans' whoever he may have been. It is very big and heavy. I intend writing a very affected essay about it.[3] When do you come back? Let me know. Yours Max

[1] Other Rothenstein letters from Burgundy following Letter 22 are apparently not extant. Max wrote the note on Henley [plate 10], for Rothenstein, *English Portraits*.

[2] After release from prison in May 1897, Wilde used the pseudonym 'Sebastian Melmoth', derived in part from a character in *Melmoth the Wanderer* (1820), a novel by his great-uncle, Charles Maturin (1782–1824). Rothenstein first asked Wilde to write on Henley but rejected his text because the writers were to be unidentified; Wilde's style, like Henley's, was 'an open secret'. For the 'interesting letters' and Wilde on Henley, see Wilde, *Sixteen Letters from Oscar Wilde*, ed. John Rothenstein, pp. 27–32; Wilde, *Letters*, pp. 631–633, 635–636.

[3] Richard Tarleton (d. 1588), Elizabethan clown, usually shown with tabor and pipe but not in harlequin dress. See Beerbohm, 'Words for Pictures.—I', *SR*, 85 (1898), 515–516; reprinted as ' "Harlequin": A Signboard, Painted on Copper, signed "W Evans, London", Circa 1820', in his *Yet Again*, pp. 283–284. See also S. N. Behrman, *Portrait of Max*, p. 40.


◇24                    Berkeley Hotel, Bognor      [late August 1897]

My dear Will

I sent you a post-card to your former address. Didn't you get it? Also, the Pinero thing was all right, and I have returned corrected proof—and will give you the M.S. safely when you come back to London.[1] Thanks for your entertaining letter. I am glad you are enjoying yourself. Here I am having a quiet, but good, time. I don't quite know when I leave—it depends on Murray Carson with whom I am to write a play.[2] Walter Sickert came down here for a day or two and made vague notes for a new caricature of me—which he has since finished and which has been taken by *Vanity Fair*. I don't know when it is to appear.[3] Soon, I hope—*you* have not appeared in *Vanity Fair*, my lad! I have been staying with the Harmsworths in Kent. Harmsworth wants to be painted by you. Furse, greatly improved, came down to make arrangements for painting Mrs. Harmsworth—and there was much talk of north-lights to be cut in the roof and a white silk dress to be made and a small stair-case to be built for Mrs. Harmsworth to stand on. The Harmsworths are very charming people—he quite amazing and interesting. Furse seems to regard you

with cordial toleration. Harmsworth has a firm belief in young men—
that being, I suppose, the reason why he wants you to paint him. He
asked me whether you charged much. I said your price for full-lengths
ranged from £5 to £15. Was I right?[4]

The weather over here is rather ghastly. Kilseen may be going on
tour with my brother Tree, but is not sure. I don't think there's any
other news. I have had a great *'succès'* with an attack on Hall Caine in
the Daily Mail.[5] I hear that Oscar is under surveillance by the French
police. I am afraid he may be playing the fool.[6]

I tell everybody you are on a sketching-tour in Burgundy. Yours

Max

[1] It was not all right. Pinero learned that Max had written this note for
Rothenstein's *English Portraits* and forced Richards to substitute text by William
Archer. Richards, *Author Hunting*, p. 67; *MM* I, 299–301.

[2] On September 11, 1897, Max and Murray Carson (1865–1917), actor and
playwright, in one of several attempts at collaboration, began writing a play. Five
months' work, during which Max's relatives fretted about his penniless state and
Max fretted about the Carsons' Spartan regime, produced one benefit matinée of a
three-act comedy, *The Fly on the Wheel*, at the Coronet Theatre, Notting Hill Gate,
London, on December 4, 1902.

[3] For Sickert's caricature, see *Vanity Fair* (London), 58 (1897), 421.

[4] Alfred Harmsworth, 1st Viscount Northcliffe (1865–1922), proprietor of *The
Daily Mail*, from 1896, and of *The Times*, from 1908; his wife, Mary Elizabeth
Harmsworth (1868–1963). Max is joking about Rothenstein's prices. When
Harmsworth finally sat to him in 1906, Rothenstein asked and received £150.
(Rothenstein to Harmsworth, June 16, 17, 1906. Northcliffe Papers: British
Museum.) This project had an accompaniment of postponements, complaints, and
apologies, and a coda of confusion over the whereabouts and owner of the portrait,
still unknown. (Harmsworth to William and Alice Rothenstein, 10 letters, January
26, 1906, to June 4, 1912. RP:HL.)

An early caricature by Max, owned by Cecil Harmsworth, 2nd Viscount
Rothermere, encountered mock resistance: 'Madame [Mary Harmsworth] says the
picture is horribly like a very nightmare of portraiture. I on the other hand am
become your inveterate enemy and if you see a stout man awaiting your ingress or
egress during the impending fog you will know that the heavy blow amid-ships
proceeds from your sincere Alfred C. Harmsworth.' (Harmsworth to Beerbohm
[1897?]. BP:MC.)

Letters to Rothenstein from Charles W. Furse (1868–1904), English painter,
indicate feelings much warmer than 'cordial toleration' (RP:HL). Present owner
of the Furse portrait of Mary Harmsworth is unknown.

[5] Hall Caine (1853–1931), author of romantic novels with religious themes.
See Beerbohm, ' "The Christian", Some Comments on Mr. Hall Caine's New
Novel', *The Daily Mail*, August 11, 1897, p. 4. An editorial note prefaces three
letters censuring Max's review: 'We have thrown Mr. Max Beerbohm to the
wolves, convinced that he can take care of himself.' See 'Onslaught on a Critic', *The
Daily Mail*, August 12, 1897, p. 4; Beerbohm et al., 'Championing a Critic', *The
Daily Mail*, August 13, 1897, p. 4.

Wilde lived in France, except for brief visits to Italy and Switzerland, until his death on November 30, 1900.

.

⋄25        48 Upper Berkeley Street [London]    [mid-May 1898]

My dear Will

I *am* so sorry about tomorrow—and I hope you won't be stranded. I have to go to see the Saturdayers tomorrow morning—also G. B. S., from whom I had a note this evening asking me to take over his business now—his foot prevents him from going to any theatre, and he is to be moved out of London as soon as possible.

So I have to go on the streets of journalism this week—an intellectual prostitute. I hope you won't pass me by and refuse to draw me for the Juniorum.¹ Any other day will do for me—after Friday. Yours Max

¹ Rothenstein addressed the dedicatory epistle of his *Liber Juniorum: Six Lithographed Drawings* to Robert Ross: 'In these days there are few who, like you, care to stand by young artists once the novelty of their début has worn off.

'I can think of nothing better to offer you, in return for your sympathy and untiring loyalty, than these six drawings—were wit reckoned, Robbie, among the arts there would be seven—of men whom both of us admire, and of whom one at least was as proud of your friendship as is Your very devoted W. Rothenstein.' The six young men are Beardsley; Beerbohm; Laurence Binyon (1869–1943), poet and art historian; Laurence Housman (1865–1959), poet and artist; Stephen Phillips (1868–1915), dramatist; and William Butler Yeats (1865–1939). The seventh man: Oscar Wilde.

⋄26        48 Upper Berkeley Street    November 19, 1898

My dear Will

I am distracted in the forlorn effort to write the Hap[py] Hyp[ocrite] which the Lyceum people want by Tuesday or Wednesday—and I am writing to cancel various engagements—as every moment of my time will have to be devoted to dramaturgy. Can you without great inconvenience get another sitter for Monday morning and another diner for the evening—I am so sorry. Please accept all apologies and offer some of them to the Harry Reeces whom I was to have met.¹

I saw Mrs P[atrick] C[ampbell] and Mr F[orbes] R[obertson] yesterday at Bedford Square—and Mr F R was so full of the way he wanted to have the Georgian dresses done (if the play were really produced) that I, a mild and embarrassed neophyte, could not introduce the idea that you ought to design the costumes. Please forgive my weakness of purpose. You are the only person who could have done the dresses really well—but I was placed in such a position that I could not make the suggestion. I will come and see you as soon as the play is definitely on—or off.[2] That will be about the middle of next week. Yours Max

[1] Beerbohm, 'The Happy Hypocrite', *The Yellow Book*, 11 (1896), 11–44; reprinted as *The Happy Hypocrite: A Fairy Tale for Tired Men*; rewritten in 1898 as a play.
[2] Because of Mrs Campbell's procrastinations, the play was off. But see Letter 30, note 1.

❖27          Thornfield, Sale, Cheshire     December 23, 1899

My dear Max—influenza has untimely invaded our house in Bradford, so we are staying on here over Xmas. I have finished my drawings & am to paint my parents before returning to Town for good—we shall be there however, for a week about the middle of January, & hope to see you then.[1] Manchester has been in many ways a pleasant place to sojourn in—in others of course impossible, & I shan't be sorry to be in Kensington again. I have many little bibelots to give you—conversational bibelots, of course—and you I trust will have a golden harvest of waving caricatures—I too have made a few that you shall see. I read your article on I. Zangwill, & now see that he has withdrawn the play with apologies to you—no wonder you critics are so arrogant.[2] Few & vague rumours of literary London reach us here; what of Zuleika & her under-graduations? I trust she is finished—as indeed she was before she was begun (not Whistler's, but the old Alexandrine theory of the creation) & that you will again delight my ears with your catalogue raisonné of her perfections, & my senses with the description of her faults.[3] You, dear Max, shall see in return, the text for the Manchester Portraits—before my suggestions, written by a local admirer of the author of Lady Granby, Bernard Shaw & Cunninghame Graham.[4]

You shall also see a volume, bound in green morocco (8 vo) from which I present you with the following extract, which I have committed to memory.
"To say the clock & ornaments for the mantel are great in value, artistic in design & form, that the bracelets are handsome & suitable for any lady, and the silver dish most appropriate for the purpose it is intended to serve, is to use words that are not fully representative of my feeling."[5]

There are two delightful daughters of Mrs Gaskell here, who say we [are] for all the world like Ricketts & Shannon, & have many of their other charming qualities & peculiarities.[6] I am trying to persuade them to wear elastic side boots & crinolines, but they will persist in their old fashioned notions of dress. They are dear old ladies—they know Herbert by the bye & have heard much of you—indeed, your brother has many friends among the Lancashire folk. Alice sends her affectionate regards to you. Will you convey all nice messages from me to your family. I hope Kilseen is well—we have had no news of her for some weeks. I hope to be settled in Town again at the end of January. Always yours, Will

[1] Rothenstein, in Manchester with his sister Louisa (1869–1918) and her husband, Louis Simon (1861–1936), was at work on his *Manchester Portraits: Twelve Lithographic Drawings. First Series.* In June 1899 Charles Rowley (1839–1933), Manchester art entrepreneur and social reformer, visited the Rothensteins during their honeymoon in France and suggested this series of Mancunian dignitaries, with text by a local writer. In July the project still hung fire. In October Rowley was impatient and also afraid of losing money because of Rothenstein's 'luxurious line of demand'. In December Rowley claimed that many sitters were too busy and too modest to sit, and he was insulted when Rothenstein asked to speak privately to the publisher. Rowley left Manchester on December 26, not to return until January 8, 1900. (Rowley to Rothenstein, June 26, October 11, December 15, 1899. RP:HL.) A projected second series was never done; Rothenstein became heartily sick of the first before it appeared: 'I spent 3 dreary months at Manchester last winter, over a book of portraits, the last I hope, I shall ever do, and I am looking forward to a less insupportable winter this year.' (Rothenstein to Margaret Woods, September 9, 1900. Rothenstein.) See *MM* I, 349. For Rothenstein's portrait of his parents, see *WR*, facing p. 112.

[2] *Children of the Ghetto*, by Israel Zangwill (1864–1926), was based on his novel of the same title and ran at the Adelphi Theatre, December 11–18, 1899. The producer stated in his withdrawal notice that the play had 'failed to interest the general public', an implied 'apology' to Max, who had described the genuine playwright as one who ' "appeals to as wide a public as any" '. See Beerbohm, ' "Children of the Ghetto" ', *SR*, 88 (1899), 763–764; reprinted in his *More Theatres*, pp. 218–221.

[3] The Beerbohm novel, *Zuleika Dobson: or an Oxford Love Story*, was begun in 1898. Some benevolent criticism from Gosse may have inspired Max to start a novel as proof that he could produce something less ephemeral than drama reviews. See Evan Charteris, *The Life and Letters of Sir Edmund Gosse*, pp. 258–260.

Rothenstein's allusion to the 'Alexandrine theory of creation' is obscure, but Whistler's theory, as stated in his 'Propositions—No. 2', holds that 'a picture is finished when all trace of the means used to bring about the end has disappeared. . . . The work of the master reeks not of the sweat of the brow—suggests no effort—and is finished from its beginning.' See his *The Gentle Art of Making Enemies*, pp. 115–116.

[4] That is, a Manchester admirer of Max as author of notes accompanying

portraits of Lady Granby, Shaw, and Cunninghame Graham, in Rothenstein, *English Portraits* [plates 6, 16, 23].

⁵ The volume in green morocco is unaccounted for, as is the florid passage from, perhaps, an unrevised text for *Manchester Portraits*.

⁶ *Manchester Portraits* is dedicated to, and has a double portrait [plate 2] of Marianne (1834–1920) and Julia Gaskell (1846–1908), daughters of the Victorian novelist Mrs Elizabeth Gaskell (1810–1865).


❖28                    1 Pembroke Cottages, Edwardes Square, Kensington
                                                                April 5, 1900

My dear Max—Alec Ross was here last night, or I would gladly have come to meet you—perhaps I shall see you on Saturday—here is a ticket for the New English, where you can see Holman Hunt & Claude Monet hobnobbing together.¹ Walter has put a title from Ecclesiastes on to his Dieppe picture. I hope his severance from Whistler has not driven him to God, for if he became religious, I have an uncomfortable feeling it might turn into religious mania: you know the extraordinary logic of his attitude. Of course it may be an excellent jest.²

I can fancy your amusement this morning as you read of the Prince's smile, not a nervous one, but a genial spreading rosy smile, as he asked if the revolver was loaded.³

Spirit of Thackeray, body o' Beerbohm, how splendid it must have been!

I am hoping to come & see your caricatures soon; the above [two lines crossed out] is not pretty, but has a kind heart underneath. Do come in & play chess again soon. My kind regards to your people—
                                                                        Will


¹ Alexander Ross (1860–1927), elder brother of Robert Ross; literary critic. At the New English Art Club show, Dudley Gallery, London, during April 1900, '*Effet de neige*', by Claude Monet, hung beside 'Portrait of Dante G. Rossetti', by William Holman Hunt.

² On the Sickert–Whistler relationship, see Sickert, *A Free House! Or The Artist as Craftsman*, ed. Osbert Sitwell, pp. 6–41.

Sickert's 'Dieppe picture': 'O ye Light and Darkness, bless ye the Lord, praise Him, and magnify Him for ever', a Nocturne, representing a street lighted from surrounding windows. The title is from line 16 of the Benedicite, *Book of Common Prayer*. Sickert's habits of re-christening and of giving away pictures complicate identification of specific works. One scholar states that 'no picture extant is known by this title and Sickert was so prolific that it is a little dangerous to jump to the conclusion that the picture must be the one Dieppe night scene of the right date of which I know. There must be other paintings of similar subjects, painted at night, which are now untraced. However, the only candidate so far is "Quai Duquesne and

Will and Max in 1893

'Will R. in Faubourg & in Quartier.'
Caricature by
Max Beerbohm, *c.* 1893

Self-caricature of Max
in top hat, 1894

Oscar Wilde.
  Caricature by
  William Rothenstein,
  c. 1893

Aubrey Beardsley. Drawing
  by William Rothenstein,
  1894

'Will Rothenstein Laying Down the Law' to Oscar Wilde on Deportment: to Arthur Pinero on Playwriting: to Lord Coleridge on Law: to the Prince of Wales on Dress: to Aubrey Beardsley on Decadence: to Mr Charles Furse on Folly: to Lord Rosebery on La Haute Politique: to George Moore on Caution: to Mr Eugene Stratton on Art; to Himself on Modesty. Caricature by Max Beerbohm, *c.* 1895

*Left*. William Rothenstein. Drawing by G. P. Jacomb-Hood, 1896
*Right*. Max Beerbohm. Portrait by William Rothenstein, *c.* 1900

'Mr W. Rothenstein
and Mankind.'
Caricature by
Max Beerbohm, 1916

'Landed Gentry. No. 1.
Mr Albert Rothenstein.'
Caricature by
Max Beerbohm, 1913

Florence Beerbohm.
Drawing by
William Rothenstein,
1915

Max Beerbohm.
Drawing by
William Rothenstein,
1915

*Top.* Will and Alice Rothenstein with Gerhart Hauptmann at Rapallo, *c.* 1829. *Bottom left.* Caricature of Will Rothenstein's hat. Max Beerbohm, undated. *Bottom right.* Max and Florence Beerbohm at Rapallo, 1921

the Rue Notre Dame", now in the Western Australian Art Gallery in Perth, catalogued as Number 102.' (Wendy Baron to Mary Lago, November 16, 1972.) See Baron, *Sickert*, figure 70.

[3] See 'Attempt to Shoot the Prince of Wales: Arrest of His Assailant', *The Times*, April 5, 1900, p. 6. See no. 7 of the Edwardyssey for the smile.


◇29                                    Savile Club      June 27, 1900

My dear Will

Next Friday I can't come and sit, I am sorry to say. I have two business appointments, one for the morning, t'other (as Henley would say) for the afternoon, and both are important. Let me come instead another day.

I was so sorry when I found that you and Albert had called this morning unseen by me. My mother came and told me when I was in bed, but I was in a state of such complete stupor (not having gone to bed before 3.30) that I could not realise *anything* but the immediate necessity for groaning and getting further beneath the bed-clothes.[1]
Yours affectionately Max
P.S. I hope the recurrence of the old Velasquez-trouble has passed off, and that you are quite well & strong again.[2]

[1] The work in progress was a portrait painting, shown at the New Gallery, London, in November 1900, perhaps the portrait of Max now on loan from Sir John Rothenstein to the University Art Collection, Hull. See *Letters*, p. 134; D. S. M[acColl], 'The Society of Portrait Painters', *SR*, 90 (1900), 679.
[2] Rothenstein had tertian fever, which afflicted the Spanish painter Diego Velázquez.


◇30                           1 Pembroke Cottages      December 11, 1900

My dear Max—we are looking forward to to-night. It was good of you to send us seats. I know it will be delightful, but do hope your mummers will do you justice.[1] I don't expect you yourself will be nervous as to the result. Success is always standing near you, eager for any excuse of approaching you—other people give it so many opportunities, but success is not so ready with them as with you, spoiled child of un-natural genius—of caricature. Your World-drawings (rather a good name for your caricatures, welt-zeignungen) grow on me daily, & as I have some small faith in your writing, you should certainly achieve a position in the world of letters, equal to, if not greater than that of Mr Gosse, so that when, in years to come, the great Nicaraguan poet shall

43

appear among us, it may be you, Max, who will preside at the dinner the nation will offer him.[2]

To-night I shall pity you, for when I shall be cosy in my stall, surrounded by the most beautiful women in London, you, in spite of your glory, will be skulking in some shameful bar, regretting that your position will not allow you to show your face, as a gentleman should, to the world. Had your life been otherwise, had you stuck to legitimate caricature instead of being led astray by the seduction of Thespis you too might have been sitting at the Royalty beside me to-night, enjoying the legitimate amusement of relaxation from honest toil, able to bear the full light of the stage without flinching.

I will, in spite of my position, give you a thought to-night, even at the moment when the well earned enthusiasm of an evening honestly spent shall rise within me, & remembering Christ's teaching, will think for a moment of the sordid bar, where I can fancy your spending an evening in the vicinity of some shameless harridan, vainly trying to drown your shame with liquid stimulants. Adieu; I do not hide from you that should such feelings of enthusiasm to which I have referred above stir me, I shall not scruple, in spite of my thoughts of you, to give full voice to my emotion. My love to you—Will

[1] Max's dramatisation of *The Happy Hypocrite* opened December 11, 1900, as curtain-raiser for *Mr. and Mrs. Daventry*, a Frank Harris play based on a scenario by Oscar Wilde and produced by Mrs Patrick Campbell at the Royalty Theatre, October 25, 1900–February 23, 1901.

[2] Eight Beerbohm caricatures as a 1900 Christmas supplement to *The World* (London); for a list of subjects, see *Letters*, p. 134.

Gosse had presided at a dinner at the Carlton Hotel on November 30, 1900, for the Danish poet, Holger Drachmann (1846–1908).

---

⟡31                    1 Pembroke Cottages, Edwardes Square
                       Tuesday midnight [December 11, 1900]

My dear Max—you are incorrigibly successful. Your play really was a great success, & people were most enthusiastic; even I for a moment forsook my habitual reserve, & clapped my hands in spite of myself, several times. You were most fortunate in your mimes, & the maskmaker was quite splendid.[1] The play seemed to me to improve steadily as it progressed, & the end is admirable. I could feel the lump in the throat of the house rising as the curtain dropped. Everyone I saw liked the play unreservedly—I think it will go better still in a few nights, when the actors make more of the beauty of the lines than they did to-night. You were called for, as a dozen people will doubtless have written you, & Mrs Pat came on & said you were not in the house, but listening at the telephone.[2]

Your people were naturally delighted. Kilseen beamed very radiant —a new cloak of wonderful make did not in any way detract from her pleasure. Alice sends her love, & many congratulations—she enjoyed the H.H. as much as I.

I saw Frank Harris, who had been behind. I think Daventry good, & Mrs Pat I admired for the first time since the first time, admired her very much indeed—but did not think overmuch of the play—did you?[3] I hope to see you soon—perhaps to-morrow. Yours always—Will

[1] George Arliss (1868–1946) played the Mask-maker. See his *Up the Years from Bloomsbury: An Autobiography*, pp. 185–189.
[2] Max was in Brighton; see *Letters*, pp. 138–139.
[3] Mrs Campbell played Mrs Daventry. Frederick Kerr played Daventry.


⋄32      48 Upper Berkeley Street      Tuesday [late October 1901]

My dear Will

Very many apologies to you and to Alice for my absence the other night —and for the feverish telegram. What happened was this. I received a messenger from Hodge during the day with a ticket for a Fabian meeting which Archer was to address that evening on the usual subject. Hodge asked me to go if I possibly could; and as I am (for reasons which I will explain when I see you) particularly anxious to oblige him just now I thought I had better go.[1] So I sent you the wire, sacrificing to duty what I certainly should not (as you know) have sacrificed to any other pleasure —no other pleasure being equal. I ought to have written later to explain all this. I did not do so because I hoped to be able to come on Saturday or Sunday to explain with my own lips. But there again duty prevented me. I have had a lot of writing to do. So pray forgive me, and many thanks for your charming letter. I *will* cure myself of the telegram-fever, if I can. It is a deadly disease, to which all are liable who live in this fated city. You must guard your son against it.[2] Have his arm injected with the glue off the back of a postage-stamp. I am going to have mine done. With love to Alice Yours affectionately Max

[1] Harold Hodge (1862–1937), editor, *The Saturday Review*, 1898–1913. Max's

first exhibition of caricatures was to open at the Carfax Gallery in November 1901;
he perhaps hoped to propitiate an editor as influential as Hodge by reporting on
William Archer's October 25 lecture, 'The English Drama of the Last Twenty-Five
Years'; see 'Fabian Lectures', *Fabian News*, 11 (1901), 34.

Max betrayed some nervousness about this exhibition: 'By the way, how about
affixing some seals [denoting sales] for the Private View. Which of the drawings
are least likely to sell? But use your own discretion. . . . I hope the Private View
will go off nicely. I have enjoyed so much all that has led up to it. You are indeed
a delightful dealer to deal with.' (Beerbohm to Robert Ross [late October, 1901].
J-P. Ross.) The Private View went very nicely; see D. S. M[acColl], 'Portraits and
a Caricaturist', *SR*, 92 (1901), 738–739.

2 John Rothenstein was born on July 11, 1901.

---

~33                             1 Pembroke Cottages       November 2, 1901

My very dear Max—your article this morning, new laid on my plate,
was indeed grateful to me with my toast.1 Were I a Prince, which the
Gods forbid, I would confer on you the right to tell fibs; for I regard you
as one of the only lovers of truth it is my luck to know. Not to tell fibs is
not necessarily to be truthful, & most people who would scorn to tell a
lie never go near the well you & I know of. I have lost all patience with
the gross stupidity of most limners & scribblers—you, my dear Max,
delight me ever more. You are just & truthful & unpretentious, dear
friend; I think I have never read a more subtle yet more direct appreciation of a man than yours of Shaw in to-day's "Saturday". It is portrait
painting as I understand the art; understand it so well that I will never
more accept a commission for work of the kind. I liked your remark on
the necessary "closeness" of good art—& your last week's article was
delicious, & you are so sure of yourself, you are not afraid to laugh.2
Were I a Prince I would do many things for you. As a mere friend, I
will confer on you my indulgence. Va, your hats may be shiny, your shoes
shinier, go dine with the worthless, countenance their shameful un-
imaginativeness, worldliness & viciousness. You are beyond their
hideous spell, & they don't touch you, *for your tie is tied upon the rock.*
Always your affectionate friend—Will

I am hanging or selecting pictures to-morrow,3 & dining out on Tuesday
& Thursday. Will you come in one day other than these?

Thanks for your amusing note of the other day, I am anxious to hear
about Hodge.

1 In a review of a 1901 reprint of Shaw's novel, *Cashel Byron's Profession*, Max
appraised Shaw's achievements. See Beerbohm, 'A Cursory Conspectus of G.B.S.',
*SR*, 92 (1901), 556–557; reprinted in his *Around Theatres*, pp. 171–175.

² See Beerbohm, 'Luck Among Theatres', *SR*, 92 (1901), 523–524; reprinted in his *More Theatres*, pp. 410–414.

³ For the Society of Portrait Painters, at the New Gallery.

⋄34          26 Church Row, Hampstead¹     April 25, 1903

My very dear Max—I know it is awful for you to be asked to do any-thing for anybody; but as none of us expect you to fall into temptation, we feel ourselves less guilty in approaching you than we would in writing anything of the kind to less conscientious & less scrupulous people. My friend Steele is in a very bad way, having lost his post as sec[retary] to the chemical society. I really forget what you thought of his lever de rideau he sent you. Could anything, think you, be done with it? Will you write me a line on the subject, & if necessary, I will gild the pill in writing to Steele.²

Alice appears to have told your people I liked your article in the Saturday.³ Can you, cher, be as innocent as they & believe it? And do I not know your Roman justice towards your friends, we scratch your back & you scratch our eyes. And would any one have you otherwise? Not even Henry Arthur Jones. Yours always affectionately—Will

We are looking forward with pleasure to seeing you all on Wednesday.

¹ The Rothensteins had moved to Hampstead. 'Will's happiness,' Alice wrote, 'seems so centered in the country.' And—an important consideration—it was 'a very easy drive to H. for any probable portrait sitters.' (Alice to Moritz and Bertha Rothenstein [Summer 1902]. Rothenstein.)

² Robert Steele (1860–1944), science teacher and medievalist, was Assistant Secretary and Librarian of The Chemical Society, Burlington House, 1894–1902; then Librarian and Curator until April 1903, when he was dismissed because of irregularities, later corrected, in Society accounts. In 1925 he received a Civil List Pension and, in 1936, an honorary D.Litt. degree from Durham University. His *lever de rideau* (curtain-raiser) was a play with a medieval setting, written in 1902. He had asked whether Max might be persuaded to read and recommend it to Herbert Tree. (Steele to Rothenstein, February 15, 1902. RP:HL.) There is no evidence that Max did so.

³ A review of Gordon Craig's production of Ibsen's *The Vikings at Helgeland* (1858). See Beerbohm, 'At the Imperial Theatre', *SR*, 95 (1903), 517–518; reprinted in his *More Theatres*, pp. 562–565. Craig (1872–1966), actor and stage designer, was the son of actress Ellen Terry (1848–1928).

⋄35              Savile Club     Sunday [May 10, 1903]

My dear Will

Mrs. Hammersley has invited me to dinner next Sunday; so I suppose I shall meet you and Alice there; which will be nice.[1] I thought your letter in the *Saturday* awfully good. Craig must be very pleased. I remember when I read my own article I thought I had not been nearly enthusiastic enough.[2] I must buy some sort of patent-pen that will run away with me. Meanwhile, floreant "qui" post "nos nostra" non dicta "dixerunt"![3] With love to Alice Yours affectionately Max

[1] Hugh Hammersley (1858–1930), a partner in Cox's Bank, and his first wife, Mary Hammersley (1863–1911). Their home in The Grove, Hampstead, was a centre for artists; among them were Rothenstein, Steer, Beerbohm, Augustus John, and Henry Tonks.

[2] See Rothenstein, 'The Vikings', *SR*, 95 (1903), 588.

Nevertheless, Rothenstein, in his efforts to help Craig, almost invariably found it 'very uphill work fighting for him as people are very prejudiced against him and what he cares for. He has always been terribly impecunious ever since I have known him, and he doesn't seem to be able to get on with people who are inclined to give him work to do. I am afraid his theoretical ideas will never be appreciated here—the English have a great dislike for anything logical; it is only in the arrangement of their lives that they accept conventions and laws—they will have none in their art.' (Rothenstein to Mary [Mrs Bernard] Berenson, December 8, 1907. RP:HL.)

In 1908 Shaw complained: 'Craig is utterly unhelpable. I daresay that is very jolly for him; but he cannot enjoy himself in both ways. His only chance, as far as I can see, is to produce drawings and to sell them. After all, a drawing is a drawing: you see it before you buy it; and you put down your money and take away your purchase without further ado. But Craig wants to be employed in matters in which it is absolutely necessary that a man shall undertake definite work, and can be depended upon to carry it out competently and punctually. As he is notoriously averse to accepting these conditions, and probably incapable of fulfilling them, he has got into his present fix. After my experience of him with Caesar and Cleopatra in Berlin [in 1906], nothing would induce me to have anything more to do with him in stage matters. Theatrical productions are like battles: they cannot be trifled with. It is a pity; but Master Teddy's demand to have the world to play with is too exorbitant.' (Shaw to Rothenstein, February 4, 1908. RP:HL.)

[3] Max's Latin is faulty here but approximates 'May they flourish who speak after we have spoken.'

⬦36                                    26 Church Row    May 11, 1903

My very dear Max—I heard the marble halls at the Imperial were papered from top to bottom, & as I admired both the play & the production immensely, I thought I would, as Wedmore says, "register" my appreciation.[1] Yes, poor Mrs Hammersley evidently felt bound to ask us, as I introduced you, although she would fain have used your presence to better purpose—however, I feel sure this is only the beginning of a long acquaintance between you, & the dear woman will have fulfilled her duty to herself & me. But you are above all to bring your caricatures, of which I have spoken with eloquence; Tonks, who is staying at the Grove, is longing to see them, & Mrs H. must own them.[2] "Maniac" was immensely flattered of course to hear he had impressed you.[3]

To-morrow I dine with the "Maccabees"—have you ever, uncircumcised, been their guest?[4]

We look forward to seeing you on Sunday. Our kindest regards to your people—always affectionately yours—Will

[1] 'Papered': filled with recipients of complimentary tickets. Frederick Wedmore (1844–1921), critic, writer of short fiction; art critic, *The Standard*, 1878–1908.

[2] Perhaps the 'Edwardyssey'; see Letter 37, note 1. Max had probably met the Hammersleys by March 1903: 'Next time I come, I shall bring the caricature of Hammersley, since you both liked it so much, on condition that Will does not instantly present it to some deserving institution.' (Beerbohm to Alice Rothenstein, March 1903. RP:HL.)

[3] Major Hubert Magniac (1858–1909), Boer War hero.

[4] The Maccabaeans, a society of Jewish professional men, founded in 1892, are still in existence. Rothenstein was a guest on May 15, 1903, at a dinner honouring the Dutch Jewish painter, Jozef Israëls (1824–1911).

❖37        48 Upper Berkeley Street    Tuesday [late May 1903]

My dear Will

Back from Oxford, and heard from Tonks, delicately, that Mrs. Hammersley "nibbles." And I have written to him, saying that £60 is the price for the Edwardyssey—I should have said £50, only an American agent the other day offered me £100, with rights of reproduction for limited sale, which I had to refuse for obvious reasons, but which raised my stomach. I don't know whether Mrs. Hammersley will shy at the price.[1] If she doesn't, then you are the fairy-godfather—and must accept, please, some sort of a commission, either in cash or in kind—the kind of caricatures that will fetch enormous prices when both of us are under the "aromatic sod." Am I indelicate? What with Tonks and Mrs H. and myself, to say nothing of Major Magniac, to whom I lent the drawings for the delectation of his brother, the invalid,—and what with Miss Brook, who admired them so much and thought me such a perfect gentleman, there is so much delicacy flying about that I hardly know where I am.[2] With love to Alice, and to John. Yours affectionately

Max

[1] Max was temporarily out of funds: 'But the god Hammersley will have

49

sprung out of the machine before the end of the month.' Two days later, Hammersley sent £60. (Beerbohm to Reginald Turner, [May 23] May 25, 1905. BP:HL.) The 'Edwardyssey', now owned by Mr and Mrs Benjamin Sonnenberg of New York, N.Y., was never exhibited until shown with the Philip Guedalla Collection in September–October 1945.

[2] Major Magniac's brother was Charles Vernon Magniac. Miss Brook was perhaps one of the daughters of Stopford A. Brooke (1832–1916), theologian and literary historian.

❧38  Savile Club, 107 Piccadilly W.  June 26, 1903

My dear Alice Mary and William and why not John, while one is about it?

I am so very sorry; next Wednesday I am engaged for a dinner and can't get out of it—I do wish I could have come. It is so long since I have seen either of you. Won't you come and dine at U[pper] B[erkeley] S[treet] some day towards the end of next week? Say Friday, or Saturday? We should all be so delighted to receive you at 7.30 on either of those days. I have just been eating a dinner in honour of dear old Sidney Colvin's oncoming nuptials. He made a charming speech—Mrs. Sitwell flitting up in the exordium, and Robert Louis Stevenson occupying the whole of the peroration.[1]

Please write to me at UBS whenever you can & will dine. Yours affectionately. Max

[1] Sir Sidney Colvin (1845–1927), Slade Professor of Fine Art, Cambridge, 1873–1885; Director, Fitzwilliam Museum, 1876–1884; Keeper, Prints and Drawings, British Museum, 1884–1912. In July 1903 he married Mrs Frances Fetherstonhaugh Sitwell (1839–1924). Both before and after marriage the Colvins were conspicuously solicitous of the welfare of R. L. Stevenson (1850–1894). Sir Sidney was Stevenson's London representative, 1887–1894, and prepared the Edinburgh Edition of his *Works*.

❧39  26 Church Row  December 7, 1903

My dear Max—I shall be most pleased to come on Saturday or Sunday, whichever day circumstances permit—& circumstances may permit of my coming on both nights, & those of the week following. It will be pleasant to see your people again—I have been unusually busy getting new work started, & also getting into a new room at Spitalfields, where I am preparing to paint "scenes of Jewish life."[1] I saw some very delicious Jacques Bull caricatures in The Sketch & shall hope to see more during the time I am dining with you this & next week.[2] Moore was comparatively payable on this visit to London—you shall hear news of him anon.[3] In the meanwhile I am yours always affectionately—Will

[1] Rothenstein's studio, in a building no longer standing, faced Spital Square. He asked Alfred Wolmark (1877–1961), one of East London's first Jewish artists, to arrange for him to paint local types there. Until 1906, he worked on eight major paintings at the Machzike Hadath, or Spitalfields Great Synagogue. Max's banter picked up the Jewish motif: 'I haven't seen Will since he went away. I hear he is just off on a flying visit to Palestine, to restore the tomb of Moses, with the profits he has made on his painting during the past year. Alice, it seems, is not properly enthusiastic about the scheme. But Will is determined to go through with it.' (Beerbohm to Albert Rothenstein [1904?]. MCT.) He wrote to Alice: 'Will arrived on his bicycle but sternly refused to cross the threshold—probably because of some Jewish feast or fast: the threshold was unleavened, or there ought to have been blood on the lintel, or something of that kind; anyhow, Will would not come in.' (Beerbohm to Alice Rothenstein, October 1905. RP: HL.) William's younger brother Albert (1881–1953), painter and stage designer, wrote about 'a sheet of delightful caricatures of you as a Rabbi—the "Mosaic Conscience" [Max] calls them—he has also done a large one of you as the "Messiah" surrounded by a crowd of Jews, you standing on a table in their midst.' (Albert to William Rothenstein [February 1906]. RP: HL.) On four of the Synagogue paintings, see WR, p. 164. A fifth is in the Johannesburg Art Gallery; a sixth is owned by Mrs Jenny Anderson; two are unaccounted for, as are most of the many studies and drawings undoubtedly done at Spitalfields. On Max's drawing of Rothenstein as the Messiah, see Catalogue, p. 122; his 'Mosaic Conscience' drawings: owner unknown.

[2] See Beerbohm, 'The Visit of the English M.P.'s to Paris', The Sketch (London), 44 (1903), 219. 'Jacques Bull caricatures' alludes to Beerbohm, Cartoons: 'The Second Childhood of John Bull'; see Catalogue, pp. 167–168, 172.

[3] The Irish novelist, George Moore (1852–1933).

◇40          48 Upper Berkeley Street          Tuesday [March 1905]

Dearest Will

The drawings are being mounted with all possible despatch; and you shall have them as soon as they are finished. I have told the framers to do them in *plain* mounts (same *size*, etc. as the *Poets' Corner* ones) without marginal lineation; for my own opinion is that the marginal lineation destroys the effect of my drawings—is too strong for them—swamps them—except when I have made *bold* work with a quill.

However, if you dissent, or if you think marginal lineation would please the millionairish eye of your brother-in-law, let me know; and the thing shall be done.[1]

It is most charming of you to have secured these drawings—to have purged, in some degree, the Augean stable which is my sitting-room.

Of course, you may object that it isn't charming of you at all. But your "deal" with Sickert the other day could be brought up in evidence against you.[2] Yours ever Max

[1] Drawings, unidentified, for possible purchase by Edgar Hesslein (1864–1938), partner in the New York textile firm of Neuss and Hesslein, husband of Rothenstein's sister Emily (1868–1961), and owner of potentially valuable contemporary paintings, many purchased on William's advice.

[2] Rothenstein's 'deals' with Sickert often involved assistance with sales through the Carfax Gallery, or five- and ten-pound payments from friends like Jacques-Émile Blanche (1861–1942), French painter and writer, associate of the New English Art Club, of the Wagner enterprises at Bayreuth, and of the Ballet Russe.

Max, however, maintained a poor opinion of Sickert's business acumen: 'The other night, walking down the hill, I tried to drive into, and to corroborate and fix and obdurate in, Sickert's mind the admirable advice that Will had given him. But I know Sickert so well, and I am sure he will have cleverly muddled away, meanwhile, such chance as he had of enriching himself through those Whistler panels. If he leaves England with a "tenner" in his capacious pocket I shall be surprised; and he will be more than pleased.' (Beerbohm to Alice Rothenstein [March 1905?]. RP:HL.)

41　　　　　　　　　　The Venice Arms, Edgeware Road [London]
　　　　　　　　　　　　　　　　Thursday [late March? 1905?]

Mister Rothenstine
Honoured Sir

I hereby returns the lone wot you wos affable enough to lone me thother night as being a man of honour myself and scorning not to be would wish a reseat for same for well I knows one carnt never be too careful in this ere vale of tears but in the hope this finds you well as it leeves me and may Heven never bless you with less bright days than at present[1] Yours respecful Max Beerbohm

[1] From a transcript (MCT) which bears an approximation of a sketch of a ragged man begging in the gutter and a young man dropping a coin into his hand: 'Beautiful Action Performed by the Young Squire', with the caption, 'I was a gentleman once, Sir.'

It is of course possible that this note was addressed to Albert Rothenstein, but about this same time Max wrote charmingly to Alice Rothenstein: 'How very nice indeed! Quite a windfall—a bolt from the blue, through the letter-box; and I, crouching on the door-mat, shoot the bolt promptly, and away slinks the wolf, howling dismally. My thanks to Will, and also to you for projecting the missile.' (Beerbohm to Alice Rothenstein, March 22, 1905. RP:HL.) Money worries were chronic at Upper Berkeley Street; Alice reported on one occasion that 'Mrs. B. is evidently very hard up, as she says "impossible ways and no means".' (Alice to William Rothenstein, n.d. Rothenstein.)

✧42                         48 Upper Berkeley Street
Wednesday night [early May 1906]

Dearest Will

Just come in and found your letter: also one to a similar effect from Stirling Lee. Flattered but frightened. And am writing to S. L. to tell the Committee how much honoured, but how bad an orator, I am. Haldane proposes: I dispose of myself.[1]

If *I* were proposing a toast, I might manage it decently enough; for then I could make an effect through preparation.

But, in *response* to a toast, no effect can be made without spontaneity —I mean, without taking up the points made by the proposer.

I have, before now, "faked" spontaneity—getting the proposer to tell me beforehand the sort of thing he was going to say. But I can't do that with Haldane—I don't know him personally. And if I went down to the War Office and sent in my card...well, you know what a lot of red tape there is at the War Office. So I am telling Stirling Lee that he must get some worthier person than myself—Edmund Gosse, for example, who, I hear, is going to be present. I should have loved to do the thing. But in me, ever, discretion "downs" vanity.

Love to Alice and to all. Your affectionate Max

[1] Thomas Stirling Lee (1856–1926), sculptor, and his wife were honorary secretaries of a committee to sponsor an exhibition by German artists at Prince's Galleries, Knightsbridge, inaugurated with a dinner at the Savoy Hotel on May 22, 1906. Rothenstein had proposed this exhibition after he had heard the German ambassador speak at the Lyceum Club in 1905; the idea was implemented as recognition of honour paid to British artists in Germany. Presiding was R. B. Haldane, 1st Viscount Haldane (1856–1928), Secretary of State for War, 1905–1912. Rothenstein proposed the toast to 'Our Guests, the German Artists'. Max was present but said nothing for the record.

✧43           48 Upper Berkeley Street     January 13, 1907

Dearest Will

Here are "the Rothensteins at home"—a sort of pendant, though a very unworthy one, to Albert's delightful picture of them abroad. Rebecca and Bertha I have had to do from "chic": they are probably much more charming than they appear here.[1] And the three persons whom I *do* know well by sight suffer obviously under my pen. But there is in the whole design a sense of a *family*, I think—something spiritually real, though not up to the mark of our old friend Giotto—(I say *our* old friend, because I regard any friend of yours as a friend of mine). What a dear little boy John is! So sunny and happy and always saying the pleasant thing to everybody: so *safe* and in that respect so unlike most other children—a great credit to you and Alice as bringers-up. At least, I hope it *is* a question of up-bringing. If his charm came naturally to him, I should be afraid he was a humbug!—such as you always accuse *me* of being.

Love to Alice Yours affectionately Max

[1] 'Rebecca': Rachel Rothenstein, born on December 19, 1903. Bertha (Betty) Rothenstein, born June 15, 1905. These drawings by Albert Rothenstein and by Max are unidentified, and present owners unknown.

⟨44    26 Church Row    January 14, 1907

My dearest Max

we were simply enchanted with your beautiful picture—merci de coeur—it is so good in these days of so-called realism & ugliness worship to find some one who is not affected by the monster modernity, & can still put into his work the dear, the human, the eternal beauty that lies in the relation 'twixt parents & children. Never, dearest friend, allow the sneaking & paltry spirit of cynicism to enter into & besmirch the fairness of your mind. Your gift will always be among my dearest & most precious possessions—thanks, again & again, thanks. I have, as have most men, met with much that is hard & selfish among the experiences of life, but such gifts as yours & the knowledge of such natures as yours, do more than any thing else to wipe out the memory of disagreeable things & make one believe in the eternal goodness of men & women, & in the triumph of kindness over evil.[1]

I loved your drawing, dear Max, & in return you shall take all this letter as a joke if you will; but just as much as you choose not to take in this spirit shall be true. Ever your affectionate friend—Will

[1] Alice Rothenstein was less lyrical but no less appreciative: 'How dear of you to make that lovely picture of us. We are all delighted—except Nurse, who says it's a wicked shame to give our lovely baby those skinny arms. We are perfectly delighted

with it. There is so much more in it than meets the eye—truly you are wicked—that cock of John's left foot makes me, for the first time in his 5½ years, pause to think of his future. Will is enchanted with the design and appears much amused at the blondness of the children.' (Alice Rothenstein to Beerbohm, January 14? 1907. BP: MC.)

Sarah Adkins (1854–1931) joined the Rothenstein family as nurse when Albert was born, and until her death was associated with various branches of the family.

∽45           6 Walmer Villas, Bradford    April 1, 1907

Dearest Max—I am writing Alice to send you the master-work, it is already mounted & framed. Albert has told me of the moving character of your latest religious picture—I burn to see it, & hope to before many days, for I return to Hampstead shortly. I predict a storm of applause for your show; you stand alone in the seriousness of your purpose & the directness of your interpretation—using the material only in order to express what you feel about men & life—not for its own sake.[1] I think Ruskin has taught me more about your art than any man, & since reading him I am getting nearer each day to a more perfect understanding of your work & of your soul—I thought of you all the time I was reading the wonderful Stones of Venice; to pass to lighter & less serious subjects, I hear your brother is taking Shakespeare to Germany. I fear the Germans may be disappointed with the English version of Shakespeare, being so used to the noble translation by Puffendorf & the less known one of Strumm.[2]

I was here interrupted by Albert, who has just written to The Times to protest against the lopping & cutting down of trees without the use of chloroform, or some previous injection of cocaine or some other compound which would render them insensitive to pain; he asks me to use my influence with you to ask you to join all those who have the interest of the arboreal world at heart in their protest against the inhuman torture inflicted by heartless brutes on their brothers; the publication of von Bliemendeck's book on arboreal consciousness should bring home to all men the barbarous atrocities perpetrated during many centuries on these noble creatures.[3] If therefore I have taken up more of your time than I should have done, you will understand that my knowledge of your quick sympathy with all that pertains to humanity will readily condone my presumption. I am, ever yours affectionately—Will

I trust you will lay my respects at the feet of your revered mother.

*new address*

11 Oak Hill Park, Frognal        Hampstead

[1] The 'master-work' is unidentified. The 'latest religious picture' was probably Max's drawing, 'A Quiet Morning in the Tate Gallery—the Curator trying to expound to one of the Trustees [Alfred de Rothschild] the spiritual fineness of Mr William Rothenstein's "Jews Mourning in a Synagogue"'; see *Catalogue*, p. 97. D. S. MacColl (1859–1948), Keeper ['Curator'] of the Tate Gallery, 1906–1911, and of the Wallace Collection, 1911–1924. Rothenstein's Synagogue painting was shown at the New English Art Club in 1906, bought by Jacob Moser of Bradford, and presented to the Tate Gallery in 1907. On the Beerbohm exhibition at the Carfax Gallery, see Laurence Binyon, '"Max"; and a Peep at the Academy', *SR*, 103 (1907), 553–554.

[2] At the Kaiser's invitation, Herbert Tree's company performed in the Royal Opera House, Berlin, April 15–20, 1907. The Royal Family and the general public were enthusiastic. Opera House personnel were antagonistic, and the deteriorating situation was meticulously reported in London newspapers.

[3] Puffendorf, Strumm, von Bliemendeck, and Albert Rothenstein's letter to *The Times*: all equally non-existent.

❖46      11 Oak Hill Park    Wednesday [early April 1908]

My dear Max—I am requested to ask you whether you will come to Cambridge next Saturday a fortnight (the 18th I think) to stay for the week end with the Darwins. Albert is to come too. Francis D. would be delighted to see you, & so would his enchanting friend W. R. who is excellent company when he is off the subjects of God, the Universe & the society for the preservation of modern buildings. There is also Miss Frances Darwin, who owns all your caricatures she can get, & whose mind, if as deep as a coal mine, is as limpid as a well. I hope you will condescend to come—there are not many people quite so delightful as the Ds & I think you would feel happy with them.[1]

We are very sorry you cannot lend grace to our house while we are away—please give my dear love to your mother; also my quite unnecessary wishes for your usual triumph at Carfax. I am looking forward to a fine entry there this afternoon. Love to all—yours ever Will

[1] Sir Francis Darwin (1848–1925), botanist, son of Charles Darwin. Rothenstein was painting a portrait in Cambridge; see Letter 47, note 1. Max did not make this visit, probably because of preparations for a Carfax exhibition, April 29–May 13, 1908. In 1908 Frances Darwin (1886–1960), poet, became engaged to Francis Cornford (1874–1943), classicist and Fellow of Trinity College, Cambridge.

❖47    Balliol Croft, Madingley Road, Cambridge[1]    May 4, 1908

My dear Max—I enjoyed your show immensely as usual; I think the

tea party at O.B.'s lingers most delightfully in my memory, & Barrie with the weeping parents & yawning children makes me perform horn-pipes in the midst of my labours. If you publish a second book you must call it "Sermons on Mounts" by Max, & dedicate it to Robbie [Ross], who has I take it looked after these accessories of your wit.[2] Like Archer, one word of warning; in one or two drawings I notice an inclination to draw like a "professional" artist; this brought tears to my eyes & misgivings to my heart; you might in time I admit draw as well as Pegram, but why not go on drawing better than anybody else?[3]

Your own sense of form is such a wonderful one & has been such a delight to all of us that you mustn't let yourself be tempted by any other—unless it be a developement of your beautiful formula for every thing which exists on the face of the world; you are one of the few people living who can give abstract qualities & forms & you must not prefer a man's gifts to a God's. A little fickleness, a flirtation with one of the daughters of men, & you go back, I hope, to Olympus. Ever yours, my dear Max, with love to all, Will

[1] Address of Alfred Marshall (1842–1924), Professor of Political Economy at Cambridge University, 1885–1908; St John's College owns the Rothenstein portrait (1908). A copy by Rothenstein (1935) is in the Marshall Library, Cambridge.

[2] Oscar Browning (1837–1923), historian and biographer; Cambridge don, 1876–1909. James M. Barrie (1860–1937), of *Peter Pan* fame (1904). Max's drawings at the Carfax Gallery: 'Mid-term tea at Mr. Oscar Browning's' and 'Mr. J. M. Barrie in a nursery—telling a story . . .'; see *Catalogue*, plates 24, 34.

3. Frederick Pegram (1870–1937), book illustrator, contributing artist for *Pall Mall Gazette, Punch,* and *The Pictorial World.*

48          11 Oak Hill Park     Sunday night [March 21, 1909]

Dear Max—I am so staggered by your letter that I cannot easily answer it. I had not the remotest notion that I had been offensive, any more than that I was so when you came, at my suggestion, to the Darwins—I believed that you would like them & I felt sure they would like you.[1] If there were any foundation of truth in my crude chaff about your written words, I could understand that you would have cause to complain; but as we all look upon you as the soundest of sound critics & as I have so long & so consistently admired & praised your work, that it never entered my head that you would view my words as being offensive.

Of course I can only express my deep regret that I should have wounded you—above all, that this should have led you to make this altogether unexpected onslaught on myself. I can only bow my head, but I would give a good deal had you not written me as you have done. If I have ever hurt your pride as you have trampled on mine, may God forgive me. There are circumstances which make your letter very cruel to me, and if I spoke to you in reference to [Augustus] John it was because I never for one moment doubted your friendship.[2] One thing I must say, that in spite of what you say to me regarding my having no friends, I am still happy in the belief that I have earned the love & affection of many good men & women, which I hope to keep.

There is something I do not understand in your letter, which shows, in spite of its ending, a real dislike to me; it is so unexpected that I cannot at this moment end mine in the same way; not that I am resentful or angry, but I am so upset & grieved & humbled that I feel incapable of saying more. It seems so tragic & unreal to me that you should ever have written me a letter of this kind, and you did not even give me a hint when I came out to the door with you of what was in your mind.

You have for so long been in the habit of chaffing me about my pedantry & bourgeoisism that I have got into the habit of assuming the part when I meet you; no one has committed more follies than I, & has less right to think himself more virtuous than his fellows; but that does not prevent me from admiring nobility of conduct, & if I expressed admiration for mid-Victorian friendships, you must have known to what I was referring. Yours—Will

[1] Apparently a visit to the Darwins in Cambridge earlier in 1909, during which Rothenstein's banter irritated Max, who seems to have said nothing until after a similar incident on March 19, 1909, at the London home of Mrs Grace Chadbourne (d. 1919), wife of New York corporation lawyer Thomas Chadbourne (1871–1938). Two crucial Beerbohm letters to Rothenstein are missing, one written on March 20, after the visit to Mrs Chadbourne, the other, early on March 23; see *Max*, pp. 256–257.

[2] On March 19, 1909, Rothenstein lectured at Cambridge on 'A Basis for the Appreciation of Art'. Robert Ross suggested, gratuitously and anonymously, that Rothenstein, when he spoke of artists 'who provoke the fretful observations from the public on ugliness', alluded to John. Rothenstein mentions him in neither the typescript used at Cambridge (RP: HL) nor the published version, but says only that the public wonders 'why the artist so often seems to go out of his way to choose the ugly. But it is the artist's privilege to see the element of hope and of beauty in much that appears sordid and hopeless. It is not that he cares for sordid things, and were it in his power to choose he would love to linger over the flowers and butterflies . . .' See Rothenstein, 'A Basis for the Appreciation of Art', *The Modern Review* (Calcutta), 13 (1913), 128; [Ross] 'Art and Artists', *The Morning Post*, March 23, 1909, p. 4.

Rothenstein's feelings toward John undoubtedly combined admiration and uneasiness; in 1899 he had written from Vattetot: 'We are all working pretty hard—myself, a charming Irishman, and a brilliant Welshman, one John of Tenby; he is very like a genius—I remember in your letter you asked if there were any new ones —he certainly has genius, but is very excessive in all his tastes, and has not yet settled down. I am praying for him, for he's a charming creature, daily.' (Rothenstein to Margaret Woods, August 10, 1899. RP:HL.) The 'charming Irishman' was William Orpen (1878–1931), who in 1901 married Alice Rothenstein's sister, Grace Knewstub (1877–1948). Max admired John's genius but found his personality bizarre.


◇49                     11 Oak Hill Park     March 23, 1909

My dear Max—I do indeed feel from your letter that your affection for me is real, & know you have mistaken my bad manners for something else. I wish I could make you realise how utterly mistaken you have been, & how bewildered I was by your letter. It was the old, old jest of the N.E.A.C. article, when you told Alice you didn't pretend to know anything about pictures, but had your article to think of, I was referring to, when I said I had heard you say it, & I thought you knew what I was chaffing you about.[1] It seems to me so mad to think I could have been so stupid as to give you so untrue a view of my feelings. I have never thought of you other than as a sort of fixed friend, & although I have always known other people amused you more, I did not think you were actually fonder of any one else. You always teased me about my "timid before the male", & my "Liverpool" side, & I you about being so truthful that I could always tell when you were fibbing, & I suppose I got into bad habits before other people, & went too far; but as for meaning to hit you in earnest, that has never entered my head; nor do I quite understand even now about the assumed superiority, & why my remark about my profession being less noble than it was should have offended you so much.[2] Surely our friendship has been close & beautiful enough, & I have always trusted you absolutely, & confided in you many times, & your house has been to me different from any house. I told you how sorry I was that I hurt you—you must know I could not do such a thing knowingly. But it seemed to me you hit me hard because I am an easy man to hit, & it was unlike you to do so just after I had shown you what wounds my friends have made, & I could not understand the fierceness of your attack, for there was *nothing, nothing whatsoever* in my consciousness to cause it. It seems odd to me that you who are so quick could think me disloyal, or patronising, to yourself. You must remember that people who are not very successful are more assertive than others;

59

my work is dull & unpopular, & the faith that is in me comes out in its basest form—I am only too well aware of that, & I am painfully aware of my shortcomings. I think if I may say a word in self-defence that I am not so self-righteous as you think; but I do genuinely admire real courage & character & virtue; because I fail I am not going to pretend those who are better men than I am are fools & poseurs & moralists, & I do feel a lack of beauty in the attitude of many of my own confrères, as Whistler called them.[3] You know I have not been unwilling to speak up for those who have seemed to me real people, whatever their morals may have been. But by nature we are inclined to justify ourselves, I don't expect we could face life if we didn't, & I am most willing to believe that you see me more truly. It seemed to me a terrible thing that this un-dreamed of difference should come between us, & that you had suddenly destroyed a feeling that had never lessened, cut at its roots & that it would scarcely be able to grow strong again. But I do believe what you write me from the heart, I am sure you feel deep affection for me as I for you, & that you would not wish to mar our friendship. I do not resent what you wrote me, nor really do I think you were wrong to be angry, only I wish I could make you understand how wrong you were in what you thought. Surely you could see when I came out with you how innocent I was of offence. But I realise that chaff in front of others is a dangerous & unkind sport, & that I am too heavy handed for anything of the kind. I feel nothing but the deepest affection for you, fraternal & unquestioning. Let us, with so much that is grey in life, keep this bright & clean. Alice knows nothing of this cloud—you were angry & have eased your heart; it has fallen in a shower of rain, & having wet me to the skin, shall not go deeper. Ever yours, dear Max, affectionately Will

[1] This letter assembles diverse and potentially troublesome themes. Max had viewed as a 'joke' his being asked to review a New English Art Club exhibition in 1903: 'The joke was obvious enough to give me a sweet sense of irresponsibility, yet not so sheerly ludicrous as to rob me of all self-importance.' See Beerbohm, 'A Gallery of Significant Pictures', *SR*, 95 (1903), 483–484.

[2] Augustus John, like William and Albert Rothenstein, was a friend and protégé of The Hon. H. C. Dowdall (1868–1955), Liverpool lawyer, Lord Mayor in 1908–9; and his wife, Mary Dowdall (1876–1939), daughter of the 16th Lord Borthwick. 'Liverpool side' is an allusion to the Dowdalls' friendship and patronage, and per-haps to the mock-chivalric idiom that both William and Albert Rothenstein employed in correspondence and conversation with Mrs Dowdall. The phrase, 'timid before the male', appears twice in an outline, written about 1909, for a sketch on Rothen-stein. (Beerbohm holograph notebook: Henry W. and Albert A. Berg Collection, The New York Public Library, Astor, Lenox and Tilden Foundations.)

[3] The lost Beerbohm letter of March 20 apparently implied that Rothenstein's

concern for high principles in the practice of art contributed to the quarrel. However, Max himself had often encouraged this tone and had implied that he found it not only inoffensive but amusing, as, for example: 'It is an appallingly long time since I sat at your feet—when may I come?' (Beerbohm to Rothenstein, February 19, 1903. RP:HL.) Sometimes he was more cautious, as when he regretted his inability to 'come to exchange silent smiles with you whilst those eminent generalisers generalised. . . . Will's pictures at the New English look very distinguished and beautiful. But I know you resent me as art-critic. So no more from [me].' (Beerbohm to Alice Rothenstein [Spring 1910?]. RP:HL.)

❖50                    48 Upper Berkeley Street      March 24, 1909

My dear Will

You can't think how I rejoiced to have your letter today, and to know that all is well between us now and hereafter—not only *well*, indeed, but *better*, so far as I am concerned; just as one realises more clearly the value of a treasure after one has been scared by chance of losing in it. We have disabused our minds of much. But it still remains for you, apparently, to get rid of a notion that "other people amuse" me more than you do. On the contrary, there is no one whose presence delights me more than yours; in a small degree because your strenuousness gives my sense of humour a chance; and in a far greater degree because your brain is so very cogent and brilliant. Also; what is all this about your work being "dull and unpopular," and about yourself being "not very successful"? I daresay you haven't all the success you deserve. But what good artist *has*, in his lifetime? Meanwhile, the Universities and the Colonies and a decent number of private persons are yours to command, and your position in art is firmly established, and acknowledged. You are one of the very few outstanding persons. Evidently you hanker after the dignity and picturesqueness and pathos which go with failure and which are so lamentably lacking to success. But you can't, dear Will, have it both ways. And personally (gross though you will think me) I am glad that you have it in the way that is vouchsafed to you![1] Yours affectionately Max

[1] Max told Florence Kahn: 'Will Rothenstein and I have *quite* made it up; and the sort of vague hostility that had for some time superimposed itself on our friendship will have disappeared for good.' A month later he wrote: 'I hear that Rothenstein was dissatisfied with the way his pictures had been hung [for an "Exhibition of Chosen Pictures" at the Grafton Galleries], and that Ricketts was rude to him, and he went away very angry, taking his picture. I feel really sorry; for he is so touchy, and people really do seem to behave rather ill to him, and he is likely to

become so embittered.' (Beerbohm to Florence Kahn [late March; April 23, 1909.] MCT.)

✧51                                  11 Oak Hill Park    May 11, 1910

My dearest Max—I have been putting off writing to you until I had a good half hour's leisure, a thing that hasn't happened to me this last week or more. The inner contemplation of you taking your ease in a country cottage, sitting at the feet of a fair wife, has been a very living image; I could have wished it gilded by rays of that May sun we read of in pre-Chaucerian poets, but at least it dances to the songs of many sweetly singing birds.[1] I send you my most ardent congratulations & hope the swift pigeon who bears them to you will drop this note at your feet. For your wife Alice & I have always felt very great admiration & sympathy, & I hope she will allow us to regard her with the same love we bear, & have always felt, for yourself. Indeed your marriage brings you still closer to us—to me at least, for you no longer will be surrounded by that peculiar & elusive distinction the bachelor holds in the married household. You are one of us, & we meet on equal terms, no longer superior to our joys & sorrows, but sharing them. You have chosen a noble lady as partner, & the privileges of such a choice you know well. Her devotion to yourself has been as clear as the daffodils growing in the grass, & Alice, with the practical instinct of her sex, had long united you both in her created world. I had been meaning to write to ask news of the Saturday decision, & now it is of course all clear to me.[2] Will the country now claim you, English country I mean, or will Italy harbour you & warm you with its sun?[3] Strange that Britain has laid claim to most earthly territories, & neglected to plant the flag of St. George in the midst of that radiant planet. From house to house we all send you our greetings, our warmest congratulations & tribute of deep affection.

Pray commend me to your wife, & say nice things of me to her, as of one who, clumsy & inefficient, yet has not on the whole an evil nature or a cold heart, & who loves the beauty of the world. Ever yours—& your wife's, dear Max—Will

[1] Max Beerbohm and Florence Kahn were married on May 4, 1910, in the Paddington Registry Office, with only Reginald Turner and Eliza Beerbohm as witnesses; the honeymoon was spent at Hythe, Kent.
[2] Max's 'Saturday decision' had been made by December 1909. His valedictory article was 'Habit', *SR*, 109 (1910), 491–492; reprinted in Beerbohm, *Around Theatres*, pp. 576–579.

62

³ When Max swore Turner to silence about the impending marriage, he warned him also not to 'mention that we *may* live in Italy. One thing is certain: we shan't live in *London*, but somewhere that is uncomplicated and pleasant and easy and unfussy and lets one be oneself' (*Letters*, p. 184).


◇52             Villino Chiaro, Rapallo¹      October 1910

My dearest Will

This is first of all to wish you a very good voyage to India, and a very happy and memorable time there. I wish your boat would set you down at Genoa on the way home, or that you would disembark at Naples and come on here, taking Horne and Giotto on the way.²

The second purpose of this letter is to thank you for the beautiful letter I had from you just after my marriage. This is rather late in the day for thanks: the thanks must seem a trifle stale to you. But your letter itself is as fresh as ever, and has always been in my thoughts. And (wretchedly bad correspondent though I am) I would have answered it long ago; only, whenever I was going to sit down and take pen in hand, I was deterred by the thought that my letter must be a very beautiful one in return, and by the knowledge that I should fall far below the mark—as I now am doing! I didn't at all agree with what you said about the "distinction" which unmarried men had in your eyes (e.g. Tonks, etc). In *my* eyes, at least, they are positively vulgar; and lamentable, also, and incomprehensible. And every day and all day I am thankful not to be one of them—though I cannot imagine that I ever would have ceased to be one of them but for the blessed dispensation by which Florence came into my life. She is even more an angel than I had ever guessed, absolutely perfect in everything, and adorable. And I am as happy as the day is long. And I think *she* is, too. And it is a great joy for us to be together in a very beautiful place, quite alone. Do come and see us—*please*.

Well, dear Will, best wishes again for you in India—and also best love to Alice—(to whom Florence is writing—not having written sooner because she was loyally waiting for me to write to you). Your loving friend Max

¹ In August 1910 the Beerbohms rented this villa beside the Genoa–Rome highway.
² In 1896 Herbert Horne had bought a house in Florence; he settled there permanently in 1912.

# PART TWO

# The Ex-Arcadians

Oh, give me legends, fairly recent legends, all the time!
Thank Heaven, we ourselves have a legendary touch
about us! We are ex-Arcadians, greatly envied by the
young.

> Beerbohm to Rothenstein
> May 21st 1942[1]

# INTRODUCTION

ROTHENSTEIN AND BEERBOHM, all their lives, maintained a remarkable consistency, a fundamental equilibrium, in their respective views of life and of the arts. Not always without regrets, but with equanimity, they accepted the demise of what had seemed Arcadia in the 1890's and in the Edwardian years. What the perceptive young of later generations envied in them was the temper of their minds and their ability to adjust, each in his own way, to the post-Arcadian world.

Rothenstein returned from India in March 1911, to a London art community that was still in a state of high excitement over Roger Fry's first Post-Impressionist exhibition at the Grafton Galleries. Fortuitous circumstances connected with Fry's second exhibition were to become a point of division in Rothenstein's career. For almost a year, he and Fry had been pursuing different interests, but relations between them were cordial, albeit in a state of delicate balance. Early in 1910 Rothenstein had declined to compete with Fry for the vacant Slade Professorship of Fine Art at Oxford.[2] When Fry was not appointed, Rothenstein wrote that he felt 'sick at heart. . . . Why is it that those who have services to render, and long to offer them so that full use may be made of their offerings are nearly always left to their own resources? I can only say to you what you say so generously to me—you are perfectly safe. Indeed, for certain reasons I believe you will do nobler work as an independent spirit than as a Professor of Art.'[3]

Fry promptly began to operate as an 'independent spirit'; he had the use of the Grafton Galleries for the autumn, and he organised the Post-Impressionist exhibition that opened there in November 1910. After Rothenstein returned from India, Fry wrote to urge a reunion, and Rothenstein replied:

There was a shower of cinders one day while I was sitting on the banks of the Ganges and one of the Juggernaut Gods is said to have been found leaning to one side—both facts were accounted for later, I read, by the Post-Impressionist earthquake in London. Yes, do come here for a night. You will find my work very tame, but when one has the privilege of drawing the Gods themselves it is very difficult not to feel such awe and reverence as to drive out any ideas but just the one of setting down as sensitively as one can what one has been allowed to look on. So you will not expect a fireworks display, will you. Nor must you expect to find me impressed by anything more than the greater conviction that all this interest is rather a getting away from the path than anything else; art is not an affair of social excitement, no one knows that better than you, and drawing room discussion does nothing any good I think. I fancy it has been a brilliant and gallant charge of the light brigade— a glorious episode, but leaving things very much what they were before.[4]

Rothenstein, temporarily blinded by the brilliance of Indian sunlight and colours, had not yet grasped the full extent and implications of the 'Post-Impressionist earthquake'; the circumstances of English art would never again return to 'what they were before'. Fry, who wanted Rothenstein's support for another, more daring exhibition in 1911, did not seem to realise how isolated Rothenstein had been in India and how little he knew about the immediate effects of Post-Impressionism in England. Nor did Fry, who was beset by private worries, art politics, public argument, and pressing practical details, seem to realise that he had dealt a second blow to one of Rothenstein's own plans. Rothenstein wrote to him:

I quarrelled with the N.E.A.C. over the very matter of the young men, and the stupidity of the N.E.A.C. realism, and tried myself to form a small society, for which you at the time rather reproved me. It was to be a society with certain aims and a certain duty, and of course I know it to be impossible to keep such a thing alive. There has always, however, remained in my mind the possibility of John, Gill, Epstein, McEvoy, myself, with a few of the more gifted young men, exhibiting together as a vague group, and we have often spoken of it among ourselves. I thought it possible something of the kind might be feasible at the Grafton, but I wanted for you to tell me just what your own plans are. . . . If you want my support, and you are good enough to say you do, you must make me feel that you are only taking work which represents something; I am too old to think there is any difference between old and new fashioned without them. . . .[5]

But Fry was hurrying away to Turkey for a much-needed holiday. He had no time to explain what he had done at the Grafton Galleries, what he proposed to do, and how he planned to use the support of the older artists; or to accept Rothenstein's invitation to spend the night and talk art. Rothenstein heard in the worst possible way about Fry's new plans: he heard them piecemeal and at second hand. After he received Rothenstein's letter of March 19, Fry explained belatedly and rather vaguely that he hoped to have 'a kind of secession show' in 1911 but had found some of the old guard from the New English Art Club unwilling to join in. 'Well,' he wrote, 'there remain John, Epstein, and yourself. John has promised to send.'[6]

Rothenstein came suddenly out of his Indian trance and replied:

There is some mystery of which I am ignorant which makes me wish more than ever that you could have managed to see me when I came back and before you went away. Robbie Ross met Alice yesterday and appears to have been under the impression that you had asked me to show my collection of Indian drawings at the Grafton and that I refused. I am very unhappy that the state of peace and joy I experienced in India should so soon be driven away by misunderstandings and gossip mongering. . . . You certainly never mentioned my drawings. MacCarthy spoke to me of a plan for getting a Russian show at the same time, a plan which seemed to me a sign of weakness, as though it were necessary to create some interest other than through that of our own contemporary work, but gave me no indication of wanting a good deal of space filled by any of ourselves. . . .

Do let us, however, get rid of misunderstandings; we are both of us working for the same thing and it seems absurd that there should be anything of the kind. I wish that I could get you to sit down, one rainy day, and write me fully as to what you propose. . . . I have strong feelings against an amateur committee of management and I feel that you should have an advisory committee of artists, quite small, but certain of their object, to manage the selection of artists and the practical carrying out of the exhibition. If such is your own idea, and you have some guarantee of continuity, I would see John, Gill, Epstein, and McEvoy, and see if we can reach some agreement.

But I don't think you realise how ignorant I am of your intentions and of your powers [at the Grafton Gallery]. . . . In the meanwhile I am being asked on all sides for my work, and am badgered by continual gossip. If you have large powers with the Grafton people and a free hand and a continuous policy there is a great chance of doing something definite, but I am most unwilling to join in a spasmodic exhibition of an ill understood movement, merely to help the usual enthusiasm for gossip which takes the place of any serious interest in art. The people who are your enthusiastic supporters look upon me as a dullard with an interesting past, who has done his best work 20 years ago. . . . The N.E.A.C. has been ruled by their own arbiters of taste and have bowed down to their own icons. If we can manage to form a really independent group and appeal to unprejudiced people I am with you, and will work with you I believe efficiently.[7]

On April 13, 1911, Fry wrote from Constantinople, explaining, still in general terms, his hopes for 1911 and thereafter. When he had found Steer and Tonks uninterested in a 'general secession exhibition of all non-academy art of any importance', he had thought of including Russian artists, since the younger English artists could not fill a gallery as large as the Grafton. He felt obliged to try to make the exhibition pay its way, and he hoped that exhibitors would trust him 'with large powers'. He made no promises but would do his best to make a Grafton show an annual event.[8]

Rothenstein replied that Fry still did not seem to realise how much he had left unexplained:

You seem to have been so much offended at my not having found the effect of the Post-Impressionists an unmixed good that you attributed a set desire on my part to oppose your plans for a continuation of Grafton exhibitions and you still persist in suggesting that I definitely refused all support. I heard, on my return, only very vague reports of your intentions, that the N.E.A.C. were not joining you and Gill clearly told me that he, John, Epstein and McEvoy were standing out. So far from joining with him I tried to convince him of the pedantry of his attitude, and I believed that it would not be difficult to break down their opposition if a really fine scheme was to be practicable. But remember that before yourself the N.E.A.C., in spite of my difficulties with them and my resignation, have, since I left their body, always treated my work with extreme generosity and I did not see how I could desert them unless I was convinced that the new association was to be on a finer and broader basis, but an equally solid one.[9]

Fry remained genuinely puzzled. 'When I asked you to join in a modern English show,' he wrote, 'I merely wanted a general consent, leaving it to be settled later what exactly you would send. I didn't *know* exactly what you had done [in India]. I thought that I had proved sufficiently my good will to your work to enable you to rely on me to give you every advantage. I was wrong and that is what has been something of a disappointment to me. . . . I'm sorry. I may under these circumstances have given you a wrong impression, but I haven't meant to.'[10]

Given the diverging nature of their interests and associations, it was inevitable that, later if not sooner, Rothenstein and Fry should follow different paths. By 1916 their correspondence would begin to resume its earlier, friendlier tone, but during the winter of 1911–12, while difficulties of every description forced postponement of Fry's second—and last—Post-Impressionist show at the Grafton Galleries, Rothenstein was in the United States. He had a New York exhibition; he met two of Florence Beerbohm's six brothers; he painted portraits and had reunions with Americans he had known in Paris.[11] Still, letters to Alice show that he was restless and sometimes irritable: 'One doesn't get much rest here, it is difficult to get out into the country, and one feels lonely and battered sometimes. I put all my passion into my drawings—I am most happy when I have sitters, but I cannot get them very regularly.'[12]

Illness forced Rothenstein to return early. During the summer and autumn of 1912 he devoted himself to Rabindranath Tagore, who was in England, and he prepared to move to Iles Farm, at Far Oakridge, Gloucestershire. 'Will's happiness', Alice had written, 'seems so centered in the country'; at Far Oakridge he was very happy indeed.[13] 'I cannot tell you', he wrote to his brother, 'how happy I am here—all my morbidness slips off me, and I enjoy the gift of life to the full. London simply disappears, and I care no fig for the things which preoccupy me there, stealing so subtly and cowardly into my brain. I warn you that I am only coming back as a visitor—this is where I live my life, the Gods being willing, for some time to come.'[14]

In 1913 Albert Rothenstein urged William to attend a New English Art Club anniversary dinner. William wrote: 'No one has sent me any kind of invitation to the N.E.A.C. dinner—I would have known nothing of it but for you. Many thanks for yours, but I cannot really afford either the time or the fare. Alice does all the coming up [to London], and I must stay here, and work, and save what I can and look after the children. I have had my dismissal from the N.E.A.C. and I have accepted it. . . . The great thing is to *do* things, regardless of indifference. Better cry out a little and work than say nothing and fritter away your

71

time. The pain and depression can be very keen, but work is the safe cure.'[15]

William did not attend the dinner, and not until 1920 did he return to live in London. He came by way of Sheffield University, where his old friend Herbert Fisher was Vice-Chancellor.[16]

In October 1916 he wrote to Rothenstein: 'You will shortly receive an invitation from the Sheffield School of Art to give a lecture in the University to the students of the School and I very much hope that you will see your way to accept it. As I told you our University Council is extremely favourable to the idea of a Chair of Art but is anxious not to seem to impinge upon the province of the Municipal School of Art. So it has seemed good to me and my fellow conspirators that an invitation should be addressed to you by the School of Art itself and that the University should lend one of its rooms for the lecture. This will enable me to go to the Council and say, "Why, my illustrious friend Mr. R. has been invited by the School of Art itself. Away then with all misgivings!"'[17]

Fisher's plan unfolded smoothly, and Rothenstein lectured at Sheffield on November 8, 1916. On February 22, 1917, the University offered him its first Chair of Civic Art. Fisher, now in London as President of the Board of Education, wrote to him: 'I am delighted . . . a splendid augury for the revival of our Provincial Schools of Art! I am sure that you are right in your view that a flourishing state of the arts and crafts in England can only be reached by the development of local Schools and local patronage. And in Sheffield you will have a rich virgin soil to till.'[18]

Schools of art and problems of local patronage occupied Rothenstein for the next fifteen years. From 1920 until 1935, again as a result of Fisher's planning, Rothenstein was Principal of the Royal College of Art at South Kensington. He arrived at a time of transition. The arts of design dominated the curriculum, but a number of new provincial art schools needed teachers of art; the College had become more of a teacher training school than a centre for practising artists. It had been, Rothenstein wrote,

a solvent on wider ambitions. Thus South Kensington has had less effect on the arts of design than was hoped.

I think the College remains the chief institution in the country where a complete education is offered to students of art. It is unfortunate that it has not always attracted the best type of student.

The presence of half a dozen gifted students will raise the standard of a whole school. Moreover, if future teachers are to get true education they should necessarily come into contact with the most gifted and mentally alert among their contemporaries, and this applies equally to those who intend to devote themselves to industrial design.[19]

This philosophy delighted the heart of Herbert Fisher, but it did not endear Rothenstein to art teachers in the provinces. How had it happened that this man, who had no academic degree or certificates; who was neither potter nor weaver nor embroidery designer; who was, in short, nothing but a painter, occupied so important a post? There were questions in the House of Commons, imperturbably answered by Fisher.[20]

Almost at once Rothenstein had his half dozen gifted students, and more, but the painting from which, at Far Oakridge, he would not spare a day, now competed with administrative responsibilities. 'How I envy your missing the things I have to do,' he wrote to his brother, 'so many of them futile. I can't help saying to myself every day—what are you doing here? I think of the farms and trees and skies, and I could be painting all day in the open. In London one waits for a late sitter, sometimes for a sitter who doesn't come, and at 5 o'clock the air is exhausted, and one must get away if one can . . .'[21]

Max Beerbohm in Italy had succeeded brilliantly in getting away, and he faced London thereafter on his own terms. The new life was as serene and un-fussy as Max had wished it to be. Florence proved to be a practical blessing to Max, who was so deft with his pen but quailed before such tasks as the doing up of brown-paper parcels. He resumed work on new drawings and on the manuscript of *Zuleika Dobson*, shelved since 1899.

Still, he needed to be in touch. 'The "Post-Impressionists" certainly ought to figure among the new drawings', he wrote to Ernest Brown of the Leicester Galleries, which planned a show of Max's work for the Spring of 1911. 'But the trouble is that I have never seen their works; and without at least a glimpse I cannot proceed! Will these works still be visible in London when I return?'[22]

He was in London on March 22—alone, since he could not afford two fares. His friends did not try very hard to hide their curiosity about whether marriage and Italy had changed him. On April 7 he told Florence that he was going to the Rothensteins: 'I shall go by the dear old Tube—with all its familiar stations, all seeming to be named after *you.*[23] On April 8 he reported, 'There were many inquiries after you from Will and Alice. Will thinks me so very lucky and so does she and so do I. He has done a great deal of work in India, and is rather obviously nostalgic—(and so am I—but not obviously, I hope).'[24]

'Max was here last week', William wrote to his brother, 'and John [Rothenstein] and I lunched at 48 [Upper Berkeley Street] yesterday; he is in many ways changed, wonderfully well and deeply happy and devoted to his wife, hating London and its ways and disapproving of things he was far from squeamish about years ago.'[25]

Florence, in Rapallo, wondered whether London would change Max. 'Do you have a desire to sleep about half past nine in the evening', she wrote, '—and are you up early as you are here—or does London undo Italy?'[26] And when he went to London in 1913, she wrote, 'I think perhaps Mr. Palmer ought not to have said in "The Saturday" that you went into voluntary exile to escape your friends—but I suppose it doesn't matter.'[27]

Max had always kept his innermost motivations to himself; the amount of subsequent speculation on his reasons for settling in Italy indicates that these, also, he did not discuss in public. But he left no one in doubt about his view of himself as a literary craftsman. When the integrity of this view was at stake, his editors found themselves in the grip of an iron hand wearing a velvet glove. In 1916 the editor of a New York periodical received this stiffly courteous manifesto from Max:

Dear Sir. I send in another envelope the corrected proofs of my two stories—"Enoch Soames" and "A. V. Laider." Every page of these is scored all over with corrections. But I am not to blame: I am not giving any unnecessary trouble. On the contrary, I am to be pitied for the great amount of unnecessary trouble that has been imposed on me. I have not added anything that wasn't in my MS.; nor have I subtracted anything that was there. I have readily fallen in with your wish that I shouldn't alter the Century Dictionary spelling—"envelop" (instead of envelop*e*), "honor," "defense," and so forth. (Indeed your wishes in this matter are mine. The one important thing in spelling is not to give the reader a "jump." In writing for an American magazine, one prefers the spelling that is most familiar to Americans.) Furthermore, the number of my corrections in these proofs is not due to any *carelessness* on the part of your printers and proof-readers. It is due merely to their crude and asinine interference with my punctuation, with my division of paragraphs, and with other details...Details? No, these are not details to me. My choice of stops is as important to me—as important for the purpose of conveying easily to the reader my exact shades of meaning—as my choice of words...Please don't think I am taking up a "high-and-mighty" attitude. I am very well aware that I am not a great or heaven-inspired writer. But I am equally well aware that I am a very careful, conscientious, skilled craftsman in literature. And it is most annoying for me to find my well-planned effects repeatedly destroyed by the rough-and-ready, *standardising* methods of your proof-readers. These methods are, no doubt, very salutary, and necessary, in the case of gifted but illiterate or careless contributors to your magazine. But I, personally, will none of them. And if, at any future date, you do me the honour to accept any other piece of my writing, please let it be understood that my MS. must be respected, not pulled about and put into shape in accordance to any schoolmasterly notion of how authors ought to write.[28]

Max reserved this unyielding tone for erring editors. Visitors to the Villino Chiaro heard it seldom, if ever. Mannie Kahn's fifteen-year-old daughter Alexandra, nicknamed Dody, has provided a charming picture of the Beerbohms at home; on condition that she write daily, her parents allowed her to stay in Rapallo from August 1921 to April 1922. 'I am afraid that you have sent your daughter to the wrong place,' Max wrote to Mannie after Florence and Dody arrived from New York. 'She is the sort of girl who should have been sent to some less appreciative household than ours. We shan't, I'm sure, ever consent to part with her. Nell and you have legal rights over her, no doubt. These will be resisted whenever you attempt to exercise them. She is a perfect darling. Eye and ear, and mind and heart, equally acclaim her.'[29]

Dody's first impression was that 'it's more wonderful than I'd ever imagined, even in my wildest moments. We got off at Genoa about eleven. It was Uncle Max's birthday, and he was at the dock to meet us; I can readily understand why he's said to be the most charming man in England—he's a dear and as nice as can be, but much older than I'd imagined. He's rather bald but not unattractively so—and his remaining hair and beauteous moustache are almost white. He's about the average height but rather slender, particularly from the waist down. He has pale blue eyes with long black eyelashes and eyebrows; a rather small sweet mouth, but seemingly lacking in strength. A really most interesting combination all around.'[30]

On September 1, she wrote: 'Uncle Max is too dear for words and we are great friends already. Aunt Florence very kindly intimated that he rather liked me more than he usually liked people. He certainly is nice to me anyway.'[31] Max's teasing disconcerted her until she caught the knack of the game: 'He told me tonight that Lady Colefax was very fair with flaxen hair. I immediately said "That means her hair is black as night and her skin olive." The funny thing was that *I* was right and Uncle Max had been teasing me as usual.'[32]

At Rapallo, Dody discovered 'the most startling fact—I've begun to grow up . . . I can tell it by the way I think and feel things. It certainly is most interesting!'[33] She proved her maturity with a series of observations on her aunt and uncle:

*September 24, 1921*

We had a funny argument at dinner tonight. Uncle Max was saying that he needed so little attention. I told him that he thought *that* because a great deal of attention had always been lavished on him in the most unostentatious way possible. Thereupon a great argument ensued at the end of which Aunt Florence and I were in gales of laughter for Uncle Max really believed what he said and maintained to the end that he was the most independent man alive. Just wait till you've lived in this household for a month. . . . Every single solitary thing from the breakfast hour to the consistency of the pudding, has to be regulated for Uncle Max. He never has to 'lift a hand' and all his wishes and wants are mysteriously anticipated. I'm not saying this in criticism—please understand—but to show you how funny it is.[34]

*October 7, 1921*

I'm reading 'Zuleika Dobson' and I am really enjoying it. But I should never dream of telling Uncle Max that. I don't want him to think that *I* too am worshipping at his shrine. The teasing is mutual now, and we have great fun. I wrote a letter to Uncle Max and signed it Mrs. Marsden, and in it I asked him to tea and told him that Lady Colefax had given me his address. Aunt Florence took it up to him and for one awful moment he thought he had to go somewhere outside of his own home. Then he suddenly decided that I was the author of the horrible (to him) document. I told him that that was my revenge for the 'apple pie bed.'

*October 8, 1921*

Aunt F. is at this moment trying to make him keep quiet because both she and I want to write, but it seems impossible for Uncle Max is determined to tell us that the London Mercury is dull this month. Now he's singing one of the songs I've taught him. Goodness! I'm afraid that this letter is entirely about Uncle Max. But he's the most important person in the house—and certainly the most talkative!

*October 11, 1921*
Uncle Max is rather 'piano' today. It seems that he is about to write something. Heaven preserve me from the perils of marrying an 'artist.' They are entirely hot-house plants, which must be carefully nurtured.

*December 3, 1921*
Heavens! Uncle Max is reading the first page of 'The Warden' to the tune of some tiresome song. Aunt Florence is nearly having a fit. *She's* reading the Bible! Oh, now he's reading the Bible to the tune of Mignon. Oh, how awful! Now it's the Italian newspaper at my suggestion. At least that's better than the Bible, because Uncle Max can't read Italian. At last, Peace.

Good friends all three remained, and others, both older friends and younger ones, took the road to Rapallo like pilgrims retreating from a society that seemed to have become cheapened, coarsened, increasingly inclined to jettison values that, in the lengthening perspective of time, took on an increasingly Arcadian appeal. Rothenstein, borrowing a metaphor from Indian mythology, wrote in 1923 that he pictured the Beerbohms in their 'shrine at Rapallo like Siva and Durga . . . watching the frantic antics of men and women in the pursuit of all save peace of mind.'[35] Max gave his friends no more information about the most secret state of his mind than he had given them about his reasons for settling in Italy, but it was apparent to all who visited Rapallo that the Villino's atmosphere, which was largely Florence's creation in response to Max's wish, was one of almost monastic tranquillity. Max's letters maintain their unhurried pace and unruffled tone. In their later correspondence, he and Rothenstein continue to practise the economy of wit and epigram that had characterised their first exchanges. Neither refers ever again to their quarrel in 1909. They look on at what Max describes as 'the old snarlings and squabblings and intriguings' of world affairs. 'But,' he concludes—and to the end of his own life Rothenstein echoes him in spirit and in deeds—'*speriamo!*'[36]

M.M.L.

¹ See Letter 121.

² See *MM* II, 210–212; *IE*, pp. 10–11; Fry, *Letters of Roger Fry*, ed. Denys Sutton, I, 327–328.

³ Rothenstein to Fry [April? 1910]. Diamand.

⁴ Rothenstein to Fry, March 19, 1911. Diamand. Fry urged Rothenstein to come to Guildford, then proposed visiting him in London. (Fry to Rothenstein, March 17, 1911. RP: HL.)

⁵ Rothenstein to Fry, March 30, 1911. Diamand. Ambrose McEvoy (1878–1927), English painter; member, N.E.A.C.

⁶ See Fry, *Letters*, I, 344–345.

⁷ Rothenstein to Fry, April 4, 1911. Diamand. Desmond MacCarthy (1877–1952), editor, *Life and Letters*, 1928–1934; chief book reviewer, *The Sunday Times*, 1928–1952; author of the unsigned preface to the 1910 Post-Impressionist Exhibition catalogue. Rothenstein told Ross why his Indian drawings would appear at the Chenil Gallery instead of among the Post-Impressionists: 'I could not give Chenil up, having agreed to show with him, but I could also not give Chenil up, to do a thing *no one but you has ever spoken about* or asked me to do, either before or since you mentioned the subject. . . . I wish I could make some one person believe that no one ever once suggested I should show them there.' (Rothenstein to Robert Ross, April 20, 1911. RP: HL.)

⁸ See Fry, *Letters*, I, 345–347.

⁹ Rothenstein to Fry, April 17, 1911. Diamand. Cf. Fry, *Letters*, I, 41–42.

¹⁰ Fry to Rothenstein, September 9, 1911. RP: HL.

¹¹ Florence's brothers: L. Miller (Mannie) Kahn (1880–1933), New York surgeon; Morris Kahn (1883–    ), electrical engineer and consultant. Rothenstein exhibited in November 1911 at the Berlin Photographic Company, 305 Madison Avenue, New York.

¹² William to Alice Rothenstein, November 24, 1911. Rothenstein.

¹³ See Letter 34, note 1. Rabindranath Tagore (1861–1941), Bengali poet, novelist, educator, philosopher. Rothenstein met him in India in January 1911 and in 1912 introduced him to the West.

¹⁴ William to Albert Rothenstein, December 31, 1912. RP: HL.

¹⁵ William to Albert Rothenstein, December 1, 1913. RP: HL. Cf. *WR*, pp. 263–264.

¹⁶ H. A. L. Fisher (1865–1940), historian; appointed a Fellow of New College, Oxford, 1910, and Warden, 1925; Vice-Chancellor, Sheffield University, 1912–1916; President, Board of Education, 1916–1922.

¹⁷ Fisher to Rothenstein, October 6, 1916. RP: HL.

¹⁸ Fisher to Rothenstein, February 23 [1917]. RP: HL.

¹⁹ Rothenstein to Fisher, June 8, 1920. Fisher Papers: Bodleian Library, Oxford. For another portion of this letter, see *WR*, pp. 308–309. Rothenstein's Sheffield lecture: *A Plea for a Wider Use of Artists and Craftsmen*.

²⁰ See Hansard, 131 H. C. Deb. 5 s, columns 2160–2161, 2181–2182.

²¹ William to Albert Rutherston (formerly Rothenstein) and Margery Rutherston, July 12 [1928?]. RP: HL.

²² Beerbohm to Brown, March 3, 1911. MCT. Ernest Brown (1852–1915), senior partner, Leicester Galleries, with Wilfred (1878–1926) and Cecil Phillips (1880–1951); succeeded in 1915 by his son Oliver Brown (1885–1966).

²³ Max to Florence Beerbohm [April 7, 1911]. MCT. The stations reminded Max of her because she had lived for a time in Hampstead.

²⁴ Max to Florence Beerbohm [April 8, 1911], MCT.

[25] William to Albert Rothenstein, April 10, 1911. RP:HL.

[26] Florence to Max Beerbohm [late March? 1911]. BP:MC.

[27] Florence to Max Beerbohm [April? 1913]. BP:MC.

She confuses John Palmer (1885–1944), Max's successor on *The Saturday Review*, with Filson Young (1876–1938), its editor, 1921–1924. See Young, 'Mr Max Beerbohm's Entertainment', *SR*, 115 (1913), 451.

[28] Beerbohm to [Douglas Z. Doty] editor, *The Century Illustrated Monthly Magazine* (New York), March 6, 1916. Taylor.

See Beerbohm, 'Enoch Soames', *The Century Magazine*, 92 (1916), 1–19; 'A. V. Laider', ibid., pp. 173–186, reprinted in his *Seven Men*, pp. 139–171.

[29] Beerbohm to L. M. Kahn, August 28, 1921. Transcript. Alexandra Bagshawe.

Alexandra (Dody) Kahn (1906–      ) is now Mrs. George Bagshawe, a resident of Yorkshire.

[30] Alexandra to L. M. and Nell Kahn, August 25, 1921. Bagshawe.

[31] Alexandra to L. M. and Nell Kahn, September 1, 1921. Bagshawe.

[32] Alexandra to L. M. and Nell Kahn, September 19, 1921. Bagshawe.

Sir Arthur (1866–1936), barrister, and Lady [Sibyl] Colefax (1874–1950), a tireless traveller and hostess, arrived on September 29, 1921.

[33] Alexandra to L. M. and Nell Kahn, September 19, 1921. Bagshawe.

[34] This and dated passages following, from Alexandra Kahn's letters to L. M. and Nell Kahn. Bagshawe.

[35] Rothenstein to Beerbohm, December 30, 1923. Clark Library: UCLA. The analogy is not quite apposite: Shiva, the Cosmic Dancer, is the Destroyer in the supreme triad of the Hindu pantheon; Durga is the stern, unyielding aspect of his divine consort, Parvati.

[36] Beerbohm to Rothenstein [late October 1931]. RP:HL.

My very dear Max—your charming & kindly letter reached me in India & it was an additional delight to get it there, where any letters from friends are doubly welcome. Such a one as yours however one does not get often in a life time, & many a time have I thought of you both, & many a time made resolutions to answer you. An affectionate family robs the traveller's friends of letters with cold blooded regularity; the letter home is the weekly task that must be performed, & once done it is difficult to take up the task again, however pleasant. The truth is that if you are travelling in a far country you either want to tell people something real about it, or keep silent; for if one once begins to talk about such a place as India one must write reams light heartedly, or a few pages with heavy care. And what idea can one give people of things they haven't seen? I have suffered too much from interminable descriptions of sunsets & other landscapes to wish to inflict a like sense of hostility to unshared beauties upon you. If I merely tell you that the academic problem as to whether the Greeks idealised what they saw, saw what they idealised, idealised what they didn't see, or saw what they didn't idealise is to be solved here by those who haven't been able to make up their minds at home, you will understand beauty is not wanting. For in spite of the terrible tidal waves which come bursting on this country from Western seas here is still the ancient world. It is not so much India & Indians I have seen, but men & women who would not be noticed in ancient Athens, Egypt or Carthage; no one would stare at them in Rome or Byzantium, & they might walk in Dante's Florence or Tizian's Venice without exciting more comment than you or I, my dear Max, in the bar of the Green Man at Tonbridge. I bless the day when I made up my mind to come to India, for I think the 4 months I spent there have been the most fruitful of my life.[1] You see it is all very well to buy Chinese bronzes, but when you find yourself in places where the Gods themselves will sit to you, so that you become the real image maker & are privileged to draw living Buddhas, you do feel that life is a precious gift. For I have been able to do this, & to walk & talk with archaic figures of the 6th century, & discuss philosophy with gentlemen who have stepped down from the niches of Chartres, & drive about in bullock carts with Masaccio's Peter & Paul & John. I will give the Rajahs & their pearls & hookahs & Palaces to anyone who wants them

—their elephants are the only decent things about them, & I blush every time I meet one of these noble relics of an heroic past world to think of the trivialities they must daily see.

I shall keep the ladies, though, if Alice doesn't mind. You may I think search the world & its museums & galleries & not find their match. You & I, my dear Max, having each of us a peerless wife cannot of course discover any new beauty to stir us, but just for a moment— supposing that we had neither of us seen our own, or one another's wives—if you could suppose such a thing—then I think you too would be likely to say that he who had not seen the women of India cannot understand the Parthenon frieze, or the writings of Flora Annie Swann & Mr Rudyard Kipling.[2]

I will also give you the nautch girl, but I will keep for myself the memory of the baker's & the candlestick maker's wives & daughters as the noblest creations of an unequally gifted Providence. Here am I, ungrateful creature, coming home 1st class on the very smartest P & O Steamer, with the privilege of seeing a live Crown Prince every day, surrounded by the fair of England & France & the Americas & have the bad taste to look with indifferent eyes on such beings. Alas, I have shut a door upon such treasures as I may never in this life behold again. In the meanwhile I have at least the comforting consciousness of having lived for 4 months among the most wonderful people & in cities of the Arabian Nights & in spite of Anglo Indian warnings of the fate that close intercourse with the native inhabitants would bring upon me, am on my way homewards free from cholera, enteric, malaria or plague & although I am I believe the only European artist who has come away without carrying off bags of rupees in payment for pearl bedecked Rajas I feel so much richer than when I left home that I feel quite sorry for the poor Crown Prince who has brought nothing back with him but a few skins, together with those of six fat Excellencies he took out with him.[3] Unless your past interests are buried so deeply in the earth that they stick out on the other side & inspire youthful Australians, you would I think be amused to see the Princely game on board; it is like reading a page of the 4 Georges which the censor would not allow Thackeray to publish. I am so glad that you feel so happy in Italy—but for wife & children I should have stayed in India, where there is no need to[4]

---

[1] On Rothenstein in India, see *IE*, pp. 27–35.

[2] 'Flora Annie Swann': an error, confusing Annie S. Swan (1859–1943), prolific

writer of popular romances who sometimes used Indian settings but never visited India, with Flora Annie Steel (1847–1929), wife of an Indian Civil Service official, who lived in the Punjab from 1867 to 1889 and visited there in 1894 and 1898.

[3] Crown Prince Wilhelm of Germany (1882–1951) spent much of a two-month Indian tour shooting and pig-sticking.

[4] Text of surviving letter ends here.

◇54        11 Oak Hill Park    Sunday morning [April 1911]

My dearest Max—you have never done nobler work than the work you show—the most recent especially. You have reached great heights & can now regard the world beneath you with serene eye, neither pleased nor angry, & your moving finger writes. Perhaps the Lord Rosebery seeing the end of all things has a more dreadful genius than anything you have ever made—it is wonderful & extraordinarily haunting.[1] The Zangwill I saw before, but I was again impressed by the touching quality of the drawing; it is a most beautiful thing & a very moving one.[2] I laughed explosively as I went round, not meaning to in the distinguished society in which I found myself—the shade of R[obert] L[ouis] S[tevenson] tickled me into a really rude outburst, which made poor dear Lady Colvin's emu feathers tremble like aspen leaves—or were they aspen leaves which shook like ostrich feathers?—& the fat head of your Royal financier was like a muffled drum playing their own funeral march.[3] But there were so many & I congratulate you de coeur. Your visit, short as it was, was a really great joy for us—I am writing you to Rapallo—this will just carry you my love & tell you how sorry we were to be prevented from going back to meet you at the show in the afternoon. Ever yours Will

[1] Max showed 118 caricatures at the Leicester Galleries, April 24–May 20, 1911. He drew Archibald Philip Primrose, 5th Earl of Rosebery (1847–1929), Prime Minister and Lord President of Council, 1894–95, and a noted pessimist, as 'Lord Rosebery, beset by the Spectre of the End of All Things'; see Beerbohm, 'Some Pen-Pricks at Prominent Personages', *The Tatler*, 40 (1911), 88.

[2] 'At last! Mr Zangwill leading the way into Zion', dedicated to the Rothensteins. See *Catalogue*, p. 161.

[3] Max drew the shade of Stevenson 'revisiting the Glimpses' (that is, the sublunary scene; cf. *Hamlet*, I, iv, 53) and finding the literary men as street-corner orators. See Beerbohm, '"Conversation Caricatures" of Yesterday', *The Illustrated London News*, 220 (1952), 811. Rothenstein's audible amusement would have outraged the Colvins; see Letter 38, note 1.

The 'Royal financier' may be Lord Burnham (1833–1916), wealthy newspaper proprietor, whom Max caricatured singly and as one of a group of financiers on their way to meet the new king. See Beerbohm, *Fifty Caricatures*, plate 47; *Catalogue*, p. 37.

◇55                                       Villino Chiaro    July 4, 1911

My dearest Will

Romeike tells me that the Craig dinner is on the 16th. Do have J. L. Garvin invited. He is a remarkable and personally very charming fellow, and a great enthusiast for Craig's work. I saw him in London, and he was very keen to be at the dinner. He lives at 9. Greville Place, Maida Vale and he had better be written to *there*; not at the office of "The Observer" to which he goes only on Saturdays.[1] I hope the dinner will be a huge success. I see that the laws which govern the universe have not in this case been suspended, and you have not been able to dispense with that permanent natural phenomenon which (for want of a better name) we call "the Duchess of Sutherland."[2] By the way, ought I to write a brief note to W. B. Yeats, the chairman, to say how sorry I am I can't be there in Craig's honour?[3] I was immensely delighted by your letter about my caricatures—(the passage about Lady Colvin is very memorable). The show was a great success financially. I hope the show of your very lovely and touching Indian drawings was a still greater. Artistically it must have been a triumph indeed.[4] Florence sends her best love to you and to Alice; and so do I. We were in Venice for some time after my return, and oh so glad to be back *here* again. Your affectionate Max

[1] Rothenstein organised a dinner honouring Gordon Craig, at the Café Royal on July 16, 1911.
    Romeike: London press clipping agency. J. L. Garvin (1868–1947), editor, *The Observer*, 1908–1942.
[2] Lady Millicent St. Clair-Erskine (1867–1956), eldest daughter of the 4th Earl of Rosslyn; wife of the 4th Duke of Sutherland.
[3] Yeats at first declined the invitation, as he had July engagements in Ireland. A change of plans allowed him to attend the dinner, but he refused to preside. (Yeats to Rothenstein [June 16] June 17, 1911. RP:HL.)
[4] Max's show brought him £400. On Rothenstein's Chenil Gallery show, see Roger Fry, 'Plastic Design', *The Nation and Athenaeum* (London), 9 (1911), 396; a review, 'Mr. Rothenstein's Indian Drawings', *The Academy* (London), 80 (1911), 757.

My dearest Will

Many thanks for your wire. In one of Maeterlinck's plays an old servitor says "Everything around this castle is so quiet that the dropping of a ripe fruit in the park draws faces to the windows."[1] *Here* life is so peaceful that the arrival of a telegram is as the dropping of a bomb that blows us straight up through the roof. We are both of us still somewhat shaken and jarred; but I have managed to write a note to Yeats; and I send it to you, because I am not sure of his address. Would you send it on to him?[2]

Love from us both to you all. Your affectionate Max

P.S. Please send Yeats a line to explain why I am writing. Otherwise he might be rather bewildered and fancy it was a spell cast by the fairies or by Shoon-na-Braugh or even by Krim-na-Hoo.

[1] See Maurice Maeterlinck, *The Death of Tintagiles*, in his *The Plays of Maurice Maeterlinck*, trans. Richard Hovey, 2nd series, p. 200.

[2] For Max's letter to Yeats [July 11, 1911], and for Rothenstein's remarks as chairman, see [Gordon Craig, comp.] *A Living Theatre*, pp. 58–61. See also, Edward Craig, *Gordon Craig*, pp. 263–64.

⋄57                          11 Oak Hill Park      July 11, 1911

My dearest Max—it was pleasant to hear from you again & to know that you are once more happily established on your roof garden at Rapallo. I always have a very clear vision of you both there, under the blue Italian sky, coloured by no London heavy shadows, but only by a sweet pink & green reflected light, like a gracious couple in a fresco by Fra Angelico—peace be on you both for long. Alice & the 3 children are at Rottingdean, recruiting after the whooping cough, while John & I lead an existence almost as idyllic as your own, picnicing in the almost deserted mansion & enjoying one another's company all the time he is not at school.

We go down to the sea for week ends & there we have all got to know the Nicholsons & to like them all very much. What charming children they are, both children & parents & how youthfully & gracefully pleasant success sits on their shoulders. Rachel & Betty adore them & Alice sits like a sundial on the beach, telling the time of day as accurately as any bronze piece, but without, I need scarcely say, giving utterance to any Latin phrases.[1]

I don't wonder your show was a financial as well as an honourable success; it is only the 19th century which has introduced any disagreement between the two & like the Archbishops & Bishops I am dead against anything in the nature of permanent divorce. You will be amused when I tell you that even I am to be tried as a possible asset for a decent firm; I am to have a show prepared in New York of paintings, drawings & lithographs by my hand, & in October next I go over with a commission to make a couple of lithographs, & the promise of some work, to try my fortune. I think the show is to be sent to Chicago & elsewhere, as well.[2] A change from India, isn't it? & you who have been & your wife who comes from there will know better than I what is in store for me. Albert is back, lively & cheerful as always, in an elegant flannel suit & with all his old talent for admiring his friends' work & commiserating with their troubles. He really is a dear & I hope life will be one half as kind to him as he is to others.[3] I hope you are writing to Yeats, who by the bye is not to be chairman I gather, because he refuses to propose the health of the King![4] Craig is over here, more abstract than ever, but always wonderful, with a very clear idea of what he means. I really do admire him more than most people, although he is called mad & impossible. I have always had a dangerous taste for the sanity of madmen—dangerous I mean for a bourgeois like myself, a jackal admiring lions at the risk of his fur. Berenson is over here & comes to lunch this week;[5] my American tour puts an end I fear to my vague plans for autumning & early wintering in Italy—I expect to leave here about the 3rd week of September, so shall be working on steadily until then. Have you by any chance the MS. play by Mme Bussy I sent you? She would very much like to have it back, if you can lay your hands on it.[6] What of Zuleika & when does she come to ravish us with her "plain" looks & her wide eyes?[7] My love to your dear wife —& when shall we meet again? Perhaps she will give me a letter to her brother, of whom she spoke to me, when I go?[8] Ever yours, my dear Max—Will

If you want to read a wonderful book, read "China under the Empress Dowager." It sounds dull, but it contains some of the most wonderful dramatic accounts of Court Life ever printed—Backhouse & Bland are the authors.

[1] Rothenstein had known the painter William Nicholson (1872–1949) since the 1890's; this was the first meeting of all the Rothensteins with all the Nicholsons. On the Nicholson children, see Letter 58, note 2.

[2] See p. 78, note 11; Letter 59, note 2.

[3] Albert Rothenstein had been painting in France.

[4] Yeats responded to Rothenstein's toast to Craig. A similar impasse was side-stepped in July 1911 at a dinner for Tagore; see *IE*, pp. 38–41.

[5] Bernard Berenson provided Rothenstein with a number of introductions to friends and collectors in the United States.

[6] Dorothy Strachey (1866–1960), sister of Lytton Strachey (1880–1932), had married the French painter Simon Bussy (1870–1954). In 1909 she asked Rothenstein to ask Max to read her play, perhaps a translation from a French work. Max spoke encouragingly about it but by 1911 had not returned the manuscript.

[7] When in London in April 1911, Max began to negotiate for publication of *Zuleika Dobson*.

[8] That is, to Morris Kahn.

◇58                    Villino Chiaro      August 28, 1911

My dearest Will

I am much excited, and so is Florence, by the prospect of your invasion of America. And I am sure you will take that place by storm, just as you took Oxford *dans le temps*, and be overwhelmed with work and dollars. It must be very nice to be on the eve of such a "walk over." Florence has written to tell her brother Morris that you are coming; and if there is anything of any sort he could do to save you trouble, he would be very much delighted. I am sure you would like him very much indeed: he is a charming fellow. No news of any sort from here: sheer unalloyed diurnal happiness and contentment—what a barren theme this is! There is absolutely nothing to be said about it. Zuleika will be with you anon. The proofs are flowing in, and the book will be out not later, I hope, than the first week in October. I am really very glad I found it impossible to go on writing the book in London years ago. I have developed since then; and the book wouldn't have had the quality it has now. It really is rather a beautiful piece of work—though it may be a dead failure in point of "sales"—and on the other hand might sell quite well: just a toss up. Heinemann evidently believes in it from his point of view, for he pays me £400 in advance of royalties—and a good many copies have to be sold therefore before *he* can begin to profit. If the binders and paper-makers don't play me false, the book will *look* nice: not like a beastly *novel*, more like a book of essays, self-respecting and sober and ample.[1] Where are you, I wonder? Still Rottingdeanising? I am so glad you like the Nicholson troupe—they *are* somehow more like a troupe than a family—Nancy standing with one spangled foot on Nicholson's head, Ben and Tonie branching out on tip-toe from his straddled legs, Mabel herself standing at the wings, holding the overcoats.[2] I said there was no news, but I forgot that the Italian fleet—or a great deal of it—was here yesterday. Is that nothing to you? The population of Rapallo went quite mad with joy, in a quiet way, and didn't at all seem to mind the general starvation by which alone such a spectacle is compassed. Florence sends her fondest love to you and Alice and the whole family, and so do I. Ever your affectionate Max

¹ Heinemann published *Zuleika Dobson* in October 1911. Max wrote to Robert Ross: 'Poor old Zuleika! She is at length to be dragged out, blinking and staggering, into the light of day. And Heinemann will be sending her to the Reform Club, to wait for you there. Be kind, be courteous, to the hag. Incline your ear to her mumblings. Pretend not to hear the horrid creakings of her joints. Tell her she does not look a day older than when you saw her or at any rate her head and shoulders all those years ago. Don't hint to her that she makes a goblin of the sun.' (Beerbohm to Ross, October 15, 1911. J-P. B. Ross.)

² Max's visualising the Nicholsons as an acrobatic troupe is apt: their affairs proceeded by inspired improvisation, and Nicholson's wife Mabel (d. 1918), a talented artist and sister of the painter James Pryde (1866–1941), came of a family incurably addicted to the theatre. Ben (1894–    ) became a major painter in his own right; Nancy Nicholson (1899–    ) married the poet Robert Graves; Tony (1901–1918) was killed in action in France; Christopher (1904–1947) died in a glider accident.

⌀59    308 West 72nd Street [New York]    November 14, 1911

My very dear Max—here have I been now for a month or more, & as in India, I have happily been able to keep out of the tourists' way & staying as I do with natives all the time, I feel I get more insight into their hearts & habits than an ordinary globe trotter. The natives here are very curious & interesting people, & New York a very exciting place. It is exciting because life is so dangerous here. There is no traffic to speak of, but things are so arranged that a clever combination of tramway & motor car gives all the effect of our London bustle, with infinitely greater danger to life, & the breathless excitement of crossing each street gives to the natives here a sense of importance & of "hustle" of which they are very proud. Apart from this, they are slow & clumsy in their management of the affairs of life, & have nothing of our quick methods & neat ways. They are slow & unpractical, but happily they are quite content to remain as they are. They have no conversation, although they talk unceasingly, for no standard of intelligence & knowledge is taken for granted; it is as though each time one played a game of tennis one had to mark out the court afresh. The most remarkable man I have met here is your wife's brother. He has judgement &

imagination, has read & thought about what he has read, & remaining outside what is called life, has been able to keep a simple & clear vision of things. He has a heart of gold & the limpidity of his mind touches me very much.[1] I fancy the best natives are to be found in the business world—those outside it seem amateurs at the game they play. Like an army in a small state, all the titles & uniforms are there, swords clank & spurs jingle, yet somehow they seem to be chocolate cream thinkers. They are, I need not tell you, the most hospitable people in the world, for the simple reason that they have warm hearts & hungry brains, & instinct tells them that with kindness they can extract enough grey matter to feed on for at least 24 hours after you have left the house, & their women are exceedingly pretty. I never seem to meet any plain young girls walking about the streets; they do not all look morally unassailable, but they wear blue serge armour of the neatest kind, which renders them so, I think, in fact. I am not making my fortune here by any means, though if flattery were golden I should carry much precious metal home with me. My old lithographs are my fortune here, such as it is, little did I think when I made them at 20 they would make me at 40! I hear your Zuleika has at last shown herself—I have tried to get her here, but so far unsuccessfully, & I burn to make her acquaintance. I hope she will bring much grist to your mill. Do write me a line & tell me how you both are. I hope you will come over to see us this spring— your visit was a great event last year. I hope too that Rapallo wears well, & that the Villino shelters two happy & contented souls. I have good news from Alice, & miss her & the children desperately. I fear I can't get back before the middle of January, as I have engagements at Boston & Chicago.[2] My love to you both. Ever your affectionate Will

[1] Rothenstein met both Morris and Mannie Kahn in New York.

[2] He did not leave for England until mid-February. The Doll and Richards Gallery in Boston exhibited 160 Rothenstein works—paintings, drawings and litho-graphs—December 8–29, 1911. He visited Boston at least twice during January 1912. The exhibition then went to The Art Institute of Chicago, January 4–28, and on January 9 he lectured at Fullerton Hall, Chicago. Harriet Monroe, editor of *Poetry*, took him to task for advocating what she thought were impracticably high standards in art; see her review, 'Rothenstein Counsels Perfection as Standard for Museums of Art', *The Chicago Sunday Tribune*, January 14, 1912, Part 2, p. 5.

◇60                    11 Oak Hill Park    April 2, 1912

My very dear Max—my only excuse for my long delay in telling you of the delight your book gave me lies in the fact that you do actually

owe me a letter—a poor excuse, but the only one I can discover to shield me. The fact is that if one didn't behave badly, even to one's dearest friends, one would find a matutinal grave, for not a moment's leisure, indoors or out of doors, would one get. It is not overwork, but underleisure, which undermines one, & so one's bad conscience serves as a paper weight, crushing down the unanswered. Still it was monstrously ungrateful, for your book came as a fierce joy to me, staying as I was in a country which provides, if Florence won't want to scalp me for saying it, rather tame ones. You have provided me with yet another picture for my mental permanent collection & that, happily, without the intermediary Lane—Sir Hugh I mean—the picture of the young Duke in his awe-ful robes cleaving the ascending crowd as he strides down to the riverside.[1] There is a nocturne too, that ravished my heart —a conjuring scene at night, a little table containing cheap tricks presided over by a delicate fairy from Paquin's spread under great chestnut trees, whose blossoms glow solemnly above the scene, mounting in narrowing layer upon layer to the sable sky. Perhaps you don't say they are chestnut trees, but the scene is a wonder. O Zuleika, with your neck of imitation marble, you wear silver bangles upon your feet, & when you walk there is music made which settles in the ears of men— bells that memory sets ringing, Lilliputian silver bells. You, Max, are Puck & Ariel combined; you have escaped from Prospero, for whom most of us still slave, & we can only turn yearning & admiring eyes towards Rapallo—we have not earned your freedom, & where you leap & run in the branches our eyes only can follow you. When, O when are you coming over to see us again? I long to see you, & it is years since we have seen your wife. Her brothers were almost as brothers to me while I was in America; they are surely among the rarest & best of men. Albert frisks about—he & George Street were here last night, & we drank your health in Touraine wine. This note merely to send you both our love & thanks & ever green memories.

Always your affectionate—Will

[1] Sir Hugh Lane (1875–1915), Irish art collector, promoter of a National Gallery for Dublin.


&#9672;61       Villino Chiaro     Wednesday [May 1912]

My dearest Will

I am so very sorry to hear you have had an operation. What a bore for you! And poor Alice, I am sure, must have had an unhappy time till all was well over. I hope you are making a quick and pleasant recovery and will very soon have your palette and mahl-stick in hand again, with the north light playing in its accustomed way on those suits of armour and oak chests with which it is your hobby to surround yourself.[1] Florence sends her love to you and to Alice, and is writing to Alice. She has been as much concerned as I at hearing about you, and hopes, like me, to hear that you are growing stronger and better than ever. I can imagine that in the course of this process, deprived of your ordinary activities, you must be *cerebrating* to an alarming extent and at an appalling rate; and I picture your day-nurse and your night-nurse as worn to shadows, both of them. And now a thousand thanks for two letters that entranced me—one about America, and the other about my "Zuleika." Even I, at the tender age of twenty-three, felt myself discommoded in very much the way you describe.[2] But it needed *you*, in the prime of life, to hit on that truly beautiful metaphor of the necessity of "marking out the tennis-court afresh for every game." We were so glad you found rest and refreshment in the company of Morris (whom I knew you would like) and Mannie (whom I know *I* shall like). It is needless to say that we heard a very great deal from them both about you and your delightfulness: they seem to have vied in enthusiasm. As to Zuleika, I don't ascribe to mere old friendship *all* that you said about her; for there were scenes in the book that I *knew* you would like when I was writing them; and one of these was the one you specially mention—the conjuring by moonlight. I have been doing a fair amount of writing—amongst other things, some new parodies (of which, with some old ones, I shall have a book out this autumn).[3] Also a good many caricatures. I am having another show at the Leicester Galleries next year, twixt April and June —about fifty drawings. Florence and I shall be in London before then. When shall you and Alice be in Rapallo? It would be such a joy for us. If there were any exclusive news about the war with Turkey, or news of any kind whatsoever, I would send it to you in a long "gossipy" letter. But there is no news, beyond what I read in "The Manchester Guardian"—which is *the* best paper and ought to have you among its subscribers. Do take it in. And now, dear Will, love from us both again, and all the best of wishes. Your affectionate Max

[1] Rothenstein's operation: for hemorrhoids. The suits of armour are probably a joke; Rothenstein's children recall no such furnishings.
[2] That is, during Herbert Tree's 1894–95 American tour.
[3] Beerbohm, *A Christmas Garland*; see Letter 20, note 2.

Iles Farm, Far Oakridge, nr. Chalford Gloucestershire

May 4, 1913

My very dear Max—it is awful to think of the stream of letters that flows from a man's pen during a lifetime, & of how few he writes of those he wishes to write de coeur, from feelings of admiration & affection. Here have I been meaning to write ever since the day I stepped into the Leicester Galleries, walking in through mud & rain & out upon air, a new joy running through my veins & a grateful acknowledgement to the Divine Power upon my lips for giving the poor human heart such easement & relief.[1] How often have I told you over the space of years how richly gifted you are; but how much more delightfully than most men you return your gifts to the Gods, through us mortals happily, in kind. Without hurting anyone you seem to observe everything, where the rest of us would be assailed as spies & hirelings, for you possess the divine art of understanding. Tout comprendre c'est tout pardonner; you are a living witness to the truth of that epigram & we murmur it as we rub the Elliman [liniment] upon our rainbow bruises.

You have never done such delightful drawings or seen more profoundly. I keep on marvelling at the amazing subtlety of the Fry drawing—the mouth & eye curling together, and the Bennett formula is equally perfect.[2] My acquisitive passion is not perhaps quite so unreasonable as it was, but I did long to carry off the whole collection bodily, to be enjoyed at my ease, with no one just looking at the drawing I want to see & read from—let no one say, after a visit to your show, that this is an age of rush & hurry. I feel humbled when I realise how quite definite & irresistible is the appeal of really finished art. The days when one considered oneself an artist by the grace of God & the public a fool by the same grace are long gone by. Some faith I still have in my own work not because I am gifted but because I care so much for what I am doing that I believe that this caring will in one way or another show itself to some few here & there, but I do exult in the richer gifts of others always & always feel under a definite personal debt to people like yourself, dear Max. Do you realise it is just 20 years since we first met? You were already so much wiser & more finished a person than myself, but I was even then alive to the existence of all the qualities you have developed so triumphantly since. It is pleasant to think that after 20 years' intimate friendship I can look upon you with an even richer & riper affection & admiration. I was glad to see red marks (Lord, have

92

mercy upon us!) on Albert's frame & mine.[3] I suppose the doors are now closed & the Academy's opened.[4] My love & homage to your dear wife. Ever your affectionate friend Will

[1] Max showed sixty-eight drawings, April 10–May 10, 1913.

[2] In 'Mr. Roger Fry', Fry appraises a wooden soldier on a pedestal; in 'A Milestone', Arnold Bennett (1867–1931) is upbraided by the heroine of *Hilda Lessways*, second novel in his trilogy that began with *Clayhanger*, for delaying the concluding book, *These Twain*. See Beerbohm, *Fifty Caricatures*, plates 37, 43.

[3] Albert Rothenstein had bought 'Landed Gentry. No. 1. Mr. Albert Rothenstein'. For 'Mr. William Rothenstein warns Mr. Tagore against being spoilt by occidental success', see *IE*, p. 205.

[4] The Royal Academy's 145th exhibition opened at Burlington House on May 3, 1913.

◇63      Villino Chiaro, Far Rapallo nr. Genoa It[aly] May 11, 1913

My very dear Will

I am not, for the most part, "psychic." But often it does happen to me that a letter suddenly arrives from a person of whom I have just been particularly thinking. On the afternoon before the morning on which arrived your welcome and lovely letter, in which you remind me that we have known each other for just twenty years, I, walking up and down our little terrace here, had realised that for just twenty years I had known you; and, realising this, I had gone into my "study" to search there among my letters for the preserved letter in which St. Cyres asked me to meet you and re-assuringly added "I understand that he speaks English perfectly." And then, next morning, there your letter was: a crown to the affectionate reminiscences that had yesterday been flitting through my head and my heart.[1] Ever so many thanks. As well you know, your belief in me has always been a great incentive to me to believe in myself; and your creative, suggestive, fertilising mind has enormously helped me, from time to time. I remember, for one example, that it was you who, at Oxford, first told me that I ought to try washes of water-colour—things of which at that time I supposed myself quite unlikely to be capable at the age of ninety. And it was you who made me see the difference between journalistic line-y drawing and drawing that had an unjournalistic grace. And it was you, later, whose advice helped me to keep within my own little *spiritual* way of expression and not to try for external accuracies. And—but I won't enumerate the

93

heaps of ways in which, to me as to so many other more important persons, you have been ballast and illumination. Merely, many thanks. Your praise of these latest drawings of mine has immensely pleased me. Commercially they have been a great success; and you make me feel that they have deserved it. But when you say, you inveterate theorist, "how quite definite and irresistible is the appeal of really finished art," and when you talk about "the richer gifts of others" than yourself, and when you profess to be "humbled" and so forth....oh *BOSH* and *TWADDLE* (though admirably reasoned and expressed)! Say that there *have* been eras in which good things in art made an irresistible appeal all round. Say that in Phidias' Athens and Giotto's Florence and Rossetti's back-garden there really *was* a public clamouring for good things and never failing to appreciate any good thing that they got. And say that in the late nineteenth and early twentieth century the tendency of artists is to regard their art as a sort of hole-and-corner parlour-game which no outsider ought to dare to look on at, and which no outsider can hope to make head or tail of.

*Granted.* But this doesn't prove that the great public in England and elsewhere is capable of "spotting" a good thing when they see it, or incapable of ignoring a good thing when they see it. I am a popular success, for the moment, because I make jokes about Lloyd-George and John Masefield and Reginald McKenna.[2] *You* are *not* a popular success, because you *don't.* I think you are right in hating the Sickert-ish hole-and-corner theory.[3] I agree that the ideal state is that in which good art is by all beloved. But I can't follow you to the point at which you have arrived: the point at which you splendidly persuade yourself that what ought to be is. And if, in your next exhibition, you sell five times as much as I, I shan't agree that this is any sign of improvement in you. I shall merely say "But of course you are and always were five times more important than I; and I am glad that for this and that irrelevant reason the worldly result has come level with the artistic reality."

Love to Alice and John and all. It was such a joy to see Alice and John in London.

Florence sends equally her love. Ever your affectionate Max

[1] The letter is no longer 'preserved'.
[2] See Beerbohm, *Fifty Caricatures*, plates 12, 22, 28. Reginald McKenna (1863–1943), Home Secretary, 1911–1915; Chancellor of the Exchequer, 1915–16.
[3] Sickert contended that 'the more an art is serious the more will it tend to avoid the drawing-room and stick to the kitchen.' Quoted by John Rothenstein in his *Modern English Painters: Sickert to Smith,* p. 50.

My dear Max—I read of your crowning with the palms—my congratulations de coeur.[1] I fear neither your family nor your army of admirers will easily consent to letting you slip away, but I do hope you may find that a day or two as an interlude between the courses will not be amiss. Then perhaps I may persuade you to come here. It would be a real joy to see you again & to have you quietly to myself. It is almost worth living in the country for the delight one's friends give when they come. There is no occasion so entirely happy—at least so it seems to me, whatever story my visitors may themselves tell. It would indeed be enchanting to have you here, & we would do our best to make you comfortable at least. My dear love to your mother.

Ever yours affectionately—Will

[1] Max was elected to the Academic Committee of the Royal Society of Literature in June 1913. He wrote to Gosse: 'It is perhaps well that, living here [at Rapallo], I shall so seldom be able to attend meetings. Some years ago I did serve on a committee (of a trivial and debased kind); and this service quickly formed in me an opinion, still held, that I am not wise in council—or at any rate that my wisdom is of so taciturn a kind that no one is a penny the better for it. Out here, my silence and my probable folly will not matter. And, for the rest, let us hope that I shall not write less well than heretofore. Honour having come to me through (what you charmingly call) the beautiful purity of my prose style I must set my face against the not unnatural impulse to say "Nunc dimittis; it is enough; henceforth I shall take the line of less resistence and wield the pen of that ready writer, that fluent old Adam, which is in all of us."

'Flesh is weak, and strong now is the temptation to show myself, after all these years, in my true colours—a splitter of infinitives and a reckless and-which-er, a verb-sap-per and caeteris-paribuster, a reliable pro-tempster and a vae-victist à outrance, a temperamental milienist [sic] with a welcome touch of sincerity (to say nothing of undeniable gifts and undoubted promise), a scarcely-too-much-to-sayer and a dare-we-adder, a haver of little hesitation in averring, and pre-eminently a ventilator of Britishers' grievances, and a voicer—a no uncertain voicer—of their most cherished aspirations, on which the sun never sets.

'But this horrid temptation I shall fight and beat, made strong by your faith in me.

'You say I must "continue to caricature the members." And this licence has a particular application at this moment. The Eternal Volatile [William Heinemann] is publishing in the autumn a book of reproductions of fifty or so of my drawings. And among the drawings which he has caused to be photographed for the book is the group, which you may remember, of the Academic Committee.' (Beerbohm to Gosse, June 15, 1913. Ashley Library: British Museum.) See Beerbohm, *Fifty Caricatures*, plate 40; Max has 'crowned with palms' all the members caricatured here.

(From William Rothenstein, artist, to
Maxwell Beerbohm, man of letters.)

—This for the censor—

My very dear Max—how are you & Florence? In mind, I feel, happier
than most of us here with this war driving one's mind this way & that
from day to day. People who are one thing, of one mind only, during
these months are to be envied. I find myself of half a dozen. The high
standard of conduct & emotion war is supposed at least to bring does I
feel certain affect people actually waging it, but I feel less sure about its
effect on people at home.

The dreadful brutality of Germany has given people what looks like
a legitimate excuse for very strong feelings. I am afraid that we who
practice the arts can never associate ourselves with one more or less
permanent state of mind & as I find it hard to condemn individuals with
any consistent severity, however much they may have sinned I find it
equally difficult to withhold all sympathy from a whole nation. The fact
is I suppose it is impossible to realise the horrors of which we read—
there are times of intense indignation & times again when something in
one's nature will have its say & if one is to see one nation all black one
cannot see others all white. At any rate the soldiers themselves are sane
& decent enough—they are dear & marvellously brave fellows & here
at least as modest & gentle as they are brave. How refreshing their
letters are compared with so many of the leader writers' stupidities!
Clutton Brock took out a patent for common sense before the war & has
been able to use it to admirable purpose during these long months &
Belloc has been very fine in Land & Water. I love to be told by con-
vincing & fine people that we are to win, to go on until we win & that
Germany is to be beaten to her knees. It is people whose own characters
I cannot trust whose sweeping denunciations I dislike. You happily are
far from all these more personal sides of the war.[1]

Do you remember, dear Max, that you promised me a note on my
drawings of Tagore? Duckworth is to publish six of them in the early
summer—could I get you to do this for me within the next few weeks?
The note need be but a short affair—& directly I get the proofs from
Oxford I will send them on to you. This will be a great kindness on
your part & it will be delightful to have your cooperation in this late
publication—I have had no portraits appear in book form since the
nineties.[2] When we were in Town last we went to see your dear mother

& found her surprisingly well & as ever touchingly kind & affectionate. Alice goes up sometimes to London but I scarcely ever; I don't feel any inclination in that direction & the taste for the life we lead at Oakridge has grown into a settled habit.[3] The children are completely happy. We share their love with a dog, a pony & a large number of rabbits; of human rivals we have none. John is just back from school—nearly 14—& is dangerously like me. He will go through difficult days I fear before he begins to look for anything in flowers save honey. Billy, who is 7, seems to have a touch of something like genius. I have never seen a child draw as he does, & if he lives & grows will put a large umbrella into my hand to shelter me from any more sun. After years of control of my own time I have suddenly a portrait to paint—Ernest Debenham, offered him by the firm on his approaching cinquantaine. A charming fellow & a delightful family to be with; his wife a niece of Joseph Chamberlain, with a very energetic & noble character & something between six & a dozen children I tell her are really as nice as our own, which is a truth which will be more pregnant for Alice than for her.[4] So the war wolf is not prowling near our door, at any rate. If you come over this spring you must really come down to us. No excuse can be fair. In the meanwhile my affectionate greetings to you both & do give us news of your doings. Ever yours—Will

If Italy makes up her mind to join us in crushing the German monster perhaps Far Oakridge will replace Far Rapallo.[5]

[1] Arthur Clutton-Brock (1868–1924), barrister; art critic for *The Times* from 1908; writer on literature, religion, and gardening. His *Thoughts on the War* achieved a ninth printing in 1915; *More Thoughts on the War* followed. Hilaire Belloc (1870–1953) wrote weekly articles for the periodical *Land and Water*.

[2] Rothenstein, *Six Portraits of Sir Rabindranath Tagore*; for Max's Prefatory Note, see pp. ix–x. Rothenstein's last book of portraits was *Manchester Portraits*.

[3] D. S. MacColl was dubious about Rothenstein's new mode of life: 'Rothenstein has become a country gentleman and paints his own haystacks (not always to their advantage). It is a very odd end for a lively wit. Let us all do more practical things.' (MacColl to Beerbohm, January 17, 1915. BP:MC.)

[4] Rothenstein was staying with Ernest Debenham (1865–1952), London store owner. Present owner of the portrait: Affpuddle and Tonerspuddle Parish Council; it hangs in the Village Hall, Bryantspuddle, Dorchester.

[5] 'Far Rapallo': see address of Letter 63.


◇66      26 Oxford Terrace [London][1]      Thursday [August 1915]

My dear Will

Ever so many apologies. It seems utterly ridiculous that I should have had to make so many bungling and promptly-to-go-into-the-waste-basket attempts to perform a task seemingly so simple. At least it must seem so to you. Even to me, with a long experience of my incapacities, it seems odd that I shouldn't have succeeded, at (say) the third attempt, in producing something not exactly calculated to make you, Tagore, me, and Macmillan utterly ashamed of themselves and of one another. And even now I am not sure that what I am sending you will "do." Read it and see what you think, and don't hesitate to say exactly what you do think. By the way, are the drawings to be a thin *book* or a portfolio? I have called them a *book*. If they are a *portfolio*, please substitute that word in the two or three cases where the word *book* occurs...But this is on the assumption that the note as a whole will seem to you all right enough. A vast assumption.[2]

How exciting, the idea of your going forth to draw the King! I can imagine beautiful results. Mind you come and see us en route.[3] Best love from us both to you both. Your affectionate Max

[1] The Beerbohms came to England in the Spring of 1915; Far Oakridge was their headquarters until 1917. Soon after they arrived, Max wrote: 'It is a relief to find things going on—superficially, at least—in the same old way. In Italy, Florence and I lived on a plane of concentrated anxiety. It was impossible to think of anything but the war. But here one realises that the world still revolves.' (Beerbohm to Rothenstein [mid-May 1915]. RP:HL.)

[2] Duckworth thought it more appropriate for Macmillan, Tagore's London publisher, to produce Rothenstein's drawings.

[3] Emile Vandervelde (1866–1938), Belgian Minister of State in 1914, asked Rothenstein to make a portrait of King Leopold, reproductions to be sold for war relief. The King was unavailable, and Rothenstein drew Ypres instead. See *MM* II, 303–306.

∻67            *26 Oxford Terrace*    Sunday [October 1915]

My dear Will

We went yesterday to the gallery and stood long before the Little Boy Lost—so called, though he was very easy to find, being in the middle of the wall that is flush with the door of the first room one enters.

```
┌─────────────────┐
│  First Room     │
│  Door           │
│      ┌┐  LBL    │
└──────┘└─────────┘
```

If anything, he looks even better in the gallery than he did in the actual barn at Far Oakridge. He brings sunshine and space instead of having to compete with them on the spot. And there was an old lady standing in front of him, nodding and smiling to herself, evidently much pleased that the dear little fellow had been found and that all was well.[1]

In the same room there is a picture of Strang's, called "A Café Bar," which is without exception the most asinine thing I have ever seen. I wish I could describe it, but I can't begin to: it needs a whole new vocabulary. It has to be *seen*. Lavatory's picture of Winston runs it close.[2] Today there is a small dim red ball discernible in the hardly discernible sky, and I take this as a token that you are out and about in a flood of sunshine, painting. We think and talk continually of Far Oakridge and all that is therein.

Love from us both to you and Alice and all. Yours affectionately Max

[1] An exhibition of the International Society of Sculptors, Painters, and Gravers opened at the Grosvenor Gallery on October 15, 1915. The title of Rothenstein's painting suggests the fantasy, *A Little Boy Lost*, by his close friend, W. H. Hudson (1841–1922). In February 1916 the Grosvenor Gallery sent 'Little Boy Lost', which depicts a figure in a sunlit, barnlike passage, to Knoedler and Company, New York, for an exhibition of contemporary British artists. Knoedler's records do not include those for 1916, and the present owner of the painting is unknown.

[2] For another assessment of the work of William Strang (1859–1921), English painter, see a review, 'Tendency in Art', *The Times*, October 16, 1915, p. 11.

'Lavatory': Sir John Lavery (1856–1941), who in 1935 gave his portrait of Winston Churchill to the Municipal Gallery of Modern Art, Dublin; it is on permanent loan to the National Gallery of Ireland, Dublin. See Lavery, *The Life of a Painter*, pp. 182, 273 [plates 25, 26].

❖68          Steyne Cottage, Bognor, Sussex     May 9, 1916

My dearest Will

I am touched and flattered by your idea that I should do a note for the catalogue of your exhibition; and nothing would give me greater delight, of course, than to do it.[1] *But*, considering the matter from the standpoint of expediency, and in a thoroughly worldly-wise spirit, I am convinced that it would be much better for your interests that I should eliminate myself on this occasion. Generally speaking, such notes do no good, and may do harm. Suppose a young and unknown artist whose work is greatly admired by an elder and famous one. A note by the latter on the former is obviously desirable. Suppose an artist of your own age and reputation. A note by (say) Alphonse Legros (specially risen from the grave for the purpose of writing it) wouldn't be amiss. Suppose a note by *me*..."Yes, yes," you say, "but that isn't the point. Of course, such a note wouldn't do any *worldly* good. The matter is purely one of senti-ment." To which I reply "True! But you musn't allow your sentiment to militate against your own interests. You *must* think of *them*. Don't forget your wife, either. Bear in mind, also, your children. The average critic wouldn't understand that my note was asked for merely as a gauge of old friendship. He would think that you and Brown *and* Phillips thought that your work needed some outside assistance. He would think that you and B *and* P were quite wrong in this notion.[2] But he would, nevertheless, be affected in his judgment—not of your work, but—of your position. This would be so even if I hadn't ever written anything at all about you. It would be the more so because he would remember that 3 months or so ago there was a note by me in your Tagore book, and that a day or two before the opening of your present show the June number of the *Cornhill* had appeared with a story by me called 'Enoch Soames,' wherein I had expressed my undying friendship and admiration and so on for you. He would say to himself 'Enough! This is the 3rd time we have had Max Beerbohm dinning Will Rothenstein into our ears. Has he no other friends and apostles? Why shouldn't *they* have a turn? Or—better still—why shouldn't W. R. stand forth alone?' I perfectly agree with this critic: you ought to stand forth alone. That is by far the best policy. Adopt it."

How we should love to come, right away, to the Farm! But we cannot. Do let us come later, instead. I am doing some writing down here, and I must go on just at present. We went from Sat. to Mon. to the Colefaxes, who are not far from here, and who had asked us 3 times —so that there was no getting out of it. I don't mean that it wasn't very pleasant when we got there. Part of the pleasantness was that dear Albert was of the party. But it was an interruption of my work, and I am that bad kind of worker to whom interruptions are an awful set-back: I find it so hard to get back into my stride. I must therefore now go on with my stride till I've reached the goal. *Then* please let us come to you. Love from us both to you and Alice and all. Yours affectionately Max PS. Albert was staying at the Colefaxes under an assumed name; but I recognized him at a glance. He told me that you might or might not be going to be a Rutherston. Let me know what you decide, so that I may not misaddress letters, etc.[3]

---

[1] Rothenstein showed fifty-six portrait drawings at the Leicester Galleries, May 27–June 9, 1916. The catalogue has no preface.

[2] 'Brown and Phillips': owners of the Leicester Galleries.

[3] In April 1916, William's elder brother Charles (1866–1928), Bradford

businessman and art collector, and Albert Rothenstein, troubled by prejudices against persons with German names, changed their surname to Rutherston. Albert argued that, although he disliked the idea of the change, 'the question of pride no longer enters in, because it is a pride which we shall not be allowed to enjoy as British citizens, nor possibly the children.' See *WR*, pp. 278–279.

William at first agreed to follow suit, but, when the moment came, found himself unwilling to do so. Albert wrote: 'I'm now Albert Rutherston, it seems odd and I'm feeling not a little sad but I know it's wisest. I signed the deed-poll to-day.' (Albert Rutherston to Rothenstein, April 13, 1916. Rothenstein.) Cf. *MM* II, 288–289.

<br>

∽69          31 Southwick Street W. [London]    June 16, 1916

My dearest Will

Here we are, back from Bognor at length, but not, alas, in time to see the whole of your exhibition. We hurried thither yesterday, and found that an exhibition of Italian war-drawings was being hung; but Oliver Brown and the elder Phillips gave us a sort of private view of your works —minus the sold and already-distributed ones; and we had a revelling half-hour. There were so very many that I hadn't seen, and all of them beautiful as *things* and masterly as presentments of the respective gentlemen's characters. I don't know which of them abide beyond others in my mind—Yeats, perhaps, and [Augustus] John, and [Ambrose] McEvoy, and—but [it] is so hard to single out any of them from the rest. Gosse, of course—(who wrote to me the other day, and was enthusiastically pleased at your portrait of him). I wish I had seen the Shaw and Ian Hamilton and various others, including myself, that had "gone." And I wish I could write a more intelligent appreciation of everything. But you know my admiration and must take my intelligence on trust.[1]

Poor Alice! I am so *very* sorry she has been having gastritis, and I can all the more sympathise because I myself had it 3 or 4 years ago. Please give her my love, and tell her how glad I am she is getting well: it is a heavenly process—getting well: I enjoyed it so much, and almost envy her: one's food is manna, and one's drink nectar, and one can't have enough of either: one isn't allowed to—and the limitation is what makes seem so divine the portion that one *does* get.

It will be lovely for us to come and see her and you and the children. Just at present, we have to be in London. But some time in *July*?

Your affectionate Max

Delighted that you liked E. Soames in *Cornhill*.[2]

101

¹ General Sir Ian Hamilton (1853–1947), appointed Commander of the Mediterranean Expeditionary Force, 1915.

Gosse wrote: 'Like Enoch [Soames] I have been sitting to the highly-remarkable Rothenstein, as perhaps you have seen. He is marvellously clever, but irregular; he does not always hit it off. In my case, I think he has hit it off superbly. You have not been so fortunate.' (Gosse to Beerbohm, July 5, 1916. Taylor.) For Gosse's letter to Rothenstein, see *WR*, pp. 274–275. John Drinkwater (1882–1937), poet and playwright, bought the drawing in 1916; present owner is unknown.

² 'Enoch Soames' had just appeared. Gosse wrote: 'I have been so immensely amused and interested by "Enoch Soames" that it would be quite ungrateful not to tell you so. It is quite perfect in your best manner, and no one else has [a?] hand so delicate and charming. You have a wonderful power of the "create [he] can Forms more real than living man, Nurseling of immortality." Poor dim Enoch is a nursling of immortality, and round him you have managed to recreate that pleasing silly gallant atmosphere of 1893 far better than any of the writers of solemn "histories." It is a kind of flashing review of H[olbrook] Jackson's rather futile and misleading book [*The Eighteen Nineties*], a hundred times better than the original.' (Gosse to Beerbohm, June 5, 1916. Taylor.) 'Create . . . immortality': Shelley, *Prometheus Unbound*, I, i, 747–749.

Max replied: 'There is no man whom I would rather please by my writings than you, and there is none whose praise can so much gratify me and encourage me; and I am as glad to have your letter as you were kind in writing it. I would have sent the "Cornhill" to you of my own accord, in the hope that Enoch would amuse you; only, in these days, one doesn't like to go on the assumption that anybody can possibly be interested, even for a moment, in any other days (and Enoch's day was so very pre-eminently "other"!).' (Beerbohm to Gosse, June 10, 1916. Brotherton Collection: University of Leeds.)

On Enoch's genesis, Max commented: 'The waterproof cape worn by Enoch was itself suggested, I think, by memory of one worn by Arthur Symons. Otherwise Enoch, as drawn by me, owes nothing to Symons, but much to my imagination of what Ernest Dowson (whom I never saw) might have been if he had been rather like Victor Plarr (whom I never had the pleasure of meeting) with a dash of Theodore Wrattislaw [*sic*] and others.' (Beerbohm to Robert Ross, June 10, 1916. J.-P. B. Ross.) Victor Plarr (1863–1929), poet; Librarian, 1897–1929, Royal College of Surgeons. Theodore Wratislaw (1871–1933), descendant of Bohemian nobility, poet in the early 1890's, Civil Servant after 1895.

◇70        Iles Farm [Far Oakridge]    March 27 [1917]

My very dear Max—what a delightful letter you wrote Billy! I do really believe he appreciated the peopling of London with Oakridge creations. As for the stamp book, ring faun is in abeyance: he will do nothing save stick in stamps & brood over their pays d'origine.¹ Have you had an answer to your National Volunteering? I am dashing up on Saturday to be interviewed by Albert's old department.² In the meanwhile I have actually got some national work to do—some lithographic drawings—which will make me busy for some weeks. If I can manage it, & you are at Ebury St, I will try to get a sight of you on Saturday, before returning in the evening.[3] We do really miss you—all the house does—& it still seems unnaturally silent & dull throughout the house. All lights go out at nine & Alice is in bed before that hour. The Russian news seems less disquieting to-day: the extremists are becoming less extreme. It is now really a question of democracy versus junkerismus, & Florence must be satisfied with America's steady decision.[4] I hope Florence is still content with our modest quarters at Ebury St: it is a pleasure to know of your being comfortable there. I want to ask a favour of you, dear Max: I want you to send me the Johnson—Will—Russell caricature. Alice doesn't like the idea of its being shown, however discreetly, at a time like the present, & I think she is right. One says things at a particular moment, wise or unwise and stupid, in intimate conversation which, being interpreted, may make mischief. And I think there are always some people who may make it, & I am rather an assailable person, having a strong spirit of contradiction always near the surface. You know my old joke anent myself—half my acquaintances disapprove of me because I am so often in the company of drunkards & the other half because I don't drink. The drawing shall be as in a safe, &, whenever you wish it, returned, or added to my own unrivalled collection. Indeed I would not hesitate to show it *myself*.[5]

John returns next week, after a couple of days in Town with his friend Tom Rowat, & there will be great rejoicing. He has come out top in literature & geography & history exams, he writes.[6] Braxton still haunts us—the children speak of him constantly.[7] They all send their warmest love to you both—so does Alice & so do I. Ever, dear Max, affectionately—Will

My typed copy has not yet come! Sheffield is clearly more prompt at delivering big guns than paper.[8]

[1] William's younger son, William Michael (Billy) Rothenstein (1908–     ), painter and printmaker. Neither Max's letter nor a unique stamp survives: 'Max made a hand drawn reproduction of the George V penny red, with my father's head on it (instead of the King) for my birthday. My father later "took care of it," in case it got lost—and lost it!' (Michael Rothenstein to Mary Lago, July 8, 1971.) 'Ring faun' is unidentified.

[2] Albert Rutherston had been at the Engineers War Service Register, Board of Trade. He was assigned in October 1916 to service abroad and was sent to Egypt and Palestine.

[3] 115 Ebury Street: the Rothensteins' London flat, principally a pied-à-terre for Alice after they settled at Oakridge.

[4] The Russian Revolution had broken out in March 1917; the United States was slowly deciding to join the Allies, and did so on April 6.

[5] 'Johnson-Will-Russell caricature': unidentified and untraced.

[6] Tom Rowat (d. 1920), who was John Rothenstein's fellow pupil at King Alfred's School, Hampstead, and at Bedales School near Petersfield, Hampshire, died in a military accident in Egypt.

[7] See Beerbohm, 'Hilary Maltby', *The Century Magazine*, 97 (1919), 445–465; reprinted as 'Hilary Maltby and Stephen Braxton', in his *Seven Men*, pp. 51–104. Max wrote this story and read it to the Rothensteins at Oakridge; see Behrman, *A Portrait of Max*, pp. 69–71.

[8] Rothenstein's Sheffield lecture; see p. 78, note 19.

◇71      115 Ebury Street [London]    Friday [March 30? 1917]

Dearest Will

Many thanks for your delightful letter. We do so hope you'll be able to snatch a brand of time from tomorrow's burning and look in on us. Of course I haven't shown that Russel[l]-Johnson drawing to any one here. It might assuredly be misinterpreted, and is most unjust. I am intrigued to know what kind of "lithographic" work you are doing for the safety of England. [1]

I received an invitation to Queen Anne's Chambers the other day, and went there on Tuesday; saw two amiable men who seemed to like me; one of them made notes about me and gave me a card from which I learn that my Enrolment Number is 131,853—so that I gather I am up against a formidable amount of competition. Nevertheless I live in hope that I may save England yet by "some kind of clerical work." [2] Best love to Alice and the children. We were delighted with Billie's letter.

Best regards to Miss Masters. [3] Yours affectionately Max (131,853)

[1] Rothenstein's wartime lithographs comprise 'Work on the Land, Set VII, Numbers 43–48 of "The Great War: Britain's Efforts and Ideals"'; and a colour lithograph, Number 10 in a blatantly propagandist series, 'The Triumph of Democracy,' commissioned by the Ministry of Information, presented by it to the Victoria and Albert Museum in 1918.

[2] 'Some kind of clerical work' was propaganda cartoons which Max declined as unsuited to his talent and therefore ineffective. In 1915 he cancelled a scheduled show of caricatures at the Leicester Galleries because he felt that his style of humour would be 'horrible in these days of sadness'. See *Max*, pp. 337–338; Oliver Brown, *Exhibition*, pp. 189–190.

Neither Colonel Charles à Court Repington (1858–1925), soldier and military writer, nor Arnold Bennett, who made separate attempts, could mobilise Max.

[3] A governess to the Rothenstein girls.

## 72

Officers' Club, General Headquarters[1] B.E.F., France

March 20, 1918

My very dear Max—I have been moving about these last days & have not had letters for some little time; but I found the last ones sent here & from something Betty wrote, I gather your mother has passed away.[2] I am sure Alice will have written me & I hope to get her letters at my last address, when I return this evening. Until then I know nothing but the bare fact; but I know how long your dear mother has been ill & that her end must have been peaceful & dignified. She was so closely associated with many years of my own life that I can evoke her presence always & see her more clearly than I can most people. You know she always made your house a kind of haven for us all—how good she was to me & to all the children & to Alice! Yours was the first house where John went to lunch out—& how many associations I have with the rooms your mother made so intimate & personal. It was her devotion to you that was always touching to me: her radiant happiness in your success & welfare, & you were able to make her life brimful of happiness & pleasure, in spite of the difficulties life brings to all of us. And as a friend I got some of her deep & ample affection & no one quite had the place in my heart which she had, & the rooms she made so charming will be stamped on my memory, so long as I have one. How we used to discuss your present & future in days long since gone by! & the delight in the weekly articles & caricatures & her pride in you—these things I shall not easily forget. I have met many people, but none with a more vivid & charming personality than your dear mother's, & I never saw her after it began to cloud.

I have a long half finished letter to you in a sketch book.[3] I have thought much & often of you since I came out, 3 months ago to-day; and I seem to have lived 3 years, so full has life been. And now it all shrinks back for many years, while I am thinking of your mother; & you are in the long low room upstairs, littered with papers, & I am coming up to you after sitting with your mother downstairs. In so many ways you are the same Max, but so much wiser & riper—yet in those days your mother thought me the wiser of the two. I should much like to see you when I come back—I am still uncertain as to when that is to be. I am deeply interested in my work here. And how often we discussed the war, & now for 3 months I have been living in it, sharing the life of the wonderful people out here & seeing with my own eyes what war looks like. The strange thing is, in so far as war concerns one's self, that the conditions are so simple & the issues of life so focussed on each day's existence, that life itself is simplified, & I find myself less irritable & more peaceful, mentally & physically, than I have ever been. Life in the army is a kind of simple State-Socialism; & an official artist a kind of official parasite, with nothing to do but draw & draw, & no material worries to prevent him working all day & every day, save such transitory things as shells. Please give my love to Florence, dear Max, & believe me ever your affectionate friend—Will

[1] Rothenstein had been in France since December 1917 as an Official War Artist commissioned to make an artistic record of England's part in the war. He had urged this scheme on the War Office, but, when he requested assignment, younger men than he had been sent first. He returned to Gloucestershire in early Summer and in July was called up for ordinary military service. He was actually on his way to the station when Sir Henry Hadow (1859–1937), Assistant Director of Staff Duties (Educational) for the War Office, 1918–19, assigned him as a lecturer in the Army's educational programme in France. Again there was delay, this time caused by French officials. Rothenstein wrote: 'I only wish I had not been allowed to waste a good part of 2 months; if Hadow had had the courage to tell me quite simply last August that the fact of my dear old father having come from a village near Hanover nearly 70 years ago proscribed my teaching in France, I should have done much more work, have gone on with my Sheffield activities and been saved much anxiety and distress.' (Rothenstein to John Drinkwater, October 23, 1918. Beinecke Library, Yale University.) See *MM* II, 303–312, 326–340. Rothenstein later joined an Australian unit at Cambridge.
[2] Eliza Beerbohm died in March 1918 after three years of failing health.
[3] Perhaps the letter quoted in part in *WR*, p. 293.

✧73          12 Well Walk, Hampstead      Tuesday [late April 1918]

Dearest Will

I was so sorry that I just missed seeing you the other day when I came to Ebury Street: I did so want to see you and hear all your adventures and also to say how deeply I had been touched by the beautiful letter of sympathy I had had from you. My dear Mother's death was a great grief for us and is a lasting one: somehow it never seemed to us that she was *really* old. I wish you could have seen her after her death. She looked *then* as young as she had always been in spirit—far younger than you or I had ever seen her look. It was most strange. One would have supposed her face to be that of a woman of thirty, literally, not more than that; and the expression of the face was all eagerness, rather than peace, like a beginning of new things rather than an end of old ones. Florence and Con and Agnes and I were with her when she died. She had not been conscious for a long time. She had had no pain. She just gradually ceased to live.

I think her life had been a very happy one altogether—though of course she had had the sorrows that are inseparable from fulness of life.

And now I hear, dear Will, that you too have suffered a grievous loss. I had heard so much about the beauty of your sister's nature, and about your devotion to each other, and I send you my deep sympathy. I wish she could have been spared, as my Mother was, knowledge of what is going on in the world at this moment. I gather that she was one of the people whom the war affected intolerably. What a period ours is![1]

Florence and I hope you will come and bring Alice to us tomorrow evening—Wednesday—and have something to eat—7.30 or earlier. I long to see your pictures. Your loving friend Max

[1] Rothenstein's sister Louisa Simon died on April 18, 1918.


◇74                              Villino Chiaro        January 1920

My dearest Will

I wish I could be at the dinner to Greaves. It would be a real pleasure. Put my name down by all means. And let me contribute to the "purse." How much are people giving? Would £5 be a correct sort of sum? If so, put me down for that, and I will send you a cheque.[1] I got from you, just as I was on the wing for Italy, *such* a delightful letter about my new book. I am immensely glad the stories seemed to you to come out well in their new form. I think I read them all to you and Alice at the farm. *Braxton* and *Savonarola* especially shall I always associate with Far Oakridge, their birthplace.[2] Your laughter, while I used to read them bit by bit from day to day, was such an encouragement. Had you looked grave, neither of those stories would have come to completion. I hate to think of your leaving the Farm—though I daresay you will both enjoy being in London. You aren't leaving it *altogether*, are you? Only *letting* it? I should like to think that you keep a firm hold on all those immemorial title-deeds and things, and can settle down again on your land when your land calls to you. Meanwhile, in London, what a whirl of committees you will inevitably find yourself in!![3] You must not overtire yourself. You must not join more than two new committees a week, nor resign from more than one. I do hope Alice is feeling better. I was so *very* sorry to hear from you that she wasn't well. It is lovely to be back

107

here with Florence. I had forgotten *how* perfect life here could be. We both send you our best love. Shan't you both ever come over here? It would be lovely if you did. What sort of studio have you got in London? I expect you will rather miss your trees and valleys—but I expect you will enjoy the opportunity of doing portraits. I liked Mrs. Albert immensely: a sort of fairy; and it was a joy to see Albert home from the wars and evermore a civilian.[4] What a nightmare the years of the war seem, don't they? Your loving friend Max

[1] Rothenstein and William Nicholson took the lead in organising a dinner to honour Walter Greaves (1846–1930), Chelsea waterman, painter, sometime protégé of Whistler; it was sponsored by the Chelsea Arts Club and held at the Florence Restaurant in Rupert Street, February 10, 1920. Lord Henry Bentinck presided; Sickert was principal speaker. Alice Rothenstein, in a long letter to Max, wrote: 'All the evening he (Greaves) kept saying to me, this is the proudest moment of my life if I live to be a thousand I shall never never forget it—we insisted on his saying a few words—he demurred—we insisted—but once he got going it was lovely—he talked and talked of old Chelsea—what times they must have been!—how you would walk right across the river stepping from boat to boat—of the crowds watching the fireworks at Cremorne, people fighting on the Bridge—the Bridge breaking—but the people still going on fighting just the same in the water and in the mud—so that in time the fireworks had to be stopped (to save the bridges and the fighting I suppose)—did we realise that now his father knew Turner?—how it takes one back! Well, he went on talking—and it made the Chelsea of Augustus John very dull indeed, absolutely colorless. . . . Walter Sickert spoke several times *most* brilliantly—but always of his own affairs—Whistler—Pennell lithographs etc. etc. and all the old Chestnuts—he did not once *refer to Greaves*—this was Walter's way of seconding the toast to Mr. Greaves. He arrived—the lower part of him correctly attired for Golfing (*very* thin legs) *and* and upper part quite indescribable surmounted by an absolutely square beard, it was cut off just—only just below his chin and stood out very wide each side and horribly disconcertingly square—it was really most embarrassing—his head seemed so short and so terribly square.' (Alice Rothenstein to Beerbohm, February 17 [1920]. BP:MC.)

Max replied that she had made it 'all so vivid that I feel I was there, *at* that dinner. And all so amusing that I have enjoyed everything much more even than if I *had* been there. Ever so many thanks. I am so glad that the dear old man was happy, and that he forthcame and abounded in his own fruity old queer vein of talk. . . . I wish WILL had presided. I took it as a matter of course that he would. I suppose he at any rate spoke in the course of the evening. These occasions "need" him—and if they get him don't need anybody else. Not even Walter Sickert, whom you record so well. I have seen that new beard of his. Quite the shrewd old farmer, up from the Midlands for the Agricultural Show: "You doan't get a noise out of I!" Also a touch of the ventriloquist's puppet—by reason of the hard sharp lines from corners of mouth down to jaw-bone. But he remains Walter. And no ventriloquist could invent the patter that *he* can.' (Beerbohm to Alice Rothenstein, February 20, 1920. RP:HL.) For another account of the dinner, see Tom Pocock, *Chelsea Reach: The Brutal Friendship of Whistler and Walter Greaves*, p. 188.

[2] Rothenstein had written: 'God blessed me above other men with a bad

108

memory. Hence however many times I see a picture or read a book it is always a new thing to me. Each of your enchanting stories [in *Seven Men*] you read to us here [at Far Oakridge], yet dear to me as they were, each was completely forgotten. Reading them brings back the sound of your voice and a refreshed memory, and the delight is the greater.' (Rothenstein to Beerbohm, November 18, 1919. Clark Library, UCLA.)

3 The Rothensteins sold the farmland but kept three cottages on the property. William, again at Fisher's urging, accepted appointment as a Visitor to the Royal College of Art.

4 Albert Rutherston and Margery Holman were married in October 1919.

◇75          18 Sheffield Terrace, Kensington     July 21 [1920]

My dearest Max—I am the most careless person in the world. Here have I been awaiting news of you for more than two months & to-day I find a letter to Conrad & one to yourself underneath a nest of papers on my desk. I admit both these were begging letters. But the one to you contained the ordinary news of our moving here, news that is now too stale to send on to you. The begging was for this—I asked you to write me 400 words (no more, a page of text only) to accompany the drawing of John Drinkwater I am publishing in my book of 24 portraits this autumn. No wonder no text came! Happily, if you are in a mood for consenting, there is still time. Who has written upon yourself must be a secret—also to whom the book is dedicated will not yet be disclosed.[1] But my friends have, willingly or with silent curses, supplied me with charming notes & I can imagine no one better equipped than yourself for a note on the owner & lessee of that cottage where you heard the starved cocks crow. No longer do we hear the crowing of starved or pampered cocks. Parker serves other masters & other eyes look across the valley long dear to us. Kensington, where John first saw the light, & Alice & myself the Registrar of marriages, is once more our home. John's cheek has changed from grey to scarlet; he is happy once more in his native air. Rachel goes daily to the Royal College of Music, leaving Betty to sit over French verbs & German nouns with Miss Conens. The house is become a haunt of musicians. Indians throng the steps & Alice sometimes leaves her bedroom, hung with golden mirrors, to walk in Bond St or Wigmore St.[2] No longer do I battle with wind and snow, & human sitters have taken the place of trees & roofs. But we still retain the long oak table & many other vestiges of Iles Farm & we hope, before long, to have you & Florence sitting on either side—for wives & husbands must not sit together.

John Drinkwater still lives at the little cottage; but he is now a man of substance. Albert has settled down to a married life of taxis & parties, Craig has appeared & has disappeared in a cloud of fire, Tagore lives near us, & where once the sweet birds sang the sound of the telephone is heard.[3] In fact we are once more normal people. I hope all goes well with you both. The family is in Norfolk, where I join them in a few days. May I expect to get my page from you? & also forgiveness for this loan? My love to Florence; I am sure she is happy in her Italy, if one can be happy anywhere in these troubled days. Ever your affectionate—Will

[1] Conrad is not represented in Rothenstein, *Twenty-Four Portraits*. In his own copy, now owned by Stanley Marcus, Max wrote beneath his note on Drinkwater [plate 8]: 'Not badly written—but too long.' Beneath his own portrait [plate 2], he wrote: 'The most completely distinguished [face?] in the England of our time. In Italy for the moment.' For his comments on himself and on Strachey, dated February 1921, from this copy, see *Max*, p. 370. For Strachey on Beerbohm, see Michael Holroyd, *Lytton Strachey: A Critical Biography*, II, 244–245, 392–394. Author of the note on Max remains unidentified. Dedication is to Max, Drinkwater, and William Simmonds (1876–1968), sculptor, woodcarver, painter, puppeteer.

[2] Winstons Cottage, beside which a neighbour kept chickens, was the Beerbohms' residence at Far Oakridge during the war. 'Parker': Iles Farm handyman until 1920. Miss Conens: governess to the Rothenstein girls. Tagore and his entourage were in London; see *IE*, pp. 267–279.

[3] The Drinkwaters rented Winstons until 1921, when their marriage began to break up; Drinkwater never returned to Far Oakridge. The American success of his play, *Abraham Lincoln* (1919), brought him, for the first time, a substantial income.

Albert Rutherston was about to launch the Oxford School of Painting and Design, at 49 Cornmarket Street, Oxford.

Gordon Craig came to England at the invitation of Claud Lovat Fraser (1890–1921), painter and stage designer.

◇76               Villino Chiaro     July 29, 1920

My dearest Will

Here is a little MS. within the prescribed limits of space. Will it do?[1] Of course I have assumed that all the letterpress, as in your previous books, will be *unsigned*; and I have written accordingly in an unsigned style; and the thing, as it stands, would be all wrong with a signature. I hope it isn't all wrong without one?? Send me a line of reassurance, if you conscientiously can. There won't, I expect, be time for the printers to send me a proof out here; so would you be so very good as to go thro' the proof sent to *you* and see that they haven't played any tricks?

I have written it all very legibly—the nearest approach to positive pot-hooks and hangers that I have ever made since I left the nursery—so that, with a little good-will, with an ever so slight reaction from Bolshevist principles, the compositors are almost sure not to go astray anywhere. Meanwhile, 1000 thanks for a very delightful letter; and also an equal number of congratulations on the fact (which you don't mention) of your new appointment. The first news I had of that was from Teddy Craig on his return here, and from him I could not glean anything very definite—merely a general notion of glory...

M. B. Oh really? South Kensington...The *Museum?*

E. G. C. No—not the Museum so much—*you* know! (with a sweep of the arm) The *place*. Whole thing. School. Telling them what to do.

M. B. I see, yes, but—telling whom?

E. G. C. Everybody. What to do and what not to do. Great fun. Students.

M. B. Ah—yes. What's the post *called?*

E. G. C. Professor—King—Director—Governor—something of that sort.

M. B. *Director*, I should think, perhaps?

E. G. C. Yes, I should think so.

M. B. And I suppose it isn't *honorary?* I mean, is there a salary attached?

E. G. C. Oh yes—surely. All the jollier!

etc, etc, etc.

I was glad, but bewildered, until a day or two later I saw the announcement (evidently *not* written by Craig) in the weekly edition of "The Times [Educational Supplement]": after which I turned for fuller knowledge to Whitaker's Almanac[k] and learned all about it. At least, not *all*—I should like to hear *all* from *you*—but enough to be sure that it would be a very congenial post for you, and you *the* man of all others for *it*.[2] If Florence and I weren't settled out here we would enroll ourselves as students. The extra £800 is a pleasant idea, too, I do hope you will have to deliver frequent lectures, as you do it so easily and so incomparably well. And I hope the Moiras and Derwent Woods and others already on the premises won't be a bother. They are very good fellows, of course. But then, very good fellows are sometimes the hardest of all to deal with: they are so apt to suspect that one isn't a good fellow oneself. However, I'm sure all will be well.[3]

We laughed long over your description of your and Alice's and the family's new doings and feelings in London. How I wish I could have sampled these myself when I suddenly dashed over to London! But I hadn't, in the intervals of all-day dealings with the printers of the book that has been compiled about Herbert, a moment in which to see any one, except some of the contributors whom I *had* to see, and Constance and Agnes. I stayed in a flat that Maud has in Adam Street—delightful rooms.[4] Give my love, please, and Florence's, to Alice and to the children. I told Alice, when I wrote some time ago from here, how very glad I was to think of Billy being at my own old Wilkinson's. But now, really, with Rabindranath Tagore on Campden Hill, it seems to me absurd that a child should be packed off daily to the lower, earthier kind of tuition that goes on in Orme Square.[5]

I hope Tagore hasn't thrown off the Christ-like phase that was so strong on him in America? I hope he does still lay his hands on the heads of little children?—and does still, at a pinch, heal the sick and raise the dead? I was greatly disgusted lately at hearing that he is not to be allowed to re-enter America.[6] It seems they *won't* trust him not to turn water into wine. Fools! Or rather, "O fools and blind!" as *he* would say. *Erratum*. For *"he"* read *"He."* Always affectionately Max

[1] That is, Max's note on Drinkwater.

[2] Rothenstein's salary as Principal of the Royal College of Art was £1,000.

[3] Gerald Moira (1867–1959), Head, School of Painting; and F. D. Wood (1871–1926), Head, School of Sculpture at the Royal College.

[4] While Florence returned to Rapallo in the Autumn of 1919, Max had stayed in London to prepare a memorial volume on his brother, who died in 1917. See *Herbert Beerbohm Tree*, comp. Max Beerbohm. Maud Tree (d. 1937) was Herbert's widow.

[5] Max wrote: 'As if I didn't know that school! I went there, as a new boy, just 39 years ago!! I was there from '81 to '85, And I am greatly glad that Billie is going to follow in those obliterated old footsteps of mine. . . . For Wilkinson himself . . . remains as boyish as ever, making me feel always like a nonagenarian in his company. . . . Mrs. Wilkinson, in those days, used to teach drawing to the boys. Hers were the only lessons I ever had: the free-hand system: . . . And what a trial I must have been to Mrs. Wilkinson! But perhaps in those days my work showed more promise than it seems to show just now.' (Beerbohm to Alice Rothenstein, February 20, 1920. RP:HL.) A bomb destroyed the building, in the northwest corner of Orme Square, that had housed Mr Wilkinson's school.

[6] Tagore was not excluded in 1920, but see *IE*, pp. 279–297.

◇77                                        Norfolk    August 5 [1920]

My dearest Max—I don't know which I should publish—your letter to me with its portraits of Teddie Craig & Tagore, or the note on John Drinkwater. As neither Craig, nor the sage, is to appear in the book the problem is simplified. You have got John's sunny & gallant nature to the life. No one was more surprised, or happier, at great success then he, or enjoys good fortune with a sincerer grace. He will love your appreciation. I am most grateful to you for your quick & generous response. I think you will like the book—the text alone justifies it. I am going to spend a little time at Oakridge—I have a number of unfinished canvases, some of which I hope to work on—so I expect to be seeing the Drinkwaters. Tagore has just gone off to accept the homage of the neutral countries. He is to go on a long lecturing tour in America in October. Having seen a book of essays by his hand illustrated by a hundred views of Tagore in America, I tried to persuade him to stay in Europe.[1] But your letter throws light on the magnetism the States exert over the good Bengali; which is the magnet & which the filings I leave it to you—& Florence—to decide. But he evidently knows nothing of any prejudice against him on the part of the American authorities. Alas, that the strong wine of praise, & the weak wine of worship, should have gone to this good man's head. It is a misfortune for a poet to be too handsome; & even the Gods sometimes take praise too seriously, not to mention the Goddesses. After all the boasting about Jupiter & Diana, the poor earthly lions really did more harm to the Christians than the thunderbolts from Heaven. Perhaps, dreadful thought, Lady Colefax has destroyed more souls than Lucifer himself. Perhaps adulation is a habit— I mean the receiving of it—like smoking, & Tagore can't do without it. At any rate, he is turning his back on the thin stream he can wash his feet in here, for the great gushing river he can bathe in in the new world.

Craig sprang in among us, asked for a million, & disappeared. I wish he would take half the sum, & stay with us. But with him, the whole is the enemy of the half, & Italy gets him—for nothing. I am by nature ashamed of *not* paying any bills, but dear Teddie always makes me ashamed of paying them, & my rent, as though, he not being in a position to keep his own golden crown at home, it were somehow wrong to earn one's own living, with so much less genius, & family & good looks of one's own & of other people to look after. Yes, I am to have a salary & Poynter's old studio at South Kensington to work in, & the welfare of a large number of young men & women to look after, & various Professors, mostly academicians, among whom to take my exercise delicately.[2] The art-masters are crying "Bolshevism" & questions have been asked in the House of Commons. If anything could convince me that the spectre of Revolution need never trouble the dreams of Englishmen, it would be the fact that this baldheaded, elderly middle class & almost academical painter, who is myself, should be hailed as a dangerous young féroce by the teachers of our artistic provincial youth. If I had some of the cuttings from the provincial press I would send them for your private comfort; believe me, the heart of England sleeps, though at times it does not perhaps beat, soundly; there is no disease; only an occasional irregularity.

I came to join the family here for a few days, & to rid myself of an-old-man-of-the-sea cold which had taken complete possession of me. The sea is already doing wonders. The family looks radiant. I came looking like a living shrimp & hope to return with the warm glow of a cooked one. Alice laughed aloud over your letter. John was not here to enjoy it—he has passed Responsions & is paying visits before going up to Worcester [College, Oxford] in October. He is an ardent Royalist, a strong Conservative, wears spats & hard linen collars & shirts & will see to it that no extra emoluments fortune may bring me will change my spiritual life.[3] Billy grows more surprisingly talented every month, but he is not very strong & gives us a good deal of anxiety. I should like you to see some of his drawings—he must send you some. All send their love; Rachel is too busy practising on a silent keyboard, & reading histories of music to write. My dear love to Florence. Ever your affectionate—Will

[1] Tagore, *Personality*, with six photographs of Tagore as tourist. Cf. *IE*, pp. 236–237.

[2] Sir Edward Poynter, 1st Baronet (1836–1919), Principal, National Art Training School, afterward the Royal College, 1875–1881; President, Royal Academy, 1896–1918.

[3] For John Rothenstein on himself at Oxford, see his *Summer's Lease*, pp. 42–95.

⬦78     Royal College of Art     October 27, 1922

My dearest Max—I don't like bothering you; but I have the less hesitation in doing this since I know that you won't easily let yourself be bothered. And if my request bores you, or is likely to cause you too much trouble, well, you will know how *not* to respond to it. I made a drawing of Teddie Craig when he was here & this is to be included in the 2nd series of 24 portraits, which Chatto & Windus are to publish in the spring. If there is one person who would be as delighted as myself to have 400 words by your hand to embellish & outradiate my drawing it would be Craig himself. And I know you to have both admiration &

affection for this dynamic personality who explodes everywhere except upon the English stage—another reason for asking your help. In return I can only offer you a copy of the book when it appears, & Teddie's eternal gratitude.[1] The book will be a kind of Liber Juniorum, with a few middle aged gentlemen who can still expect to be cast for youthful rôles. We rejoice at the success of the lovely P.R.B. drawings.[2] All send their love to you both. Ever yours & Florence's—Will

We heard, with astonishment & admiration, of your adventurous journey to Florence. I hope the Royal Geographical Society will ask you to lecture on your exploration. If you went to Settignano you must come & speak at the Alpine Club.[3]

[1] Max is not listed among authors of notes for Rothenstein's *Twenty-Four Portraits: Second Series*; the author of that accompanying the drawing of Craig [plate 5] is unidentified. 'Teddie [Craig] of course I saw when he was here,' Rothenstein had written, 'as one sees a Zeppelin visiting London—enchanting to see, a little precarious to observe without an angle.' (Rothenstein to Beerbohm, October 1, 1922. Clark Library, UCLA.)

[2] Max's twenty-three drawings of the Pre-Raphaelite Brotherhood and associated figures, done at Oakridge, 1916–17; exhibited at the Leicester Galleries, September 1921, as 'Rossetti and His Friends'; published as *Rossetti and His Circle*. Present owner of the drawings: Tate Gallery.

[3] Max's journey emboldened him at home: 'Florence and I have become globe-trotters: we have recently returned from an extended tour, embracing Carrara, Lucca, Pistoia, and Florence. We much enjoyed it. I have become a percher aloft on precarious ladders, a painter of domestic frescoes.. I have done a fresco in the embrased arch over the green door of the spare bedroom, and another above the high-up fanlight in the hall. I think they look very jolly and Giottesque. Florence is not so sure about them; but there they are, to impress posterity; and I meditate some other designs for other eligible gaping and inviting spaces on our premises. Have you ever worked on the top of a ladder? It is exhilarating, bracing, and great fun. One may fall and be fractured or killed at any moment. One faces death but sees only one's art. And one *sings* all the time. Perhaps one doesn't sing accurately, but one sings loudly and with joy. Accuracy, as you may remember, was never my strong point in song.' (Beerbohm to Alexandra Kahn, October 19, 1922. Transscript. Bagshawe.) On the frescoes, see *Catalogue*, pp. 60, 165.

Beerbohm to William and Alice Rothenstein

⌖79            Netherton Hall, Honiton, S. Devon        June 9, 1923

My very dear $\begin{cases} \text{Alice and Will} \\ \text{Will and Alice} \end{cases}$

From each of you I have had a letter, full of thoughtfulness and kindness and delightfulness; and this letter is to thank both of you ever so much.

I am glad you really liked the exhibition, and glad you thought I did well in subtracting the pictures about which there was such a fuss. I had foreseen that these pictures would make the injudicious grieve; but I hadn't guessed that the heathen would rage furiously together. As their rage (mostly simulated though it was, I suppose) seemed likely to infect the general public, and perhaps to lead to "incidents" in the Leicester Gallery, I decided to do what I did. Some people seem rather to regret that I didn't ignore the whole agitation. But I'm sure I was right, and glad you are sure too.[1]

Florence and I are coming to London on Monday, and we will hasten to come and see you, and seeing you is the thing that we most of all look forward to.

We have been having a very pleasant and restful time here with the H. G[ranville]-B[arker]s.[2] Dear old Thomas Hardy and his wife spent the day here yesterday. He is younger than ever, and was lately much pleased that a poem which he had sent to the "Fortnightly," and which he did not think really very good, was "put in" by the Editor.[3] Fond love to you and to all from your loving Florence and Max

[1] The Beerbohms went to Devonshire on May 25; the Private View of Max's Leicester Galleries show was on May 29. Many viewers were outraged by nine drawings of King Edward VII: the eight 'Proposed Illustrations for Sir Sidney Lee's Forthcoming Biography', and 'Long Choosing and Beginning Late'; see *Catalogue*, pp. 60, 61. Sir Sidney Lee (1859–1926), Shakespearean scholar and an editor of the *Dictionary of National Biography*, wrote, at the request of King George V, *King Edward VII: A Biography*.

Dody Kahn had written: 'Uncle Max is at present doing a series of caricatures of Edward VII. They are terribly amusing, and the last one—of him in heaven—is perfectly awful: an enormously fat, entirely bald old man in the funniest costume— suggested by me—is playing some sort of lyre. I'm sure it couldn't be found in any musician's instruments shop, but as Uncle Max says, "Who can prove what sort they use in heaven?"' (Alexandra to L. M. and Nell Kahn, November 8, 1921. Bagshawe.)

[2] Harley Granville-Barker (1877–1946), actor, producer, playwright, then married to American heiress Helen Gates Huntingdon (d. 1950).

[3] Thomas Hardy (1840–1928) and his second wife, Florence (Dugdale) Hardy (d. 1937), whom he married in 1914. The poem most recently 'put in' was 'A December Rain-Scene', *The Fortnightly Review*, 110 (1921), 881.

◇80                     Royal College of Art     November 7, 1924

My very dear Max—John speaks with unwonted enthusiasm of the days he spent with you. I need scarcely say how grateful we are for the welcome you gave him. I hope he did not keep his foot too long in his neighbour's house. He tells us you were unfailing in your hospitality—however wearying at times the young may be you appear to have asked him hourly what conversational liqueur he would have! and what is greater than this kind of generosity? It happens that John has always looked on you as his model; without his dropping any coin in the slot, true wave ruling Britania (I robbed the lady of an n) or despised two sou piece, his hero appears to have functioned ideally. Thirsty as we were for news, he could not give us enough to satisfy us. But he gave a Boccaccio-like account of your rare visits to the city—of the inhabitants' respectful salutations, of the care you devoted to your dress, of the gracious feelings you extend to your not too proximate fellow citizens. He tells me you gave him wise & ready counsel. For all this I am truly grateful. Kindness & sympathy for one's children, be they worthy or erring, is dear to a parent's heart, & yours, dearest Max, to John will not readily be forgotten.[1] Ever your devoted—Will

[1] John Rothenstein, recuperating from a throat ailment, was at the Villino from September 24 to October 19, 1924. 'Quite a chip of the old block!' Max wrote to Florence, who was in America. 'He looked very grey and travel-stained on arrival, but fresh as a rose next morning. He is *extremely* intelligent, and keen and sane and entertaining and nice. . . . . John's overcoat, hanging in the hall this morning, looked extremely out of keeping with the surrounding scene—an epitome of London: damp fog seemed to be exhaled from every fold of the herring-bone tweed.' John's visit left Max acutely aware of a generation gap: 'I think he enjoyed his visit very much. As did I too—tho' 30 years is a wide gulf to span, and it somehow chills one to have to explain the difference between H. B. Irving and Henry Irving. J. seems to know a good deal about the 16th and 17th centuries (having read about them for his Schools at Oxford), but about the 19th his mind appears to be a complete blank. The first decade of the 20th also finds him at a loss. As to the 19th, by the way, I must except the 'nineties: about them he is not indeed very knowledgeful, but is (or was till I rather threw cold water on them) extremely enthusiastic. . . . I think he is one of the people for whom Oxford is no great good. He loves it dearly, but I don't think it enriched him with much beyond some expensive friends and habits. Very good manners I think he would have had in any case; and of course a sense of humour; and various other qualities that make him well worth one's effort across the aforesaid gulf.' (Max to Florence Beerbohm [September 25, October 19, 1924]. MCT.)
H. B. Irving (1870–1919), actor and criminologist, son of the actor-manager Henry Irving (1838–1905).

Villino Chiaro      November 12, 1924

My very dear Will, What a charming letter from you! But quite undeserved. It is you, as John's begetter, that should be thanked by *me* for

his stay here—you and dear Alice. And ever so many thanks to you both herewith for what I immensely enjoyed. I hope the young man wasn't inwardly bored much. I claim only that I did my best to make his visit pleasant. I wish Florence had been here. The weather was good at any rate; and the air, which is *always* good, must have been helpful to his tonsils after the London air; and the early hours—how appallingly early he will probably have told you!—may have been good, too. As for "conversational liqueurs"—that is all nonsense. It was *he* that provided these. I was but a barrel of old, flat, but not, I hope, unwholesome, beer, which he was so good as to tap with polite regularity. The memory of this chaste beverage must soon have vanished from his palate under the cascades of fiery yet mellow Teutonic brandy poured down his throat by Gerhart Hauptmann—who doesn't, I believe, speak English: no matter: I conceive John's jaws being held open by the English-speaking son of the Poet and Master.[1] But I seem to be writing a great deal of nonsense. How are you and Alice and all?—especially dear Rachel? I was so very glad to hear that she was making good progress to real and complete recovery. Give her my love. And love to Betty, the shaper of shapes.[2] And love to Billy, who, I conceive, will cut all the young men out, so soon as he is of age to hold an exhibition of his own. If I were you, I wouldn't let him contribute anything to any general exhibition. Just keep him dark, and then suddenly *burst* him into the light, all alone. Great fun, this would be. But I am afraid you'll think me vulgar. And I plead guilty.

What I'm *not* vulgar in, what I have a real high fine spirit about, is the appalling state of the Art Schools in Rome. John told me that there was a likelihood of your coming out officially, in the Christmas holidays, to inspect these Schools, for the Board of Education. Do! My reason for asking you to do this isn't *merely* that you couldn't reach Rome without passing through Rapallo and couldn't do that without being compelled by Florence and me to sojourn here on the way. You might like to sojourn here; but I know you of old: the things you would like to do are not the things you would see fit to do: a Mosaic man; a Cromwellian man; a splendid man, deaf to all but duty. Thus it is that I base my plea *not* on the fact that Rapallo is nice and that Rome (which with Florence I saw for the first time last Spring) beats everything for wonder and grandeur, but on the state of the Roman Art Schools. They are unbelievable. They cry aloud aloud to Heaven and to the B. of E.—Mrs. Strong's especially, alas! Most of her pupils have fallen away. She herself turns up fairly regularly, but *never* sober. She encourages what

118

pupils she still has to use india-rubber. "A little stippling and then a great deal of india-rubber, and then a little more stippling," she says to them, with a tipsy leer. She has done good work in her time. But, my dear Will, she is *past her work*. The British Embassy, the Quirinal, even the Vatican, are all for her, still. She is strongly entrenched; she'll take a lot of moving. You are the only man to tackle the job. It's a job that will test even *your* strength and probity. But you can fortify yourself for it here *en route*. Duty, and probity, and dignity, and decency, and sense of what is internationally needful, all combine to indicate an Italian journey by you.[3]

With dearest love to Alice—and *couldn't she* come too?—Your affectionate Max

[1] The German poet and playwright Gerhart Hauptmann (1862–1946) spoke no English; his son Benvenuto (1900–1965) was to arrange for John Rothenstein's travel to Agnetendorf, Silesia.

[2] Betty Rothenstein had won a sculpture scholarship at the Royal College of Art.

[3] Eugénie Sellers Strong (1860–1943), archaeologist, antiquarian; Librarian and Assistant Director, British School at Rome, 1909–1925. In 1925 the School was reorganized and Mrs Strong replaced. Max's comments are predated by a sympathetic letter from Rothenstein to her, to which she replied: 'Your more than kind and understanding note moved me to tears—in no figurative sense. It seemed to break that barrier of ice and misunderstanding that has surrounded me ever since I heard of this lamentable affair. . . . Tho' Mr. Shannon who represents the Royal Academy happened not to attend the fateful Committee, and only heard *here* [Rome], 10 days ago, a little more of the impending changes.' After she had left the School, she wrote: 'I cannot help smiling at your speaking of my "retirement"; what could give you that impression? You know that I fought the word last summer, and even wrote to the kind promoters of the dinner that if it were used on the cards, I should not be able to accept the honour they proposed to do me. . . . The Committee must face the fact that they chucked me out for reasons of their own; . . .' (Eugénie Strong to Rothenstein, October 24, 1924; February 11, 1926. RP: HL.)


◇82      Kay's Crib, Little Sheet, Petersfield, Hampshire

August 27, 1925

My dearest Max—John sent me on your letter, & the delightful preface you have written for his book.[1] I hope the riddance of the millstone is some compensation for having to endure its discomfort. I need not say how happy I am that you are to be godfather to this bulky venture. I wished for no other; & had you not found it possible to carry out this task, there would have been no preface. Any one but yourself would have been unthinkable. I much wanted to inflict myself, as well as my drawings, on you both this summer. I am not, like dear Albert, a collector of doctors. But discomfort sending me to Harley St, I was told I have been for long overworking, & was sentenced to rest for a couple of months.[2] Since there appeared to be no appeal, I thought at last I might invite myself to Rapallo. But I was not to be treated even as a political prisoner—I was forbidden to leave the country. So I joined Rachel, & we recline together, side by side, on chaises longues; each indignant at the other carrying a cushion unaided. I confess, delightful as it is to be with her, that I find resting, either during the day or the night, very wearisome. I am to be allowed to paint again in a few weeks' time; but I begin to doubt whether, if I go on resting all the time, I shall really be fit for work. I wish I could have joined you both, idling first at the Villino, then joining you on your travels.[3]

John finds his labours greater than he anticipated. He has now daily work, having a place with a literary agency, & tracking & cataloguing drawings seems to need years.[4] I have a decoration to do for the Houses of Parliament this next year.[5] But I shall probably have to give up the College which, though it has proved too much for me, keeping my own work going, has given me in many ways much happiness.

I will wait, before sending you more proofs, until John's book is out, when of course you will get the complete work. I think of you constantly. Nor is there any need to bring up your name—your praises are sung almost daily by some one. When I get back I want to send you both some odd drawings I found of Florence, when going through my drawers & portfolios. Give dear Florence my love. I still hope to see you both in your bower, & wish it could have been this long summer—a part of it, I mean. Rachel too sends her love. Alice is at Oakridge with Betty & Billy. Ever your devoted Will

[1] For *The Portrait Drawings of William Rothenstein, 1889–1925*, comp. John Rothenstein, pp. xi–xiv. Max took so long over this Introduction that Arthur Waugh (1866–1943), Director of Chapman and Hall, threatened to go to press without it. (Waugh to Rothenstein, July 3, July 8, 1925. RP:HL.)

[2] Albert Rutherston was not malingering; his health had been poor since his military service in Egypt. William himself was seriously ill; discomfort that he thought was indigestion was now diagnosed as severe heart damage. 'I sit in the Library of the Athenaeum [Club],' he wrote, 'the only old gentleman under 80, in the afternoons now, and read. I forgot, my dear Teddie, that I was in the fifties, and went my way, very unwisely, I think, as though these working days were still the 'nineties.' (Rothenstein to Craig, September 18 [1925]. Gordon Craig Collection: Bibliothèque Nationale, Paris.)

[3] The Beerbohms had visited Bologna.

4 John was with the firm of A. M. Heath. Max wrote: 'And I am excited at hearing that you, John, are lending lustre to the premises of a literary agent. Are you handling and placing MSS. of your own and charging yourself monstrous percentages and accusing yourself of robbing yourself and hotly resenting the imputation?' (Beerbohm to Rothenstein, August 20, 1925. RP: HL.)

5 'Sir Thomas Roe's Embassy to the Court of Jehangir, 1614': one of a set of murals for St Stephen's Hall, Westminster.

◇83                Villino Chiaro     September 8, 1925

My dearest Will, I am so glad and relieved that the Introduction doesn't find disfavour in your sight. I should have liked it to be ever so much more interesting, etc.; but I haven't an Angel's pen, nor even one of gold: just my old steel one, which I ply as best I can. I have just corrected the proof and am posting it to Henrietta Street for the printers.

Why, oh why, aren't you, of all people in the world, bloomingly well and strong? It never had occurred to me that *you* could ever have anything at all the matter with you. You have always appeared to me such an exquisitely-adjusted dynamo, warranted to work forever without trace of friction. I suppose this is how you have appeared to yourself too—with the result that you've never allowed yourself that easing-off which every human being, howsoever dynamic, needs now and then. I imagine you must be a very bad patient, the despair of Harley Street. But I am sure poor dear Harley Street won't have to cope with you very much: your native strength will soon restore you to your native health—provided, of course, that you don't treat the advice of Harley Street with disdain. Relax a little. Lie back in your chair. Complain that the cushion isn't soft enough. Say what a lovely day it is. Say you wonder whether it will rain to-morrow. Say what a clever man [J. L.] Garvin is. Say what a lovely day it was yesterday. Smoke a cigarette, saying nothing. Having finished the cigarette, say that you wonder how Tonks is, and repeat that it's a lovely day. In fact, try to behave a little more like us others. Then, but not till then, you will be all right, dear Will, I am sure. What fun if you *had* been able to visit Italy this summer! Later on you must appear here.

Love from Florence and me to you and Rachel.

Your affectionate Max

✧84                    13 Airlie Gardens     January 13, 192[6]

My dearest Max & Florence—it seems wonderful that we are to be with
you in a few days' time. I hope we have not been putting you to undue
trouble. Dear Max, I did appreciate your letter, & I am grateful indeed
to Florence for looking after our rooms. Rachel is rejoicing at the idea of
coming to Italy. I think you will both like her. Long illness has given
her a thoughtfulness & self-reliance, without diminishing her natural
gaiety & interest in things & people, which makes her the most charming
& helpful companion. A year ago I took her to Switzerland, acting, as
well as I could, as her nurse & guardian. Now she is bringing me to
Italy, a charge under her care, an energetic & resolute young person,
whom no one would imagine to have been through long & serious illness. She has been learning Italian, to help me in my ignorance, & she is
looking forward to having Florence as a guide to the beauties of
Rapallo. Rapallo—the Times speaks of scarcely any other resort: I am
a little alarmed at the notoriety this home of yours is acquiring. Why
didn't the severe & virtuous Austen go to Porto-Fino?[1] That we can
take refuge sometimes in your Villino is a great relief. You too will be
relieved to know that my talking powers are very decidedly limited at
present, & I think I may claim for myself that I am now as good a
listener as you will ever have, & that I am become as idle & as restful
as any Cistercian—is that the order which neither speaks nor toils? I
shall not ask to climb mountains, nor to refute heresies. But to be with
you both will be a deep happiness, & a refreshment to the body & spirit,
with Rachel by my side, & I hope to find you both well & as free from
care as man may be. Heaven forbid that we should add to the natural
difficulties which beset us all! We hope to greet you at Rapallo next
Tuesday, before noon. Ever your affectionate—Will

    [1] Sir Austen Chamberlain (1863–1937), Secretary of State for Foreign
Affairs, 1924–1929, had just led the negotiations for the Locarno Pact of Security
and Peace, at the conference in Locarno, Switzerland, October 5–16, 1925. It was
signed in London on December 1, 1925, and Chamberlain arrived in Rapallo,
ostensibly on holiday, on the 19th. In fact Mussolini visited him there on the 29th,
and in January 1926 the Fascist Party and other dignitaries came to see him.

✧85  Hotel Bristol [Rapallo]    Friday morning [February 26, 1926]

Dearest Max—I left yesterday without thanking you properly for that

Max at Rapallo, 1921

William Rothenstein at the
Royal College of Art, *c.* 1930

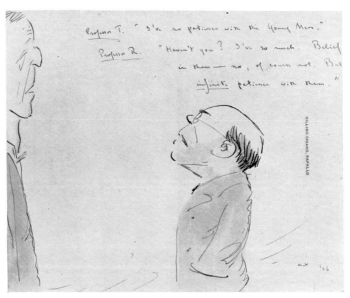

Henry Tonks and William Rothenstein.
Caricature by Max Beerbohm, 1926

This, and the succeeding eight pictures form the Edwardyssey sequence by Max, inspired by Edward VII's European tour in 1903.

Marianne Calypso dallies with him—The sailors grow impatient. Says Marianne

'A ce moment c'est un Monsieur Loubet qui m'entretient. Mais je voudrais bien être honnête femme . . . C'est vraiment vrai que t'es pas bourgeois—toi aussi! Tiens! T'en as l'air. Mais c'est un gentil gros bête . . .' (Emile Loubet; President

*Top.* Edwardysseus will not hearken to the Syrens. 'His Majesty then ate a piece of cake and drank a glass of port wine a hundred years old, while four nuns sang Kathleen Mavourneen.' Daily Mail April 17 describing the visit to the Convent of Dom Successio.

*Below.* Meanwhile Carlos the Cyclops detains Edwardysseus in his horrid cave (King Carlos of Portugal)

*Left.* Leo Circe tries her vile incantations on him (Pope Leo XIII)
*Right.* After many other curious, lamentable and delectable adventures,
Edwardysseus is washed ashore on his own island. To him appears, in
the guise of a Highland shepherd, his mother, Pallas Victoria, and puts
him on his way

*Left*. Edwardysseus reaches Windsor Great Park—but is unrecognised by the faithful Eumaeus-Knollys, by George-Telemachus, and by Jacko-Argus (Sir Francis Knollys: the King's Private Secretary. George: the Prince of Wales, later George V. Jacko: a dog)

*Right*. Edwardysseus smiles his well-known Hanoverian side-long smile, and is instantly recognised by the faithful Eumaeus-Knollys, by George-Telemachus, and by Jacko-Argus

Penelope–Alexandra is here seen, grievously beset by those pushful ones who covet the throne of Edwardysseus. In the background, resentful but helpless, stand George–Telemachus and Jacko–Argus. (The suitors: Sir Ernest Cassel, Sir Thomas Lipton, Lord Burnham, Joseph Chamberlain, Alfred Harmsworth, Hall Caine, Winston Churchill, Wilson Barrett and Lord Rosebery)

The Happy Ending—
'Whosoever shall smoke
the cigar of Edwardysseus,
him will I wed.'

William Rothenstein
in uniform, *c.* 1940

Max and Florence Beerbohm
at Abinger Common, *c.* 1941

joyous gift. It was delightful to be reminded again of those drawings, which I saw with you at the Leicester Gallery. I spent a happy evening with them after we left you. And what an honour to be included among them! I was again struck with the likeness to John, the cheek & mouth especially, (alas, poor John) of the old self. I can't help feeling envious, even of the new self. Did you, as children, sometimes put emptied eggs upside down in one another's egg cups? I feel so like one of those eggs— I *look* alright at the breakfast table. But when I enjoy your drawings, & gaze across the bay towards Porto Fino, I still *feel* like a real egg. Your legends are perfect. The scene is unmatched. Of the last I can only take memories away with me. But I can take your book, of which all at home will have a share. And it will endure longer than my memories.[1] I hope dear Florence is better. We meet anon. Ever yours Will

[1] The 'joyous gift' was a copy of Beerbohm, *Observations*, which includes the drawing of Rothenstein (plate 47) from 'The Old and the Young Self' series, first exhibited at the Leicester Galleries April 17–May 16, 1925.


⋄86          Villino Chiaro     Sunday night—after seeing you off—

[February 28, 1926]

My dearest Will—Just merely to wish you "bon voyage" again—and to say the sort of thing that I tried to say on the platform to you, the sort of thing that my inhibiting Charterhousian cramping upbringing makes so hard for my lips to say while my heart is imploring them to say it. The heart said, "O lips, be unsealed! Express *all* the joy that Will's and Rachel's visit has been to Florence and Max! Say something about the fact that Max has known Will for almost 33 years! Touch lightly on all the illumination that the former would have missed, and all the fun, and all the everything, if the aforesaid former hadn't known the latter! I, being but a heart, can't express myself well. And you, lips, being Max's, are also at a disadvantage. But Max is supposed to write well. I rely on his golden pen."

And here that pen is writing about the "former" and the "latter" and indulging in just the sort of dull twirligigs that I hoped it would just for once avoid.

My pen is as bad as my tongue for purposes of friendship. But your brain, dearest Will, will be aware of what my heart is driving at. Love to Alice and all—Your affectionate Max

My dearest Max—though replies to reviews are generally vain & tedious, I could not, in the case of the Times Lit. Sup. article, refrain from a gentle pulling of the reviewer's leg. I hope none of my drawings is quite so solemn & conscious as his writing. You, he says, began it— so if I walked on the scene with my old baggy umbrella under my arm—neither rapier nor tasselled cane would be in the character—& I hope you don't think I was making *you* ridiculous.[1] John, in the same number of the Sup[plement] has a curtailed review of the Venetian Glass Nephew.[2] Mrs John Lane recently sold some MSS & letters: among these was a note from you to Conder about some verse I seem to have written, with a caricature of Will R. as bard. Young Symons wanted it, & bid up to £10—it went for guineas & his rival was prepared to go up to 20 for it.[3] You must put up your prices, dear Max! Although I clean my glasses every day & rub & rub, I cannot get odd reflections of the Villino, of the cypresses & olives of San Moritzo, of Porto Fino, of you & dear Florence & the Hauptmanns out of the glass, & the Craigs will keep passing across too. I must visit the occulist, & see what he can do.

Did you read Raleigh's letters: they are brilliant. Of course he speaks of you—who doesn't?—& of others, with quick affection or prejudice, & of affairs with that peculiar Scottish wit characteristic of Scots who have been rooted, for a century or more, in English soil.[4] Mrs Dowdall has written a most amusing book on manners & deportment.[5] But I miss your select library, & its librarians, more than I can say. Our libraries here contain everything, & one doesn't know what to ask for. I still sigh for a city like Porto Fino. London is too big, & too full, for me. Even at Easter, & in August, when the railway companies try to empty it, it seems as full as ever. I wonder the companies go on trying—but they do, with true Western grip. If only you could exert your ambience & auras here—but no, they would be dissipated, soaked in petrol. Better they should make of Zoagli an Eden—I hope dear Florence won't mind —do assure her Eve in my eyes has always been fully dressed.

Rachel asks me to make up some form of intelligent greeting to you both, just when I am *delving* into the recesses of my mind for all my natural stupidities in the hope of winning some kind of reputation as an artist before I leave this world. Ever, dearest Max & Florence, your devoted—Will

If the dear Hauptmanns are still at Rapallo, my affectionate greetings.[6]

[1] Max, that is, in his Introduction to *The Portrait Drawings of William Rothenstein, 1889–1925*, 'began' the comparison between the qualities of his own drawings and Rothenstein's. See a review, 'Character and Temperament', *The Times Literary Supplement*, April 15, 1926, p. 277; and Rothenstein's reply, 'Mr. Beerbohm's Drawings', *TLS*, April 22, 1926, p. 303. Rothenstein's 'tasselled cane' appears in three early Beerbohm drawings of him as Paris boulevardier; see *Catalogue*, p. 121.

[2] See Elinor Wylie, *The Venetian Glass Nephew*; [John Rothenstein] 'The Venetian Glass Nephew', *TLS*, April 22, 1926, p. 300.

[3] The note, addressed to Conder's wife Stella and dated February 7, 1906, is owned by Stephen Greene. A. J. A. Symons (1900–1941) was collecting 1890's materials.

[4] Sir Walter Raleigh (1861–1922), Professor of English Literature, Oxford, 1904–1922. See *The Letters of Sir Walter Raleigh, 1879–1922*, ed. Lady Raleigh, II, 334.

[5] The Hon. Mrs. [Mary] Dowdall, *Manners and Tone of Good Society*, tongue-in-cheek advice to the English on everything from dress and table manners, to perfecting the art of being a foreigner.

[6] The Hauptmanns were in Rapallo at least until May 13, 1926.

❖88          Waterlane House, near Stroud, Glos.          [August 1926]

My dearest Max—here we are, within a mile of Iles Farm, having a holiday, where John Drinkwater's ancients drive their waggons home, & his maidens have such pretty ankles but no desire for service.[1] Dear Rachel wanted to have a last romp with her & Betty's friends, her notion of a romp being to get me in & out of basket chairs, to bring me my medicine & to look after the whole house. She envisages her coming operation with the utmost cheerfulness, which I confess I don't. Betty has won the travelling prize for sculpture at the College, which will give her several months in Italy next year. Did you write to Shaw? At last he is being honoured in his adopted country—a poem in the Times! & a dinner at the House of Commons. I wrote to pay my homage, of course: I told him, inter alia, that his 2 hundred years sojourn in Ireland was all very well, but that he was really a Scot, & had been canny enough to retain his vigour of mind & body by extracting ultra violet rays from lime light.[2]

You, on the other hand, can do this by merely living in Rapallo. The Hauptmanns wrote me a long letter one eighth of which I can read. Of you G. H. says: "Du hast uns mit Beerbohm in Berührung gebracht, und dafur nimm noch besonderen Dank. Auch er ist gehört zu den Goldkönnen [Goldkornen], die im Liebe [Siebe] zurückblicken [zurückbleiben]. Wenn mich Rapallo anzie[h]t, so ist Beerbohm ein wesentlicher Faktor geworden mit seiner Gleichmassigkeit[,] seiner

Philosophie und seiner vorbildlichen Daseinsform. Die Stunde[n] in seinem Hause[,] zu vieren an seinem runden Tisch, behalten in Gretens und meiner Erinnerung tiefe Bedentsamkeit."[3]

I hope there is nothing in this to trouble Florence—there are 2 or 3 words I can't understand. I wrote to Richard Sickert on his marriage, but no reply. Albert has an enchanting cottage near here, & a really lovely baby; we are driving to the Biddulphs this afternoon.[4] I go back to work next week, & then will take a second holiday in September. Alice isn't so well as I should like her to be; you can imagine she has had trouble enough these last 4 years. We have all enjoyed being back here—our love to you & Florence from our simple & your princely countryside. Ever yours—Will

[1] 'Drinkwater's . . . services': see John Drinkwater, *Collected Poems*, II, 6–7.

[2] Parliamentary Labour Party members honored Shaw on July 26, not at the House of Commons, but at the Hotel Metropole. See H. S. S[alt], 'On Mr. Bernard Shaw's 70th Birthday', *The Times*, July 26, 1926, p. 15. Rothenstein wrote to Shaw on July 24. (Shaw Papers: British Museum.) If Max wrote to Shaw, the letter is not in this collection.

[3] On January 26, 1926, Rothenstein, in Rapallo, introduced Max to Gerhart and Margarete Hauptmann. Additions and corrections bracketed are from Hauptmann's holograph text: Rothenstein added the verb '*ist*' in the second sentence. *Translation*: 'You have put us in touch with the Beerbohms, and for that my very special thanks. He also belongs among the gold grains that remain in the sieve. If Rapallo attracts me, then Beerbohm with his evenness of temper, his philosophy and his exemplary mode of life has become a decisive factor. The hours in his house, with the four of us sitting at his round table, remain in Grete's and my memory with deep significance.' In his preceding paragraph, Hauptmann had written: 'The older one becomes, the less remains in the sieve with which one strains the sand. But the gold that remains is therefore all the more valuable.' (Hauptmann to Rothenstein, July 21, 1926. RP:HL.)

[4] On June 4, 1926, Sickert, who now used his middle name, married his third wife, Thérèse Lessore (1884–1944). The Hon. Claud Biddulph (1871–1954), second son of the 1st Lord Biddulph; and his wife, Margaret Howard Biddulph (1880–1970), lived at Rodmarten, a large 'post-Morris' house at Cirencester.

<><>89　　　　　　　　　　　　　　　Villino Chiaro　　April 20, 1928

My dearest Will—Florence has just been writing about the umbrella. I take her seat at the writing-table, to chime in with all the 1001 apologies that I owe you. Peccavi! It was so like me to be thinking of *you* and not of your umbrella. I had said to you a few minutes before the train came in that I must not forget to hand the umbrella to you. But *you* came in, as well as the train; and it was only as you both went out that I remembered my awful lapse. I do hope to Heaven there will be no rain to-morrow at Boulogne or Folkestone. As soon as you are in London you will be all right of course and can await calmly the arrival of the thing which will of course be dispatched to-morrow. I say "all right"— but on reflection am not so sure; for John is in America;[1] and I suppose that Alice's and Rachel's and Betty's umbrellas are of that queer stunted modern kind, with a 12 inch circumference; and Billy, I'll be bound, has *no* umbrella and would be pained by the thought that such things exist. However, I trust you to win through—however wet the weather may be pending the arrival of what we send you. I don't mean that you would rob one of your students. I only mean that at The Athenaeum next Monday at luncheon time you would have the choice of the umbrellas of the Archbishops of Canterbury and York.

And meanwhile, dearest Will, this letter is to say how much our thoughts are with you, and what a joy it has been for us to be again in close daily touch with such a mind and heart as yours. Love to you and Alice and all from Max

[1] John Rothenstein was teaching art history at the University of Kentucky in Lexington; see his *Summer's Lease*, pp. 149–170. In January 1929 he married Elizabeth Smith, of Lexington.

Beerbohm to William and Alice Rothenstein

◇90                          Villino Chiaro     May 9, 1929

Dearest Will and Alice and All

Here we are. And you will be glad to know that I had wronged the Channel, which turned out to be a millpond—a mirror—a lamb lying down without a lion.[1] I felt slightly guilty in its presence—guilty but glad. I felt rather as I did when I first met W. E. Henley. Rap[allo] is decidedly cold, but the drought of the past months doesn't seem to have had awful results, and our little garden looks quite decent—though of course il faut cultiver notre jardin. To-day is the private view day, and I wish I were again at the Goupil, amidst those grand pictures. I always feel and say that I don't at all understand oil-painting; but I was conscious that I did at the Goupil have sharp bright glimmerings of intelligence, in the midst of very keen sensuous pleasure.[2]

1000 thanks for all our lovely Sunday evenings with you, and for all the brisk and shining processions of interesting, gifted, good-looking, young, middle-aged, old, male, female, cordial, graceful, well-mannered, heartening people that passed by. And another 1000 thanks for our stay under your roof—a lovely finale to our English visit. Fondest love to all 5 from us 2. Max

[1] The Beerbohms came to England late in November 1928, for Max's Leicester Galleries exhibition entitled 'Ghosts', November 30–December 29, 1928. They returned to Rapallo in March 1929.

[2] A Rothenstein exhibition at the Goupil Gallery, May 10–30, 1929. Response was poor and made him feel so much outside contemporary currents in art that he thought of leaving the New English Art Club again. He confided this to MacColl, who dissuaded him; see *WR*, pp. 344–347.

◇91          Nauheim     August 14, 1929

Dearest Max—here am I, once more averting my eyes from most of my fellow men—& women. For in Nauheim come together not only the halt & the lame, but the fat & the fatter. God, when he said, let there be short skirts, forgot Nauheim. But the young children are lovely, with their flaxen hair & bright dresses & on Sundays young peasant girls come into the town, wearing dresses, & their hair, as Dürer & Cranach painted them nearly 400 years ago. That is the charm of Germany—she combines the very new with the very old. The small towns round here are enchanting—like the pictures in Struwwelpeter. The tall houses have something Gargantuan, big & jolly, breaking out into carbuncles of carvings all over, in the very spirit of Rabelais. I am sure you & Florence would love them as I do; and the villages have the same charm. Just now it is beautiful to see the fields, all gold, covered with antlike peasants, reaping & binding & carting until night falls. The country scene moves me more than the city always; I feel as though I have wasted 3/4 of my painting life, working in a studio. You, dear Max, found yourself at once, & never deserted yourself. I have been trying to draw you in the early days, draw you in words this time; a failure of course, but all sorts of memories bubble up when the mind is directed to a single point, & certain clear visions. I have been pencilling notes fairly regularly, during resting hours, & have got to the Oxford days. I wish I had your memory; & writing, with me, is like painting—what I first put down needs constant simplifying.[1]

I have just had the last 6 proofs of the new portraits: yours is one of the best, being drawn simply in black. The more elaborate drawings come less happily; Kessler, who has been here from Hamburg to see me, says they should have been done in Germany.[2]

128

You shall have a copy of the book in the autumn. Alice & the girls are in the Tyrol; I join them next week. Where are you & Florence, I wonder—at Acqui again? I can't visualise you there, but at Rapallo, in that little wrist-watch of a home—so small, so perfect, polished & dustless, its works so flawless, hour hand & minute hand alike so trustworthy, I can see you better.

I should like to walk up & down, up & down that little terrace of yours again sometime, & look at that sky, so like an Italian primitive, growing pale as it joins the hills, but without the least sign of a crackle—all purity.

Billy is in Suffolk; he has fallen over head & ears in love with the English landscape, & swears he will never love another—nay, never so much as look at another. But I am old, & can look on the bright, warm South with delight, yet without lust; your little garden, with its lemon & orange & fig trees, has a place very near my heart, dear Florence; but perhaps you will come back to England yourselves this spring, & look out on to our chillier garden. My love to both of you. Ever yours—

Will

[1] John Rothenstein, during his father's illness and recuperation in 1925–26, had suggested that he begin writing some recollections, and William had done so. In 1928 Richard de la Mare (1901–    ), then a Director, now Chairman, of Faber and Faber, broached the subject of publication, and the project was put in hand. Rothenstein suggested as a title, 'Figures and Shadows: A Painter's Memories'. Another hand added a note: 'Men and Memories'. (N.d. Faber and Faber.)

[2] Rothenstein was dissatisfied with reproductions of his *Twelve Portraits*, and de la Mare wrote: 'I am most unhappy about the portraits—I hate to think that you are disappointed and dissatisfied with them—yet what can I do! I do hope that the fact that the book has been praised universally by those to whom I have shown it already is some consolation.' (Richard de la Mare to Rothenstein, October 22, 1929. RP: HL.) Count Harry Kessler (1868–1937), diplomat, arts patron.

◇92                              Villino Chiaro      October 1929

My dearest Will

It's a lovely book—say what you will against it! In course of reduction in scale, and of printing, some delicacies and subtleties must needs suffer; but really and truly it seems to me that in an imperfect world this latest book of yours should satisfy even the man whose work it enshrines. Of one thing I am sure: these latest drawings of yours are absolutely your best. I don't know which are my prime favourites—possibly Shaw, T. S. Eliot, and myself, and, oh, well, the other nine. Very many congratulations.

You gave me an enchanting account of Nauheim; and I was quite sorry to think of your having to tear yourself away. Still, I like to think of you in the sequestered glades of Airlie Gardens and amidst the sombre columns of the Ath[enaeum]. It seems a far cry from here to the Ath.; to Ramsay MacD. and D. S. MacC. e tutti quanti. How famous MacD. has become! I have a flair in such matters, and I felt, when first Florence and I met him at your house (less than a year ago!) that he was somehow destined to go far, though he was at that time a mere obscure Leader of the Opposition—his very name unknown to all but the few readers of Parliamentary debates; shy, ingenuous, innocent; anxious to make a favourable impression, but loth to thrust himself forward; blushing, stammering; pathetically grateful for a kind word or look. And now!

Do you remember, by the way, that when you and he and I were lunching together at the Ath., you asked him how his tour through Lancashire had gone, and he answered, "I was afraid." "Of what?" you asked. "Well," he said, "the enthusiasm was so great that" etc. We were moved by this high sense of unworthiness and these noble doubts. But it afterwards occurred to me that what he really had been afraid of was that the Socialist party might be going to sweep the country. Had this happened, he would of course have been compelled by his wild men to try and wreck the country; and this he wouldn't have at all liked. However, all's well. He's on clover, and likely to stay there for a goodish time.

Your Paris memories were very vivid, very tender and acute; and I am sure the whole book of memoirs will be a very valuable and fine one. I look forward eagerly to the next instalment. I wonder how I shall like the look of myself 35 years ago! Not much, I fancy—unless you shall have grossly flattered me.[1]

I have done a scribble apropos of something you say in the Paris section, and will post it to you separately.[2]

My fondest love to Alice and to ALL. Affectionate Max
PS. I thought Galsworthy's O.M. was exactly right. Neither Shaw nor Wells, the only other two men worthy, would have been suitable. Wells is a Republican and wouldn't have accepted the gaud. Shaw is really too irresponsible in his public utterances, and seems to grow more and more so. I daresay he would have accepted, on some principle of his own. But

he would certainly have made a point of guying the whole thing to the first interviewer who came along.

Now here is an idea that occurred to me yesterday. Do turn it over in your mind and, if you like it as much as I, do, please, in your suasive, authoritative way whisper to MacD. that a man very fit to be recommended for an O. M. is

C. P. Scott[3]

No precedent would be created; for there never again will be an editor-proprietor of the Scott kind (nor indeed has there been one in the past). This would be one point to put to MacD. Another is that the honour would be approved as warmly by Socialists and Tories as by Liberals. Another is that it would be a rebuke[4] to all Rothermeres and Beaverbrooks and kindred men. But the main argument, of course, is that C. P. Scott deserves the honour as well as any living man. N.B. He is *very* old; so there's no time to lose. Do, if you agree with my feelings, suggestionise MacD. *soon*—so that he can consider the matter well before he has to present his recommendations for the New Year honours. (And of course meanwhile COMPLETE SECRECY is needful.)

Forgive me for bothering you.

PPS. Florence has already written.

---

[1] Selections from the in-progress *Men and Memories* appeared in *Artwork*, edited by D. S. MacColl. See Rothenstein, 'Recollections', *Artwork*, 5 (1929), 77–88, 170–184.

[2] See 'A Recollection: Oscar Wilde, Charles Conder, Max Beerbohm, and the Writer [Rothenstein] at the Café Royal, by Max', in *MM* I, facing p. 220.

[3] C. P. Scott (1846–1932), editor, *The Manchester Guardian*, 1872–1929. John Galsworthy (1867–1933) was cited 'for services to literature and the drama', in the Birthday Honours, June 3, 1929.

Max felt strongly about the O. M.: 'Barrie got the O. M.,' Dody Kahn had written from Rapallo, '—and Uncle Max was perfectly furious when he heard it. He thinks it only right to go to men over seventy, and that Barrie has had enough honors. Aunt Florence of course thinks that Uncle Max should have had it—and an earldom—and the Nobel Prize, and—and—and etc. without end.' (Alexandra to L. M. and Nell Kahn, January 6, 1922. Bagshawe.)

[4] Max wrote, then struck out, 'rebuff'.

◇93      13 Airlie Gardens  November 3, 1929

My dearest Max—your generous letter, & that glorious drawing, arrived together, the latter received with shouts of laughter & admiration by the whole family. What a lovely thing it is—& how marvellously you have brought yourself back. How can I hope to portray Max sober

131

as you present him drunk? I must look to the pictures to bring life into the book; I shall certainly make a heavy call on your drawings, dear Max. Nonetheless I was heartened by your kind references to the scraps MacC[oll] printed. I do a little before breakfast most mornings, & most evenings before supper. How I should value your counsel! but I must get it, later perhaps. No one can help me as you can. I am vain enough to think that, when in the mood, I can evoke images in talking; but my pen lags & gets dull; I don't seem to get the water out of the ink. But I fear you won't appear in Artwork—(what a dreary name for the brilliant D.S.M.'s review!) since Faber & Faber, who propose to publish the book, won't sanction any more borrowing.

I am relieved at your & Florence's reception of the 12 portraits: I have been really distressed over the book. You, Steer & Einstein are reasonably good, MacD[onald] fair, Shaw, Eddington & Baldwin painfully bad. But as you say, probably few will notice the difference. And in any case, so few people buy my books of portraits—I got, to my amusement, a 1st cheque, for 4/2 from Macmillan's for the 6 drawings of Tagore, published more than 12 years ago!

Florence, dear, you did write me a charming letter. The children are constantly talking about your visit. I don't know about the dead, but the living certainly speak across time & space—or else, like       , your ghosts haunt Airlie Gardens.[1]

I haven't, naturally, seen Ramsay MacD yet: he is only just back, his brows, I should think, still reeking of roses & laurels. It has been pleasant to witness the reversal of popular feeling, now so strong in his favour. Poor Austen; even though he retired to Locarno, he wouldn't have much notice taken of his monocularity. Perhaps his garter comforts him; I hope it does.[2]

I agree with you about C. P. Scott. But is there a vacancy among the O.M.s? In whose coffee should poison be dropped; I plump for Barrie's. But perhaps the little man wouldn't like the attention of Death to be drawn to him, he always so shy & retiring. But think how modestly he would respond to the Freedom of Hades, when it was conferred on him, as it would be, inevitably.

Mrs Craig has been here, worrying about Teddie; can I get Melchett to subsidize The Mask?[3] Alas, I can't (vide the last no.) & isn't it tragic that it should, after all the offers, come to this again? Mrs C. says, too, can I get him a manager, do I know of anyone etc. etc. And both of us really believed, 6 months ago, that this time Teddie was staying on his feet.

I will write you again soon: this to let you know at once that the drawing reached me safely, & how uproariously it is appreciated. My love, as ever, to you both. Will

[1] Rothenstein's omission: for the 'ghost'.

[2] Ramsay MacDonald (1866–1937), Prime Minister, 1924, 1929–1935, was 'just back' from conferences in the United States and Canada. Austen Chamberlain, now out of office, was made a Knight of the Garter in 1926, after his negotiation of the Locarno Treaty.

[3] Craig is not mentioned in letters to Rothenstein (RP:HL) from Alfred Mond, 1st Baron Melchett (1868–1930), industrialist and patron of the arts. *The Mask*, Craig's theatre arts journal, was published in fifteen volumes, 1908–1929.

✧94                    Villino Chiaro    November 25, 1929

My dearest Will

This is no answer to your dear and delightful letter. It is merely *propaganda*. Do, please, remember and "push along," as only you could, that notion of the O. M. for C. P. Scott. It would be so right that he should have it. My impression is that there are one or two vacancies (thanks to H[is] M[ajesty]'s fastidiousness in the matter). R. MacD[onald] would of course have to explain to H. M. who C. P. S. is: a not Socialist man; a Liberal man; but a man of whom all Socialists and all Tories—all of them, at any rate, who know a good thing when they see it, and have been seeing it for 40 years or so—are unanimous in admiring and revering; a man over whose 80th birthday dinner that sound northern sportsman and statesman, Lord Derby, enthusiastically presided; etc., etc.; a man whom H. M. could go in no possible fear of; a man after the Queen's own heart (if she too were told about him). Do, Will, *do, please*, bring the beautiful stroke off. I am perfectly sure that a few *oral* words from you to R. MacD. would do it. I am sure that he would after a moment or two see the rightness of the idea.

Time presses. New Year's Honours are announced on Jan. 1.

I will write a real letter to you later. Meanwhile, love from Florence and me to you all. Affectionately Max

PS. Of course don't let anybody know of the idea (barring Alice and the family)—in case nothing came of it. Special point to be made to R. MacD.: that no precedent would be created, inasmuch as there will never be a similar case.[1]

[1] If Rothenstein approached MacDonald, nothing came of it. Scott was not on the New Year's Honours List.

Dearest Max—Savonarola went beautifully. Playfair was amusingly bustling as introducer & the actors fooled delightfully. The Pope was most impressive, & my little sister the poisoner as lovely as a Borgia— really lovely. Had I been young, or Savonarola, I would have tumbled fatally in love with her; she had a small head, like a beautiful Pre-Raphaelite snake, & a long, lithe body. Leonardo was the one blot: he should have been like L. (there is the one remarkable drawing)—but he looked like a comic super. They all said their lines well—much better than if the play had been a real tragedy. If I were training mummers I should take Sav. Brown, instead of Hamlet, as a stock exercise. Alice & I both enjoyed ourselves—& I remembered how I sat with you all when the Happy Hypocrite was produced by Mrs Pat.[1]

You will, I know, be proud to have helped preserve a bit of Oxford— which bit, I wonder?

I was there a couple of weeks ago, staying with Fisher at New Coll[ege], where I met a distinguished member of the Common Room, one Albert Rutherston. Do you mind you of a lunch at the Ath[enaeum] with D.S.M[acColl] when Schwabe was suggested as successor to Tonks, & you said, since I backed him, 'twas settled? I laughed to-day when I saw his appointment announced.[2] A[lice] tells me that Florence is going off motoring with Mrs Hardy: I am sure they will both enjoy themselves. My dear love to you both, & if Mrs Hardy is still with you, mes hommages to her. Ever yours affectionately—Will

[1] A dramatic version of Max's story, ' "Savonarola" Brown' (in his *Seven Men*, pp. 175–219), in a benefit matinée for the Oxford Preservation Trust, at the Haymarket Theatre, February 26, 1930. Nigel Playfair (1874–1934) was producer and 'Introducer'. For the full cast, see a review, 'Oxford Preservation Trust: "Savonarola",' *The Times*, February 26, 1930, p. 12. On Mrs Campbell's 1900 productions see Letter 30, note 1.

[2] Randolph Schwabe (1885–1948), Slade Professor of Fine Art, University of London, 1930–1948. On May 13, 1929, Albert Rutherston was appointed Ruskin Master of Drawing at Oxford; Rothenstein wrote: 'What next in the way of the unexpected? He is very pleased and as active as a tornado in a harbour.' (Rothenstein to Beerbohm, June 23, 1929. Clark Library, UCLA.)


⋄96                    Chequers, Princes Risborough, Buckinghamshire

                                               September 28, 1930

Dearest Max—excuse this note paper: it was the only paper I could lay my hands on.

Can you sup with us this evening—we have no one coming: just ourselves & the Prime Minister. Ever yours Will

TELEGRAMS
BUTLERS·CROSS
STATIONS
LITTLE·KIMBLE·1·MILE
WENDOVER·2½·MILES
PRINCES·RISBOROUGH·3½·MILES
TELEPHONE WENDOVER·78-77

CHEQUERS
PRINCES·RISBOROUGH
BUCKS

28·9·30

Dearest Max – excuse this note paper: it was the only paper I cd lay my hands on. Can you sup with us this evening – we have no one coming: Just ourselves & the Prime Minister.

Ever yrs
Will

◇97    Great Western Royal Hotel, Paddington    February 14, 1931

My dearest Will

I have read Men and Memories straight through now. And I shall use no other. Any other (and there are so many of them!) would seem

135

flimsy, and dull, and ill-balanced, and lacking in vividness. You know how I delighted in all the separate pieces that you showed me in typescript and proof, and how sure I was that this was a fine work and would moreover be immediately *and permanently* a success of a rare kind. But now, having read it in the only right way, from the outset onward, without a glance at the insidious index, I am surer than ever. One of your great "pulls," of course, is in being a painter, a user of eyes: you *see* men and women and places, and you remember the sight of them; and thus the reader undeservedly shares your power. Also, you aren't, as are most of the few memoirists who are aesthetically susceptible, a mere receiver, a mere liker or disliker: you are such a good *judge*. Your summings-up are as impressive as your impressions are clear. They are never pompous; and really one wouldn't mind if they were, for they always strike one as being right and final.

And how good the actual *writing* is, all the time! And, when you are *moved* by memory or by thought, how beautiful!—as, for instance, on page 76, or throughout Chapter xxviii.

It is a queer sensation, to renew one's youth by reading a book. Really I had quite forgotten what I was like at Oxford and in the years near after it. But there I am, rather absurd, but rather pleasant and promising. I have enjoyed the meeting. And also the meeting with all those other young and now elderly, or elderly and now dead, pirouetters on the human stage.

The book is *great fun*, besides being a great book. And thank you, dearest Will. Your affectionate Max

<br>

◇98                    13 Airlie Gardens      February 15, 1931

My dearest Max—never has anyone written me so generous a letter as yours. I can't believe that I deserve it. But I know your rich & kindly nature, richer & more kindly each year, & your unchanging loyalty to your friends. I wish I could believe the book one half so good as you say; but of course I am glad that you approve—no one's praise is so precious to me as yours. I tried to write portraits as I paint them; but writing is a more dangerous business. How to keep clear of offence, & yet give some truth to the drawing, is a difficulty. You overcame it; & re-reading certain parts I wish I had studied your spiritual technique more carefully. Yet I know that one cannot escape one's own shadow—& mine can never have your grace, & your large charity. Can shadows have charity?

I think yours has. In vol. 2 I hope to show that I have learned from your example. Meanwhile my thanks de coeur for your heartening words. They have been as champagne to Alice, & will hasten, I believe, her convalescence. Florence also said the kindest of words in my ear—to her too my thanks. Ever, dearest Max, your faithful & devoted—Will

✧99                                                            [early March 1931]

My dear Will

Couldn't you contrive to be a little more real?[1] Max

[1] Max sent a press cutting, 'Literary Notes', *Inverness Courier*, February 24, 1931, p. 3: 'Mr. William Rothenstein, whose book "Men and Memories", came from Faber and Faber last Thursday [February 19], is a character in Max Beerbohm's story, "Enoch Soames".' If Rothenstein did not contrive to be real enough, at least one bibliographer assumed Enoch's reality: see *British Diaries*, comp. William Matthews, p. 293. Max was at Edinburgh University to receive an honorary D.Litt. Max stayed in England until March 15, 1931: 'Max returned to Rapallo on Sunday; we shall miss him much; he was at his best and most genial, and so kindly, that one almost fears he may divest himself of his sting, and remain a pet wasp. But he has adopted a new, and no less charming, style of drawing.' (Rothenstein to Reginald Turner, March 19, 1931. RP:HL.)

✧100                          Rezzola, Pugliola, Prov. di Spezia     April 3, 1931

Dearest Max—I haven't yet written to thank you for the lovely letter you sent D.S.M[acColl]. I was busy putting back the dust-covers over the gilt & scarlet.[1] Then I got ready to go to Nauheim; but my doctor, who turned up in London, wouldn't hear of my taking the baths so early in the year. This means, alas, the wreck of my summer's painting. Needing, so everyone said, a holiday, I decided to come on here with Alice, in search of warmth.

Is it warm in Rapallo? Here it is icy; did we take the wrong train & go north instead of south? But no, we are so clearly in Italy; though can anything look colder than vines & fig trees, bare & budless, on a sunless day? And here are the elderly water-colour painters, wandering, like disembodied spirits (I wish they were) from coast-town to hill-town, from tea-party to tea-party, who tell me I am once more in Italy. We passed Camogli on the way, & I thought of that golden day when Florence drove us there, & Rapallo, where I half hoped I might get a glimpse of you both, & Chiavari & Sestri. The scene here is wider, &

137

grander, than the Rapallo landscape, but so like, that on the road I think constantly, at the next turn I shall see the familiar Villino. Alice is better; but her cough hasn't yet gone. I am longing for warmth, for her sake. Thus do little men expect the infinite to serve their needs. We were greatly grieved at Bennett's death; he was so completely of this world, so genial & friendly & human. Death seems somehow fitting for a Tennyson, a Victor Hugo, but unnatural in dear Bennett's case. We had got to care for him a great deal during these last years.[2]

I hope dear Florence is well, & not too beset with the cares of the new annexe. We hope to see you both before we return—A[lice] is sure to be writing Florence about an hotel—*not* the Bristol, the approach is too steep for me. Ever yours affectionately Will

[1] Rothenstein's knighthood was announced in the 1931 New Year's Honours. Max wrote: 'I am getting slightly tired of your knighthood and want you to be a baronet.' (Beerbohm to Rothenstein [January 28, 1931]. RP:HL.) D. S. MacColl, Randolph Schwabe, and Max arranged a dinner in Rothenstein's honour at Kettner's Restaurant, Soho, on March 21, 1931. Max, who had returned to Rapallo, sent a 'Max Vobiscum' message, not, unfortunately, included among MacColl's papers in the Glasgow University Library, or among Rothenstein's papers.

[2] Arnold Bennett died on March 27, 1931.

◇101                                    Villino Chiaro      April 10, 1931

My Dearest Will

How lovely it will be to see you both! Ever so many thanks for your charming and amusing letter. I had heard already from D. S. M[acColl] how much everybody had enjoyed the dinner; also from Ellis Roberts.[1] I gather that your speech was a very beautiful thing—but of course it *would* be. How I wish I could have heard it! Mannie Kahn, who is with his wife at the Bristol, awaiting his daughter Dody and her bridegroom, told me that your book has been having enthusiastic notices in America. I expect it will have great "sales" there—the geographical area being so huge. One thing is certain: that on both sides of the Atlantic the book will continue to be bought and read as long as civilisation lasts. How long that will be one has of course no means of knowing. Already, after all, from the standpoint of persons born in 1872, there are but remnants —plenteous and bright remnants, I admit—of civilisation. Machinery and democracy have ground away the greater part of what one loved. To the young, of course, everything is as loveable as it was to us. But no!—

that isn't quite so, alas. The young do seem pathetically aware that all's not well. And that is one of the reasons for the great success of M[en] and M[emories]. The book gives the young a panorama of a time in which they take a yearning interest. Let us be sorry for the young, in this their time. *We* didn't take a yearning interest in the eighteen-sixties. We refused to know anything about them, and shone in the forehead of the morning.

I do hope the weather at Pugliola has reformed itself. Here, during the past 4 days, it has been perfect; and I feel that in that period dear Alice's cough will have disappeared.

Florence and I both think that the hotel you would like best is the *Marsala*. Alice may remember it. She and F. and I lunched there once. It is *in* Rapallo, on the sea-front—without one single step up to it. F. and I have known it well for years. It is purely Italian: no cosmopolitan efforts of any kind—except towards cleanliness. This sounds as if the place weren't quite clean; but it really is. And the proprietor is a charming man; and so is the head-waiter.

What a joy it will be to see you! A joy for me alone, though; for, as you will have known from Florence's letter to Alice, Florence will have already started on her Pirandello journey to England.[2]

Most loving messages from both of us. Max

P.S. Benvenuto is at this moment engaged to be married to an English girl. But don't mention to the Hauptmanns that I told you this; for I am not sure that it isn't a secret.[3]

[1] Ellis Roberts (1879–1953), journalist and biographer, wrote to Max: 'It was an "occasion". You were missed more than any one present was noticed, and your letter set a standard for the speeches which none of them fortunately attempted to follow. I expect you will have heard fully from the Victorian Guest or from MacColl but I doubt if either of them will tell you how amiably each spoke.' (Roberts to Beerbohm [April 2, 1931]. BP: MC.)

[2] On May 11, 1931, Florence Beerbohm appeared at the Theatre Royal, Huddersfield, in a play by Luigi Pirandello: *The Life I Gave You* [*La Vita che ti Diedi*] (1925), trans. A. C. Roberts. Her appearance was arranged by Alfred Wareing (1876–1942), Director of the Theatre Royal, 1918–1931; appointed Librarian, 1931, Shakespeare Memorial Library, Stratford.

[3] Benvenuto Hauptmann was engaged to a young lady identified, in his father's notes, only as 'M. M.' (Hauptmann Archives: Staatsbibliothek, Berlin.) No marriage followed this engagement.

◇102    [13 Airlie Gardens]    [mid-October 1931]

. . . that line of Ernest Dowson—"shepherd, the old towers fall," returns constantly to my mind. Last week our beloved old nurse Adkins, who brought Albert into the world, died in her sleep.[1] Then Orpen, too, died in the same way & now Ricketts has gone. How brief life seems, when one looks back on the beginning & lives to see the end of a man's career. Time is shortened, like a telescope; I see Orpen & Ricketts as they were as very young men, but while Ricketts retained much of his early character, Orpen's older self was quite surprisingly like his young self. I wished I had shown him more affection, & that I had cared more for his art. He remained a sort of playboy, without [Augustus] John's profundity or Steer's sincerity. Yet I was much affected by his death; & when we saw, on the easel in his studio, that during his last days he had returned to his old drawing of the Happy Hypocrite, that from a photograph, enlarged, he was transferring it on to canvas, Alice & I were both deeply touched. The young Orpen, in his little engineer's jacket, with his modest unassuming ways, was foremost in our minds, & the rather bloated, less intelligible figure we knew during the last years faded into the background.[2] Poor Shannon still has 2 nurses to look after him; he is difficult, I gather, at times.[3] You will be sorry I know to miss these figures of a past which lengthens, & shortens, like a figure in Mickie the Mouse.

We thought of you often this summer, when we returned to the cottage at Oakridge. I found Gloucestershire lovelier than ever; so unspoilt, such quiet valleys & sleepy old villages tucked away; but alas, a countryside that, compared with the busy Italian scene, seemed asleep, like the villages. Now the political doctors, having left their patient to the panel doctors, are busy about his bed, great specialists, quarrelling in the parlour, in the Hogarthian manner, as to the symptoms, & the cure. Difficult days, dear Max; & I think of your prophetic John Bull, with his wreath for "them poor decaying Latin nations."[4] My love to you both. Ever yours—Will

[1] 'Shepherd . . . fall': unidentified, but not a published Dowson line.

[2] Max wrote: 'I had not seen Orpen often in recent years—only sometimes when I was asked to lunch by someone at the Savile [Club], where he was such a popular figure. But the fact of not seeing often a man whom one likes and admires doesn't make one grieve the less at the thought that one will not see him again. I am deeply touched about the "Happy Hypocrite" painting, and am glad that through my work I must have been in his thoughts.' (Beerbohm to Alice Rothenstein [October 1931]. RP:HL.) For Orpen's 'old drawing of the Happy Hypocrite', see *Sir William Orpen*, ed. Albert Rutherston, plate 32. The work on the easel at the time of his death was an oil sketch, now owned by Diana Olivier.

[3] Charles Shannon died on March 18, 1937.

[4] See Beerbohm, *Cartoons: 'The Second Childhood of John Bull'*, plate 4.

13 Airlie Gardens    March 13, 1932

My dearest Max—I am not, like you, a perfect letter-writer who doesn't write, but a careless one, who does put pen to paper habitually. So it has gone against the grain to remain a silent friend. The fact is, with the burden of vol. 2 about my neck, I have had to devote myself entirely, after getting back from the studio, to my unnatural task. Now the last sheets are sent away, & I have some leisured moments: the first to whom I write, who but yourself?

The Ellis R[obert]s gave us some news of you both, but not enough.[1] But since *you* have no committees, & don't go far from the Villino & get your amusement at home, I can, without mental strain, imagine your daily life, no cross word, but only crossword problems, a glass of golden wine, the only perfect cooking that remains, a walk on the flagged terrace, a look over the birth of Venus sea, a glance at the lovely garden, with its figs, & vines, its lemon & orange trees—but I mustn't go on—nostalgia for Italy comes on me! How I longed to join you when, after pneumonia, I was ordered away: I enjoyed the cold & the fogs at Broadstairs, & then the cold & the mists at Paddockhurst. Happily the secret of dear Rachel's ordeal was kept from me. And Alice, who had to endure the agony of waiting again, became utterly exhausted, more so than I have ever known her to be. Even in Switzerland, where she went with Rachel, it took her long to recover. Doesn't it seem strange that Rachel should be the only person known to her doctors who has survived what she went through? And yet, a few weeks later, she was skating & ski-ing! Her indomitable will to live saved her; and now, we are assured, she will be stronger than she has been, & healthier, these dozen years. Billy is living his queer solitary life, doing beautiful things. None would understand them better than you & Florence.[2] John is writing industriously—a good deal of notice was taken of his last book.[3]

I hear nothing of Teddie [Craig]—nothing. I hated Lytton Strachey dying—one tilted at him, but he was one of the real men of his time. I saw more of him since he joined the Ath[enaeum] & then suddenly I heard he was ill. He had the same trouble, I gathered, as Rachel. And we miss Arnold Bennett.[4]

Did MacColl send you his book? I think it remarkable—and surely as a writer merely, D.S.M. is among the first. He is fighting hard for Waterloo Bridge; but it is a lost battle—the National!! G[overnmen]t has given in to the L[ondon] C[ounty] C[ouncil]—I succeeded

Ricketts as the painter on the Royal Fine Art C[ommission], so hear much on the subject—it is scandalous that this noble remnant of true London is to be destroyed.[5] They pulled down the house in which you wrote your Saturday articles, then Regent St, now Waterloo Bridge: next it will be Adelphi Terrace, the Temple, & then St Paul's. One charming link with a vanished past I came across last week, when I went with one of the Russells to see Cavalcade: we drove past the front of Drury Lane, to a private entrance; the Duke of Bedford's, with its own staircase, sitting room & lavatory, along with the family box.[6] I thought of *your* Duke, in Zuleika. Was it you, I wonder, who proposed Guedalla for the Ath[enaeum]? I haven't seen him there yet.[7] But I am asked almost daily when you are to return.

I met Lady Desborough yesterday, who asked affectionately after you. I had to go round with the King & Queen, to show them the mural paintings done by Indian artists at India House:[8] was pleased to find the Queen indignant about Waterloo Bridge. I hear that your annexe, dear Florence, is a delightful place, as I expected it would be.[9] I send you both my dear love. Ever your affectionate—Will

[1] Ellis Roberts and his wife Harriet (d. 1972) were at Rapallo in January 1932.

[2] Rachel had had a serious relapse. Michael Rothenstein had a show of drawings and paintings at the Warren Gallery. Max wrote to the poet Siegfried Sassoon that they were 'very fine—very original and strong, with no nonsense about them—no Bloomsbury formalisation and arid mechanisation about them—and with genuine beauty throughout them.' (Beerbohm to Sassoon, February 25, 1931. George Sassoon.)

[3] John Rothenstein's 'last book' was *British Artists and the War*.

[4] A year later, Rothenstein wrote: 'It is long since I heard of, or from Craig— he has become a tragic figure, far off, in a Byronic gloom.' (Rothenstein to Florence Beerbohm [1933]. BP:MC.)

In 1931 Max proposed Lytton Strachey for Athenaeum Club membership, and Strachey wrote: 'I am beginning to feel rather excited about the Athenaeum. But at the same time I entirely sympathise with the electors and their druggist friends, so that if they firmly refuse to have anything to do with me I shall not be particularly horrified. If the rules were reversed, should *I* elect them?' After his election, he wrote: 'Your efforts have been crowned with success, and I've been elected to the A. under rule 2! It was really most noble of you to take this trouble. I am delighted and very much obliged. I haven't put my nose in yet. I wish you could be there to show me round. I shall feel rather like a New Boy at school.' (Strachey to Beerbohm, March 27, April 15, 1931. BP:MC.) Strachey never made use of the Athenaeum; he died on January 21, 1932.

[5] MacColl's book: *Confessions of a Keeper and Other Papers*. The Royal Fine Art Commission, to which Rothenstein was appointed on November 27, 1931, advised preservation of Waterloo Bridge, opened in 1817. In June 1932 its survival seemed assured, but in 1938 it was demolished; a new bridge was opened in 1944.

[6] Miss Flora Russell (1869–1967) was a cousin of Bertrand Russell. Noel Coward's *Cavalcade* opened at the Drury Lane Theatre on October 13, 1931.

[7] Philip Guedalla (1889–1944), historian, owner of a notable collection of Beerbohm caricatures; see Letter 37, note 1.

[8] Four Indian students at the Royal College of Art painted murals for India House, London headquarters of the Indian High Commission. See SF, pp. 172–175; *IE*, pp. 299–302.

[9] The 'annexe' was a cottage, which the Beerbohms called the Casetta, at the top of the Villino's steep garden.

◇104                                    London     June 11, 1932

My dearest Max—little did you think that, through you, I should become as a character from "Crime & Punishment," or I, that I should commit murder. But so it is. No wonder you do not write me. And I live in dread of the day when you make the dire fact public, for you alone know it. Alas, that it should have been a child of yours I murdered; & I, who owe to you so much! Those four lines on Housman! Three errors in four matchless lines. How could I have done it? Even confessing, I have no hope of forgiveness. Only in a 2nd edition can the crime be condoned; & that may be, never. Did I think, when I did one murder, it would be repeated four thousandfold? Alas, no; does any murderer realise the extent of his crime?[1]

Ah me, from you, for ever silence. I implored Oliver Lodge, who was here. But he can only make those who have passed talk, not the living write. From Rapallo came not even a rap.[2]

So I go my ways in grief & darkness, trying to do my daily task, & to hide my sin from men's eyes. I draw & paint, & teach the young (he, teach! you will bitterly exclaim) go to the Athenaeum, attend lunches, dinners, meetings, mechanically, lifelessly, dutifully—for the days must be lived through, however heavy the heart.

But yesterday, I re-read The Dragon of Hay Hill.[3] And the knowledge that never again sha

Here I broke down. I do not expect forgiveness, or pity; do not mistake me, it is not for that I write. But out of a black heart cometh ink. Your contrite, your wretched & forever miserable—Will

[1] See *MM* II, 343. The errors were corrected in the Rose and Crown Library edition (London, 1934): 'these grim two' for 'this grim twain', and 'supplies' for 'prefers'.

In Max's copy, Rothenstein wrote: 'Dearest Max—not that you will ever forgive me: at least you will find (see page 343) the gross misquotation amended. Never again will I trust to a vague, rickety, senile, tuneless, faulty memory.

Though I have not cut off my right hand I have cast my pen, instrument of my sin, into the flames. But even death will not drive the blush from my face—twain indeed!' (BP:MC.)

[2] Sir Oliver Lodge (1851–1940), psysicist; Principal, University of Birmingham, 1900–1919; member, Society for Psychical Research.

Rothenstein wrote to Craig: 'As for Max, he is alive, but he behaves as though he were already a classic—as silent as Hazlitt or Lamb. Not a word have I had from him since he left [in March 1931], and so many sent him!' (Rothenstein to Craig, May 19, 1932. Craig: Bibliothèque Nationale.) Max wrote, however, on April 25, 193[1] and in [late October, 1931]. (RP:HL.) His dereliction, nevertheless, was chronic, and in 1935 a note written jointly with the Hauptmanns was signed: 'Max—who owes so many letters and is always trying to write a letter worthy of one of Will's—and *will do it tomorrow.*' (Hauptmann and Beerbohm to Rothenstein, March 3, 1935. RP:HL.) Tomorrow's letter, if sent, does not survive.

[3] Beerbohm, *The Dreadful Dragon of Hay Hill.*

◇105                          13 Airlie Gardens          October 20, 1932

Dearest Max—what a long, long silence! Not a word for months from the Villino—Florence as silent as you. It is as though no boats went out with their sails spread to catch fish in the bay, no wind were in the trees of the gardens, no soul in the narrow, shaded streets of Rapallo. Such silence—not a note from a bird even. It was a relief to find Richards' book on my table, & to hear, in my ear, the authentic voice.[1] And a few days after, looking across the room at a reception in Arlington St, I caught sight of a familiar colour, & a familiar line.

So I know that all is well, generally. But I prefer the particular—your abstract welfare is poor news.

So much happens that nothing seems worth telling, if time becomes four-dimensional. Well, we are back in London again—the cosy season. I like London best in the autumn—when the days are long I always feel ashamed to be doing nothing in the late afternoons, knowing what I would be at in the country. The 8 years at Oakridge made a permanent mark on my conscience. After Nauheim I had a lovely time sitting in front of places for 6 weeks; among others at Kenilworth—did you ever go there? At Stratford we went to call on the good Wareing, who talked of course of Florence. And again, we stayed a night with a friend at Huddersfield, & heard more of her. I went back, too, to Haworth—the vicarage where I used to have tea with the Vicar's sons is now a Brontë Museum. I found Haworth little changed; only the mill-girls, then be-clogged & beshawled, now have bobbed hair & silk stockings.[2]

We last heard of you from the Ellis Roberts. What delightful people they are! Among the friends we have made later in life, we count them as the most precious.

We saw John & his wife at Leeds: he is happy in his work, & absorbed by his new duties. He gets little time at present for writing, but later I hope he may have more leisure.

I am at work again, enjoying it while I may; this is as well, for few enjoy anything I do. 'Tis all the young, or Sickert, who now looks at nothing, but squares art, & the camera does the rest. Heaven knows I am unhappy at no man's well being & good fortune: but this admiration is a depressing portent.[3]

Forgive this scrappy letter: it will show that we are alive, if nothing else. Ever yours—Will

[1] Grant Richards, *Memories of a Misspent Youth*, with a Rothenstein pastel of Richards as frontispiece; preface by Beerbohm, pp. vii–x.

[2] Haworth, the village home of the Brontës, is a few miles from Bradford. Rothenstein's impressions in 1932 echo earlier comments on the Bradford–Haworth area: 'Bradford though depressing is full of interesting things. If one could but keep outside one's friends' houses it would have an almost barbaric character. The factory girls, with their heads completely covered by their great plaid shawls have a mystery which has something quite Spanish—do you know Goya?—a mystery, alas, that they quite cast off on Sundays, when they parade the streets in violent mufti. There is a market here, where they hang out wares of such crudity, that taken together, they attain something very near to beauty. . . . And the sweet shops, exhibiting the utmost ingenuity in colour and shape, are the most mediaeval things I have ever seen. Morris—William Morris I mean, would rave over them. . . . I think you would find the sinister dreariness of their work and the higher coloured vulgarity of their pleasures, of extreme interest. But over the gentlemen and ladies of the town I will draw a curtain—of their own manufacture.' (Rothenstein to Margaret Woods, December 30 [1899]. RP:HL.)

[3] Rothenstein, a believer in painting from life and from Nature, was appalled by Sickert's latter-day practice of painting from photographs. See *SF*, pp. 275–276.


◇106          13 Airlie Gardens     December 31, 1932

Dearest Max—we are hoping that the N[ew] Year may bring us a visit from you & Florence. The feeling is growing that only Florence can do justice to a Shakespearean woman. All Florence's friends have agreed to this belated sense of what is needed; the Old Vic wants her, Wareing needs her somewhere else, but that she must come is clear. But without you she is unlikely to move, so we look to see you both. Indeed a visit is overdue; t'will be none the less welcome.[1] We have John & Elizabeth with us over the holidays: John seems to have made great changes at Leeds, & with Elizabeth to have gained many friends. They curl in front of the fire here like dogs after a long run, enjoying the warmth of social London. We have just spent a couple of days with Albert & Marjorie; their 2 boys are enchanting creatures. On our way back we came through Oxford. It may tickle you to know that your portrait is now in the Ashmolean—one of my drawings of you & another of Robert Bridges were purchased for the gallery from a recent show I had at Agnew's.[2]

I have just been rung up & asked for a portrait of Sickert: this can mean but one thing—a knighthood on Monday. I know this will rejoice his 72 years' old heart. Most of the news of the world has been held up, these last months, by accounts of his doings. All the painters are wondering whether they have wasted their time all these years painting from life when they might have saved themselves endless trouble by squaring up photographs, or copying the drawings of Dicky Doyle in oil colours.[3]

I was glad to see you among the protesters against the destruction of Carlton H[ouse] Terrace. We have had a difficult time on the R[oyal] Fine Art Commission because Blomfield is one of our members; but I think the threat will not now be carried out. For once public opinion has been emphatically roused.[4]

500 people gathered at small tables in honour of Squire, who, himself sitting at one, was invisible to the company until he rose to reply to the speeches.[5] I suggested Maurice Baring be elected to the Ath[enaeum] under Rule II, & I hope it will happen next month.[6] Ramsay MacD[onald] always asks affectionately after you whenever I see him. But then, who doesn't?

I send you & Florence all my voeux for the New Year. We hope to have you with us soon. Meanwhile ever yours affectionately—Will

[1] Alice Rothenstein, the Ellis Roberts, and Wareing hoped to persuade Lilian Baylis (1874–1937), lessee and manager of the Old Vic and Sadler's Wells Theatres, to bring Florence Beerbohm to London in a Shakespearean role. (Wareing to Alice Rothenstein, December 3, 1932; to Lilian Baylis, copy [December 1932]. RP:HL.)

[2] In 1932 John Rothenstein became Director of the City Art Gallery at Leeds. The Beerbohm and the Bridges portraits are still owned by the Ashmolean Museum.

[3] Sickert was not knighted. Richard Doyle (1824–1883), cartoonist, illustrator, designed the famous cover of *Punch*.

[4] Sir Reginald Blomfield (1856–1942), architect and member of the Royal Fine Art Commission, designed an office building to replace Carlton House Terrace. His *Memoirs of an Architect* stops short of this episode. For his design, and for protests by Max and others, see 'What Public Opinion Says: Carlton House Terrace', *Architectural Review*, 73 (1933), 11–16.

[5] J. C. Squire (1884–1958), journalist, playwright, critic, poet; editor, *The London Mercury*, 1919–1934. He was honoured at a subscription dinner.

[6] Maurice Baring (1874–1945), poet, critic, essayist, playwright, novelist; a leader in popularising Russian literature in England.

◇107                    Far Oakridge      December 30, 1935

Dearest Max—if your person was absent, your authentic voice was with us for 20 minutes yesterday, to the delight of everyone. No one interrupted your talk, nor disagreed with your conversation. The only disappointment was your leaving us; Alice, Rachel, Betty, Billy & his young woman all listened entranced. I am glad at least it was to "good, warm Paddington" that you retired—our station. We return to your Hell to-morrow, with regret.[1] Shall we see you & Florence before the 10th? Billy gets married on the 7th—in the self-same Registry Office where you witnessed our marriage.[2] Do you remember the man who brought in the rabbit pie in the middle of the ceremony? Our dear love & all our good wishes to you & Florence for the New Year. Ever, dearest Max, affectionately Will

I have just heard from Mrs Cust that *Jan. 9th* is the night of our dinner.[3]

[1] See Beerbohm, B.B.C. broadcast, 'London Revisited', December 29, 1935, in his *Mainly on the Air*, pp. 3–11.
Siegfried Sassoon wrote that he 'adored every word of it, and felt the wisdom of the ages in it, and the glory of exquisite art and the affirmation of exquisite courtesy—everything was there which I love and value deeply. It was "the Real right thing", as far as I was concerned. But then, you see—it was you, Max,—and you always do things perfectly. The BBC. is your foot-stool and your hand is stretched out over Fleet Street.' (Sassoon to Beerbohm, December 29, 1935. BP:MC.)
[2] Michael Rothenstein and Betty Fitzgerald were married on February 7, 1936, in the Kensington Registry Office.
[3] 'I recently painted a portrait of a Lincolnshire squire', Rothenstein wrote, 'and renewed acquaintance with his sister, Mrs. Harry Cust. Do you know her? One of the original souls, and looking like one still, slender, exquisite, and swathed in delicate veils. She lives with the memory of her husband, scarcely liking it disturbed by company.' (Rothenstein to Margaret Woods, December 23, 1935. Rothenstein.) The 'squire' was Sir Charles Welby, 5th Baronet (1865–1938). Present owner of the portrait: Sir Oliver Welby, 6th Baronet. Not Nina, but her husband, was one of the high society intellectuals dubbed the 'Souls' in 1889. See note 3, p. 23

◇108               High Point, Highgate Village [London]

                         Early morning, April 9, 1936

Dearest Max—a line before going to Oakridge. Never have I enjoyed a play more—beautifully conceived, written, acted & staged as is the Happy Hypocrite. So beautifully staged that the actors find it hard not to be too solid & objective in the fanciful scenes, in the wood perhaps especially, where the jarvey & the woodman seem right while Lord George & the Mere are, physically, a little out of the lovely picture: a matter of dress only. For in the last cottage scene there was no such feeling. And how well that last scene was played! And how delightful was Cupid—a real creation on the part of author & mime: both the immortals in fact had the element of fancy of the original source of the play. I thought Viola delightful & Ivor Novello perfect, both as rake & reformed lover. Every one round me was bubbling with enthusiasm— Alice longing to get round, but feeling you would be overwhelmed with congratulating, adulating visitors.

I scarcely hoped Miss Dane would manage to preserve the spirit of the Ur-story, but she did, & this is a great achievement.[1]

My memory went back to so many nights in the old theatre— indeed, a lump came into my throat when I saw Lady Tree sitting alone in the box.[2] But why, O why, will they paint theatres brown, blue— anything but red & white & gold?

An enchanting evening, dearest Max—& may crowds sit enchanted for a thousand nights.

My love to you both. Ever yours—Will

[1] Max's story, *The Happy Hypocrite*, was revived on April 8, 1936, as a three-act musical with dialogue by Winifred Ashton [Clemence Dane], music by Richard Addinsell. For the full cast, see a review, 'His Majesty's Theatre: "The Happy Hypocrite"', *The Times*, April 9, 1936, p. 12.
Despite the clear affinity between *The Happy Hypocrite* and Wilde's novel, *The Picture of Dorian Gray*, Max, in connection with a later American enterprise, wrote to Florence's brother: 'The Happy Hypocrite was published in England and in America in 1896, and has been on sale ever since. Two dramatic versions of it have been produced in England. To the best of my knowledge, no critic, nor anybody else, has suggested that the idea on which it was based—the idea of a bad man assuming a saintly mask, and wearing it for some time, with the psychological and physical result that his face became a counterpart of that mask—had been used by somebody else. The idea was conceived by me in my own mind, and has not until now been plagiarized.' (Beerbohm to Sam Kahn, May 11, 1944. Constance Kahn Starr.) Sam Kahn (d. 1958), staff member and City Editor, *The Commercial Appeal* (Memphis), 1905–1955, was Max's agent in the United States. Cf. Wilde, *Letters*, pp. 575–576; Felstiner, *The Lies of Art*, p. 50.
[2] Lady Tree: Maud Tree, Herbert's widow.

Dearest Will, It is a lovely piece of work—a model of insight and delicate justice, as one would expect. I have made a few punctuational changes, being a born busybody, and one or two suggestions of a technical kind—which you can ignore to your heart's content![1]

What a strange thing to be a supereminent genius and hero as Lawrence was, *plus* such streaks of sheer silliness (e.g. the marginless reproductions, and the excuse for them; and the view of the Odyssey; and the translation of it...I have read various extracts from that translation—read them with gasps. And I would rather not have been that translator than have driven the Turks out of Arabia).[2]

We are off to Edge on Saturday morning, pausing to spend 2 days with Berners; and we shall be rusticating for 3 weeks or so.[3]

Our fondest love to you and Alice, and warm thanks for your kindness and delightfulness to us. Your affectionate Max

[1] See *T. E. Lawrence by his Friends*, ed. A. W. Lawrence, pp. 252–258. Rothenstein had asked Max to read his piece with a 'hard and ruthless eye'. (Rothenstein to Beerbohm, May 6, 1936. Clark Library, UCLA.)

[2] See *The Odyssey of Homer, Newly Translated into English Prose*, trans. T. E. Shaw [T. E. Lawrence], a controversial book suggested and designed by Bruce Rogers (1870–1957), Printing Adviser to Cambridge University Press, 1918–19, and to Harvard University Press, 1920–1928. For a typically diplomatic review, see 'The Odyssey in Prose', *The Times Literary Supplement* (London), November 17, 1932, p. 854. See also Lawrence, *The Letters of T. E. Lawrence*, ed. David Garnett, pp. 586–590, 814.
For the 'marginless reproductions', see Lawrence, *Seven Pillars of Wisdom: A Triumph*; the list of illustrators, of whom Rothenstein was one, pp. 19–20. Lawrence gave his 'excuse' in a letter to Rothenstein after *Seven Pillars* was privately printed in 1926: 'For the brutality of the plates I must plead guilty. The politeness of margin makes me very angry. Kennington's huge pastels could be ruled down, so, into normal pictures: but by running them out to the edge they jumped out of the book, and re-became monstrous, as their originals. John and the rest (including you) had to follow suit, in self-defence. It was my deliberate intention to make the pictures appendices, not illustrations, and to rouse with them just the feelings you expressed. Regard my *Seven Pillars* as a protest against the illustrated book, and you'll feel what I was driving at.' (Lawrence to Rothenstein, May 5, 1927. RP:HL.)

[3] 'Edge': site of Highcroft, the Ellis Roberts' Gloucestershire home. Gerald Tyrwhitt-Wilson, 14th Baron Berners (1883–1950), diplomat, painter, patron of the arts, who lived in Berkshire.

Dearest Max but what a delightful surprise! for us, of course, for you &

Florence knew 2 weeks ago. And how right & proper & altogether cheering, and, incidentally, a brotherly support to myself, who had to bear your congratulations 8 years ago, when I knew how much more fitting it would have been for you than for me. Do you remember that we lunched together on the day? And now dear Florence is Lady Beerbohm—the real & authentic name, for Herbert's wife bore another. And now *your* friends will be wondering whether to address you as Sir Max or as Max only, until you have knelt before your Sovereign! And it is, once all is said, a charming thing to happen, for no one confuses the tradition of Sir Anthonys & Sir Joshuas with the Aldermanic brand. I am sure Florence is pleased, too, & among your countless friends there will be rejoicing. But I cannot believe any are more pleased than we, dear Max.[1]

It was so lovely coming on you the other day. I am to be at the Ath[enaeum] on the 19th for a day or 2. Is there any chance of your being in Town? We must meet & drink bruderschaft. Miss Jungmann rejoices too & has written off at once to the Hauptmanns.[2]

My love & congratulations to Florence. Ever yours affectionately—
Will

[1] Rothenstein wrote to his brother: 'Yes it was delightful, and surprising, to read of Max's knighthood, the more so since, when it happened to me, Florence said of course Max would never accept anything of the kind. It is altogether right and proper that this should be, if not the O[rder of] M[erit] or the C[ompanion of] H[onour]. And to my amusement, to escape letters, Max goes off sans address.' (Rothenstein to Albert Rutherston, June 11, 1939. RP:HL.)

[2] Elisabeth Jungmann (1897–1959), Gerhart Hauptmann's secretary at the time of his meeting with the Beerbohms (Letter 88, note 3), became Max's assistant and secretary after Florence Beerbohm's death. In 1956 she became the second Lady Beerbohm.

◇111        Abinger Manor Cottage Abinger Common[1]

[June 22, 1939]

Dearest Will

Thank you for your very beautiful letter, which has touched me deeply: the latest of so many wonderful letters of yours. You are many things, but not the least of them is that you are the modern male Mme. de Sévigné; and some day all the world will know it—though France, characteristically, won't admit it. I shall take modest rank among those who would have been Polite Letter Writers of the Second Class if they hadn't suffered from permanent Writer's Cramp. Meanwhile I am a Knight at any rate, and you can't precede me in processions: we shall walk abreast, shoulder to shoulder, in step with each other, in front of furious lesser dignitaries.

I remember that you once wrote to me, when I was in Rapallo, pointing out that we had known each other for *twenty years*; and this span seemed to me tremendous, hardly credible. And now we have known each other for forty-six years; and this doesn't seem to me odd at all: merely *very delightful*. Your always affectionate Max

1 In the autumn of 1938 the Beerbohms left the Villino in the care of servants and neighbours and came to England for the duration of the impending war. In January 1939 they moved into Abinger Manor Cottage as neighbours and guests of Sidney Schiff (1858-1944), translator of Proust; novelist who used the pseudonym Stephen Hudson. He and his wife Violet Schiff (1876-1962), lived in the Manor at Abinger Common, Surrey. From this new perspective Max surveyed past and future: 'Without aristocracy of one kind or another there certainly can't be anything of the kind that you or I can regard as civilisation. But (here is a point that does occur to me [and there's nothing new about it!]) there can't be any sort of aristocracy without slavery. Slavery has, thank heaven! existed in England in our time, our beloved time. And now it is ceasing to exist, alas! I say "alas!" not with my *whole* heart. In a rather remote corner of that organ I am pleased that the lives of the majority of my fellow-creatures are happier than they were. You are much kinder-natured and more philanthropic than I am, and I expect you can derive from that difference greater comfort than can your affectionate Max.' (Beerbohm to Sydney Schiff, March 15, 1939. BP: MC.) The brackets are Max's.


◇112                    Far Oakridge    [early July 1939]

Dearest Max—we were all delighted with your letters. You will have been overwhelmed with tributes of admiration & affection. I wanted to send you the galleys of my 3rd vol., to invite your comments & counsel; but coming as they did at the time when you were beset with correspondence, I refrained from bothering you. Then came a letter from Fabers bidding me send the corrected galleys to the printers, with as little delay as possible. So I did what I was told. Would you care to have a set, while I am awaiting the page-proofs? I should value any opinion from you.1 And I hope you will not too much disapprove of my reflections on yourself. Sending away MS is like sitting down after making a speech: one thinks of many things one should have said.

We had been hoping to see you & Florence this month: now Harriet [Roberts] writes she is to spend many days resting, & they are not to be at Edge until August. Can we persuade you both to come to us for a while? It would be the greatest possible pleasure to us to have you; & I can promise quiet & the simplest possible life. I say quiet, for I have become accustomed to the aeroplanes which pass over our heads. At least we are away from those who have the latest inside information, from the F[oreign] O[ffice] or the War Office or a Cabinet Minister. I bless the day when we got rid of our flat in London. And we have no parties to go to, no visitors & no visits to pay, & the garden to entertain us when we want to potter about. If I go up to Town I stay at the Ath[enaeu]m. Lately we did go to Walter Sickert at Bath: it was his 79th birthday & he played the centenarian beautifully, going upstairs to fetch his teeth before lunch, & descending the steps down to his garden on his backside, dressed in bright orange clothes, with a coloured neckerchief instead of collar & tie, & a Dieppe sailor's peaked cap cocked over his eye. His beard comes up to meet his cap, so there is not much of his face to be seen. They were a hardy lot, the members of the N.E.A.C.: Bate, Brown & Clausen are over the nineties, & Steer, Walter [Sickert] & MacColl entering on their eighties. You & I are youngsters by comparison.[2] But I am quite proud of being nearish to 70! We have had the family with us, with their wives, babes & husbands: all except Elizabeth who is on a visit to her parents in America. All will be gone at the end of next week. So can we persuade you & Florence to come on to Oakridge for a while?

I wish you had let yourself be elected to the Literary Society: it is a pleasant monthly gathering with much good talk.[3] I shall be at the club on Monday & Tuesday, when I have a drawing to make. My love to Florence. Ever yours, dearest Max—Will

[1] Rothenstein, *Since Fifty*, in progress.
[2] Sickert was seventy-nine on May 31, 1939. Rothenstein wrote to Wyndham Lewis: 'I went to see Sickert yesterday at Bath. It was his 79th birthday. Also, his memory is beginning to fade at the edges; but he is a wonderful old man. He was fierce about the R[oyal] A[cademy] "that old place built on a dunghill." No, I said, on nothing so fertile! He has the richest memories of the 19th century painters; most of these will be lost, for he had no Boswell.' (Rothenstein to Lewis, June 2, 1939. Cornell University Library.) See *SF*, pp. 324–325.
Wyndham Lewis (1884–1957), painter and critic, novelist and writer of short fiction. Francis Bate (1858–1950), painter and lithographer. Frederick Brown (1851–1941), head, Westminster School of Art, 1877–1893; Slade Professor of Fine Art, University of London, 1892–1917. George Clausen (1852–1944), Professor of Painting, Royal Academy, 1904–1906.
[3] A private dining club. Max did not become a member.

Dearest Will

Ever so many thanks for a delightful letter which reached me this morning at Charing X Hotel. Florence and I return to Abinger this afternoon. In your letter you said you would be in London on Monday. But meanwhile I have seen John at the above address; and he had a wire saying you would be in London tonight, by change of plan. Thus you will not be at home to receive what will have been sent to you this afternoon, from Bristol, by Moray McLaren, of the B.B.C.; to-wit, a typescript of a broadcast play based, by Douglas Cleverdon, on my story *Enoch Soames*. In that version you appear, saying the sort of things that in that story you said. Well, McLaren and Cleverdon would not of course, nor would I, dream of allowing you thus to appear, unless you gave your full authorisation.[1]

Would you, or wouldn't you, object to being represented in the play by some actor or other who would of course be instructed to give an approximate idea of your clarity and precision and briskness of utterance?[2]

*Or*, would you or wouldn't you, in your heart, prefer that the name of *William Rothenstein* should disappear, and the character be given some imaginary name?

I, at first, when the idea of the broadcast was mooted, wasn't sure that I wouldn't rather that an imaginary character should be substituted for *Max Beerbohm*. But, after some moments of pondering, I decided that I had no objection. But don't let this influence *you* for one moment.

Say *yes* or *no*, exactly as you feel.

And would you not mind saying it soon enough for Moray McLaren to know by Monday morning? He started this morning for Bristol, where the rehearsals are to be held.

The simplest and easiest thing for you to do would be to ring up the B.B.C., ask for Mr. Moray McLaren's secretary, and utter your decision. She would then ring up M. McL. at Bristol, and all would be well. If you could ring him up tomorrow (Saturday) morning, so much the better.

John will tell you more about the matter, if you want to know more. I showed him the beginning of the play, where you come on. You don't, I think, say *anything* that you didn't say in the actual story.

I have written into the typescript the following directions to whatever actor might be cast as impersonator of you.

"Voice. Very brisk, unhesitating, clean-cut utterance. Consonants well-defined. A sympathetic voice, but with *no nonsense about it*." Correct?

How lovely if we could come to Glos.! Our plans are on the lap of the gods.

I will write again. Love from Max

Please, please, let me see the exciting galleys! How joyously would I devour those foretastes![3]

[1] Moray McLaren (1901–1971) in 1935 became Assistant Director of B.B.C. Features and Drama. Douglas Cleverdon (1903–    ), B.B.C. radio writer and producer, 1939–1969. 'Enoch Soames' was rehearsed on July 29, 30, and 31 in Bristol and broadcast in the London Regional Programme on July 31, 1939, with a recorded repeat on August 7, 1939. It was performed during World War II and in September 1947 with different casts, except for Dennis Arundell (1898–    ), who played Enoch in all performances.

[2] Rothenstein stayed in the script, but Sickert was substituted for Beardsley. 'The substitution of *Walter Sickert* for *Beardsley* which interested you,' Max wrote, 'was made because W. R. never liked A. B. so much as most of us did (though the two were quite passably good friends.)' (Beerbohm to Cleverdon, July 21, 1939. Douglas Cleverdon.)

[3] Galley proofs of *Since Fifty*.

❖114                Abinger Manor Cottage        July 20, 1939

Dearest Will

First of all: I vaguely remember having said to you about vol. 2 that it was as good as vol. 1, tho' it must have been more difficult to write. Vol. 3 must itself have been, for obvious reasons (almost everybody being alive, etc.) more difficult than vol. 2. *But* it is, most assuredly, every bit as good. Many congratulations and thanks before publication. The narrative and the criticism, the constant interweaving of these, rejoice my heart, all the time. My only reservation is that you really are *too* indulgent in your many references to the present writer. Thank you all the same.

Know therefore that on galley *85* in paragraph the fourth, I have deleted the words "who painted a portrait of his wife and later attacked both the Schiffs in his *Apes of God*." I didn't know that Wyndham Lewis had attacked them. (I did once look into the book, but it disgusted me so much that I only read a few pages.) I only knew that the Schiffs had befriended W. L. And I would much rather those loveable creatures should not be reminded of the result.[1]

On galley *89*, I have substituted *illustrious persons* for *royal personages*. And *the illustrious person* for *Queen Mary*. Also I have very slightly elaborated the Guedalla-Wright-G.O.M.-and-me anecdote.[2]

I hope all this is clear? It can't be other than tedious.

The radio affair is on the evening of July 31. I am passing on to Douglas Cleverdon—passing it on as my own precaution—the right pronunciation of surname (tho' I'm sure they would get it right anyhow).[3]

Love to Alice and all from us both.

And again CONGRATULATIONS of the warmest kind. Your affectionate Max

[1] Compare *SF*, p. 136, on the Schiffs and Lewis. Galley 85, with Max's emendations, is missing from this set (RP:HL). Letters from the Schiffs to Lewis (Cornell University Library) show that they bore uncomplainingly a good deal of recrimination in return, for Lewis felt that they had not been generous enough as patrons and caricatured them as Lionel and Isabel Kein in his *The Apes of God*. On the Lewis–Schiff relation, see also John Rothenstein, *Brave Day, Hideous Night*, pp. 70–71. For the Lewis portrait of Violet Schiff, see Walter Michel, *Wyndham Lewis: Paintings and Drawings*, plate 69.

[2] Compare *SF*, p. 142. Before revision by Max, this anecdote on galley 89 read: 'Only the other day I was speaking to Philip Guedalla of Peter Wright's gross impertinence in accusing Gladstone of being governed by his seraglio, when I suddenly remembered my own early series of caricatures of Gladstone, equally unpardonable.' (RP:HL) 'G[rand] O[ld] M[an]': W. E. Gladstone, Prime Minister, 1868–1874, 1880–1885, 1892–1894. See Peter Wright, *Portraits and Criticisms*, pp. 152–153. Max's 'unpardonable' early series: eleven drawings, 'Mr. Gladstone Goes to Heaven': see *Catalogue* pp. 66–67.

[3] Max instructed Cleverdon that 'the name Rothenstein must of course be pronounced in the English way: Roe-tn-stine (not with a broad German *o* or a German *sht* for *st*)'. (Beerbohm to Cleverdon, July 21, 1939. Douglas Cleverdon.) Felix Felton played Rothenstein; V. C. Clinton-Baddeley was Max.

⋄115            Far Oakridge    July 22, 1939

Dearest Max—I cannot thank you enough for the trouble you have taken in reading through the galleys. I have of course taken all your emendations. The small mistakes of stops & spelling I had already corrected. In fact there are various changes throughout the text. Fabers will send the 2 sheets to the printers—MacLehose of Glasgow: I am sure you will have improved them. I will, if I may, send you the page proofs as they come to me. I would not for anything cause pain to the dear Schiffs. I referred to Lewis's uncalled-for attack by way of reproof to him; but I quite see you are right—it is best not to remind them of an ugly case of ingratitude. I know your kindness & loyalty to your friends, so I take your praise as it is meant.

But I know how pedestrian the pages are; and as you say, to write about the living is profitless & needs qualities that are not mine, while romance gives form & colour to figures, such as Oscar's, Whistler's, Verlaine's, which have become legendary. But as Herbert said about Hamlet: 'it's a good part,' so I say, your letters, & those of others, are the best part. Alice & I are coming up on Monday until the end of the week. If you & Florence should be in Town, let us meet. Our address is 10 Devonshire Place: Alice's flat. My love to Florence and to the Schiffs. Yours—Will

◇116          Abinger Manor Cottage     July 28, 1939

Dearest Will

"Pedestrian." Yes, you're that, right enough—in the sense that you plant your feet upon the ground and make swift sure progress on them, straight ahead, or around by-ways, according to your choice, and reach your destination every time, with us at your heels—us grateful, us enlightened. A much better performance than (say) the performances of non-pedestrian W. B. Yeats who (admired by you) floated about with his feet a few inches above the ground, with a dimly impressive grace, nowhither.

I wonder how you conclude the book? I don't mean, of course, "Do you sum up and point the moral?" Merely "On what wise gentle note do you recede?" Best love from your affectionate Max

PS. I wasn't quite satisfied with "it is Hardy, not Meredith, who has survived." Meredith is out of fashion, but he'll come in again, believe me, sooner or later (it doesn't matter which), on the strength of his earlier novels, and of the poetry of his prime. He was quite as great a man as Hardy.

PPS. The "Soames" broadcast will be, as I said, next Monday. I don't know at what hour of the evening; but this will of course be announced in the broadcasting column of *The Times* on Monday.[1]
          Do listen in.
          Station: Regional.

[1] After the 'Enoch Soames' broadcast, Rothenstein wrote: 'But since when have you acquired the BBC voice? I scarcely recognized you. The Devil [played by Brian Cummins] spoke rather indistinctly: I suppose, being a foreigner, one could

scarcely expect clear diction from him. I wept for Enoch Soames—how sad a case!' (Rothenstein to Beerbohm, August 1, 1939. Clark Library, UCLA.)

Max, also, professed being close to tears: 'I thought the whole thing fault-less. . . . And the whole cast shone—especially that member of it who had the principal chance of shining, Mr. Arundell. I had always regarded Soames as a well-made synthetic specimen of a type that I had known well and had been annoyed by. I had never thought of him as a real human being, a pitiable fellow-creature to whom one's heart ought to go out. Mr. Arundell didn't bate one jot of Soames's dismal absurdity, but he did make flesh and blood of him—insomuch that at the back of my head I rather wished the play could have a happy ending! I was, quite honestly, at the words "Neglect, failure," not far from the verge of tears; *moi qui vous parle.*' (Beerbohm to Cleverdon, August 1, 1939. Cleverdon.) Mr Arundell recalls: 'From a dramatic-technical point of view it is interesting that the first time I had personally so much sympathy with the character that it was rather senti-mentally sloppy: the third time I tried to think as Soames would have about Beerbohm—with the result I have told you of [i.e., Max's approval of his per-formance].' (Arundell to Mary Lago, February 3, 1973.)

◇117    Abinger Manor Cottage    [postmark: November 21, 1941]

Dearest Will

So *very* sorry to hear from dear Alice that you aren't well. I do hope that when you have quite recovered you won't proceed to be so tremendously active as you have been during the past year and more. Regard me as a model. Copy out carefully my life-long motto: *Restfulness.* Florence and I so constantly wish to see you and Alice, and to talk and laugh, in these rather unlaughable-in days, with you both. Life here goes on very much as when you were last here. The white posts aren't quite so gleamingly white as of yore, nor is the grass quite as freshly mown; for the Schiffs' head-gardener is now in the Home Guard. Sydney and Violet have been much better in health throughout recent months. No more doctors' visits to them. Leo Rau (as perhaps you know) is now an Army doctor. He came here a fortnight or so ago—*un*medically—and looking very English in his khaki.[1] Which reminds me that I haven't seen you resplending in your pale steel blue; and that I want to, but not until you are really strong again, dearest Will. Florence is writing to Alice to-night. She goes often to Mrs. Carpenter's school, and children some-times come in here to master the French language, and will no doubt be revelling in Proust before they are many years older.[2] I do so immensely look forward to seeing your Airmen drawings. The specimens that I have already seen are lovely. *And* your writing, to that I look forward with equal eagerness. I was reading again lately a great deal of Vol. III with intense pleasure in the manifold fine qualities of your mind. I do

157

hope there will be real good news from Libya to-day or to-morrow. The American strikes aren't charming, are they? Rooseveldt, I think, has only himself to blame. In spite of his immensely powerful position after his third election, and his intense sympathy with England, he failed to do the obvious thing: he didn't raise the moral issue, merely the material one. Had he said, "Are we a great nation? If so, shouldn't we behave as such? Are we to allow England to do all the fighting on behalf of civilisation? What will posterity think of us if" etc., etc. Americans are immensely susceptible to anything in the way of Gospel. I am convinced that Rooseveldt could have swept away all opposition. But now—who knows?

Well, dearest Will, I will gabble no more, for the moment, but merely send fondest love from us both to both of you.

Your affectionate Max

¹ Dr Leo Rau was Florence Beerbohm's physician. In 1939 Rothenstein again asked to be an Official War Artist. Again there was delay: 'There is a chance of my being taken on by the Air Ministry to make portrait drawings of the eminent, but I gather there is much intrigue over war work, . . . (Rothenstein to Albert Rutherston, August 26, 1939. RP: HL.) He then 'volunteered to make records of R.A.F. units for the Air Ministry, by which we are surrounded here [at Far Oakridge], and I am awaiting a decision. I have of course offered all drawings I may make to the Ministry. I get numbers of letters from artists offering to work for the Ministry of Information, but no one there seems to have had time to consider this side of propaganda which proved fruitful during the last war.' (Rothenstein to Margaret Woods, October 5, 1939. Rothenstein.) His offer was accepted in 1940, and he worked until 1944; see John Rothenstein, *Brave Day, Hideous Night*, pp. 158–160.

² Mrs Mary Carpenter came to Abinger Common School in 1914 as Head Teacher.


Beerbohm to William and Alice Rothenstein

◆118                25 Highpoint [Highgate]        January 28, 1942

Ever dearest Will and Alice

Thank you both for your letters. I hoped you would perhaps be listening, so that I might be addressing you personally. The singing was rather a daring move; but I was always rather a wild sort of fellow, of the nothing-venture-nothing-have type; and I am glad you approved.¹ I do hope that you, Will, are having a *thoroughly* restful time; *and* you too, Alice. Florence is doing that here, in Rau's flat. She and I had been going to stay here for 2 or 3 days after my broadcast (for which we stayed at the Berners Hotel, near the B.B.C.); and when, on the morrow of the broadcast, we came up here, Florence had bronchitish symptoms and a high temperature, and it was lucky we weren't down at Abinger, with snow-bound roads, etc. She has made a good recovery, but is still weak, and we shall be remaining here for some little time. She has a *very* good and pleasant nurse; and Rau is here from his regiment two or three times a week. He is perfectly satisfied with her progress. It was rather an anxious time, just at first. But now all is well.

I wish Winston weren't so intransigent about his dear old pals. It's a lovable trait, but cuts no ice, and is doing him harm.

Also I wish Germany were already conquered. Japan also. This is England's "greatest hour" without doubt. But how nice if one could telescope time!

Sydney and Violet have been in much better health this year, I'm glad to say. Fondest love from Florence and from your ever devoted

Max

¹ These Rothenstein letters do not survive. See Beerbohm, 'Music Halls of My Youth', in his *Mainly on the Air*, pp. 33–42, a B.B.C. broadcast on January 18, 1942, during which Max burst into song.

Siegfried Sassoon wrote: 'Max's broadcast was a lovely thing. It brought tears to my eyes—for personal reasons, but also because it was so touching in its courtesy and courage—who else is there who could have given us such a half-hour of civilised humour (and wit) combined with the finest sense of artistic values? But I need not praise Max to you! We both realise that he is one of the few really great men alive now in England. I think, however, that he has an extra significance in these times, through being so exquisitely civilised. Never were such people so needed (*and* wanted!). It is delightful to think of Max being so enormously popular on the wireless—even though the majority of his hearers will probably never read a word of his published writings.' (Sassoon to Rothenstein, February 1, 1942. RP: HL.)

✧119     25 Highpoint     February 3, 1942

My dearest Will

My mind had idiotically post-dated your birthday. *What* a mind! But the heart is another matter, and with the whole of that I send you all best birthday wishes and love, and in these Florence joins from her bed of convalescence. It is sad that you too are laid up at this time, and I do hope it will be very soon that you are up and about again: *up* more especially, and not yet insisting on being *about* so tremendously much as you have been in the past year and more. Don't despise repose. I like to think that you are finding a charm in it, with the chess that you are playing and the books that you are reading in the midst of it.

By the way, the date of a man's birth-certificate is no criterion of his age, which is a thing to be determined rather by the use he has made of his life. You, having done so much as you have done, and done it all so splendidly and with such success, are about a hundred and forty, according to my reckoning. Certainly not less than a hundred and twenty.

I telegraphed yesterday in answer to dear Alice's inquiry about Florence. Rau says she is now out of the doctor's hands: must merely stay here for a fortnight or so of complete rest.

Please give our love to Alice, and to Rachel, if she is with you, and to every one in the family.

My heart looks back so fondly on all the years of our friendship. Almost half a century. Or rather (for friendships, like lives, should be measured by their intensity) almost a century. Your devoted Max

✧120                                            Far Oakridge      April 3, 1942

Dearest Max—I hope Florence has been enjoying the kindly warmth which has followed on to the icy days which probably kept you both indoors, as they did me. The usual miracle of the crocuses & primrose is being performed, without the aid of priest or saint, to be followed by that of the almond blossom. Soon we shall be enjoying the oncoming spring at Oakridge. Alice left to-day & I join her there on Monday, after being away since October. We had good news of you both from Miss Russell. I gather that you & Florence care for those 2 charming sisters as we do.[1] They likewise seem delighted with you both; but you will miss Diana for a time—she seems to be making remarkable progress. Alice went up on Wednesday to see John's new acquisitions for the Tate, but she was too tired to talk to the many people she met there; the meager rations, after the ample ones she had at Baslow, have left her seriously undernourished, insisting, as she does, on my getting more than my share.[2] You probably heard that Miss Russell offered a recent painting of mine, of James Stephens, to the Contemp[orary] Art S[ociet]y which they passed on to the Tate, a generous act on her part.[3]

Did I tell you that Stafford Cripps has taken a small farm house, to which he has added a wing, just below us? What an astonishing reversal of opinion towards him—Browning's "Patriot" à rebours![4]

Did you hear that your old Rapallo neighbour Ezra Pound, is now the Italian Haw-Haw broadcasting to America? Alice met Alys Russell in Town who told her that the Berensons are in no wise suffering through remaining in Italy: I have heard nothing of the Lubbocks.[5]

I have been reading among other books old Sir George Leveson Gower's 2nd vol. of reminiscences, which I think you would like—only they give one only too vivid a sense of the difference between the past of yesterday & to-day's present. He was a charming letter writer & moved in the pleasantest circles & has many amusing stories to tell.[6] While staying here I came upon David Low's "Rake's Progress." Do you know this series? They give an astonishing picture of the decline of Pre-war society, with its debased & debasing girls & old women, delineated to perfection. And such brilliant compositions too.[7] I came too by chance upon a book with some Dicky Doyle drawings, which I began to read out of curiosity—Piccadilly. Have you come across it? it is by Laurence Oliphant, a familiar name, but of whom I know nothing, & has some curiously interesting—& bold—satire on the time at which it appeared— the early 70ies.[8] There is no biographical work here in which I could look him up—he certainly roused my curiosity. I have also, inspired by Sydney [Schiff]'s enthusiasm, read a couple of books by Thornton Wilder, & have returned too to the Barsetshire series. Forgive this wandering about books, but reading at present is my sole recreation— not quite, for I play chess when I can find a partner. My love to you both. Ever, dear Max, yours—Will

[1] Flora Russell wrote: 'Sir M[ax] says it causes him great irritation to hear an Englishman talk German very fluently—apropos of Harold Nicolson and Hauptmann—I think.' (Flora Russell to Rothenstein, March 30, 1942. RP: HL.) Her sister was Miss Diana Russell (1874–1971). Apropos of Max and Nicolson, see Nicolson, *Diaries and Letters*, 1930–1939, ed. Nigel Nicolson, p. 166.

[2] John Rothenstein had become Keeper of the Tate Gallery in 1939. This exhibition attracted such crowds that he had to ask the police to help organise them.

[3] Flora Russell hoped to present this painting, begun in 1937, of the Irish poet James Stephens (1882–1950), to the Tate: 'I am going to acquire your portrait of James Stephens on the *instalment* plan and hence the small cheque I enclose. Was there ever such impertinence on my part? But you know what collectors are when they want something! I have a lovely plan of where it is to have a home, . . .' The Tate Trustees met on March 19. 'I hope,' she wrote, 'they will behave . . .' (Flora Russell to Rothenstein, February 11, March 18, 1942. RP: HL.) They behaved nicely and accepted the portrait.

[4] In 1940, Sir Stafford Cripps (1889–1952), British Ambassador to Russia, 1940–1942, bought Frith Hill, a farm near Stroud.

[5] William Joyce (1906–1946), Brooklyn-born Irishman, broadcast pro-German propaganda to the Allies, who nicknamed him 'Lord Haw-Haw'. Ezra Pound (1885–1972) began broadcasting over Rome Radio in January 1941. The Pounds had settled in Rapallo in 1924: 'The Ezra Pounds came today,' Florence Beerbohm wrote to her brother in 1933. 'I had met him in Rapallo and told him laughingly what you said—"that you would travel across Europe to talk to him." Well I (Max is speaking: Florence has handed me the pen) rather fear that Ezra

may have been inclined to take those words rather less 'laughingly' and lightly than they were meant; and that the words may have raised hopes rather higher than hopes ought to be. He is writing to you. If there is anything you can do for him or for 'Globe' [Milwaukee], do please do it—, dear Sam; for he is a good fellow, and a gifted one, and disinterested, and not (who is?—who that matters, I mean) rich. BUT, oh BUT, of course you must not do for him anything that would in any way be difficult for you or prejudicial to the *Commercial Appeal!*' (Florence and Max Beerbohm to Sam Kahn, November 9 [1933]. Starr.)

Alys Russell (d. 1951), American-born first wife of Bertrand Russell. Percy Lubbock (1879–1965), literary critic and historian, husband of Lady Sybil Scott (d. 1943), daughter of the 5th and last Earl of Desart and former wife of Geoffrey Scott (1885–1929), architect, first editor of the Malahide Castle Boswell papers. The Lubbocks were living at Lerici.

6 Sir George Granville Leveson-Gower, *Years of Content, 1858–1886; Years of Endeavour, 1886–1907.*

7 Twelve colour plates inspired by a resort encounter between cartoonist David Low (1891–1963) and the Prince of Wales. 'I had a handsome offer to buy the whole of the "Rake" but I refused,' wrote Low, 'because of a vague feeling that their proper place was in some London Museum, where they might have some small value as a kind of panorama of the London of the 30–40's—now gone for ever. (Perhaps I shall have to build the museum myself, though.)' (Low to Rothenstein, March 23, 1942. RP: HL.) See West and Low, *The Modern 'Rake's Progress'*, with commentary by Rebecca West. Present owner of the drawings: Prudence Rowe-Evans.

8 Laurence Oliphant, *Piccadilly: A Fragment of Contemporary Biography*, with eight illustrations by Richard Doyle.


Beerbohm to William and Alice Rothenstein

✧121                        Abinger Manor Cottage        May 21, 1942

Dearest Will and Alice

You may possibly have overlooked, in *The Times* of a few days ago, the picture that I enclose. At first glance I thought it was the floor of some warehouse, with a lot of crates standing about on it. So this is Kharkov! And any number of other towns all the world over now. Not *all* the world over. England hasn't anything quite so extreme as yet. But she will toe the mark later on, I'm sure.

Forgive this dismal opening. Let me hasten to say how pleased and flattered I am by the picture of you, Alice, reading "Seven Men" aloud to you, Will.[1] "Braxton and Maltby" was written in Winstons Cottage; also "Savonarola Brown"; so you have savoured them on their native heath. But I don't imagine they pleased you half so well as I have been by "Men of the R.A.F." What a very splendid collection of drawings!— "in form, in moving, how express and admirable!" The sitters, so very various in age and kind, seem to have a common denominator, revealed by you; something that somehow distinguishes them from other men, from earthmen; an aëreal look; haven't they? And how you have revelled in having, at last, sitters who aren't cursed with the universal dreary drawback of a neat turned-down collar, a neat sailor's-knot tie, and a neat pair of lapels to a neat lounge-suit! All those impressive helmets or head-pieces and cords and streamers and mufflers and jerkins and gadgets have a life of their own, and you have beautifully made the most of them. Nor have you ever written anything better than your tale of your adventures and of your impressions. How fresh and strong, and wise and vivid, all the pages are! Many congratulations.[2]

You must, both of you, be immensely glad to be home again at F[ar] O[akridge]. I do hope that you, Alice, are not continuing to eat too little, and that you, Will, are learning the art of leisure. Florence is regrettably averse from that art, but she does consent to practise it in moderation. She is much better and stronger than she was at the time when she fell ill. Miss Flora and Miss Diana are a source of great delight to us. The former motored us to the latter a few days ago. What a lovely house and gardens! We hadn't been there before. The invalid looked very well and blooming, as invalids so often do. It is a great disappointment that the bone of her hip has not joined properly, and she will not be able to walk without a stick. We all talked much of you both.

What good reading you have been having! Byron's letters are, I think, the best ever written—the fullest and most spontaneous. So many of the most celebrated and admired sets of letters aren't letters at all in what seems to me the true sense. They are literary compositions, and one can't imagine them in *manuscript*: they seem inseparable from print. "Piccadilly" I have never read. I now shall. I had always been meaning to. I wish Laurence Oliphant had existed in our own time. But no, I don't. For if he had, I shouldn't be so delighted as I am by the legend of him. Oh, give me legends, fairly recent legends, all the time! Thank Heaven, we ourselves have a legendary touch about us! We are ex-Arcadians, greatly envied by the young.

Have you ever read Trollope's *political* novels? Phineas Finn, Phineas Redux, The Duke's Children? To me they seem as good as the Barchester ones.

"But I have detained you long enough," as Victorian statesmen on platforms used to say after speaking for two hours and three quarters. And I hear no "(cries of No, no, go on!)" So with all fondest love

I am your devoted Max

¹ Described in letter from Rothenstein to Beerbohm, May 12, 1942 (Clark Library, UCLA).
² Rothenstein et al., *Men of the R.A.F.* 'In form . . . admirable': Shakespeare, *Hamlet*, II, ii, 296–297.
Rothenstein wrote: 'These last days I have been going down to see the planes off to Norway—they go in the evening and return in the night and early morning. There is something acutely moving in these young people going off in their planes, dressed like Knights on a quest so different from any the knights could ever have dreamed. . . . I have been asked, if I hate war, how I can find satisfaction in recording those who make it. Form is a permanent reality, war an accident in time. An airman is only dropping his bombs at odd times; most of the time he is an ordinary human being, a son, husband, lover, father. One of the young pilots I drew failed to return and the gratitude of his relatives for the poor record I made of him touched my heart.' (Rothenstein to Flora Russell, May 4, 1940. Mrs Noel Blakiston.)

◇122                          Far Oakridge    August 22, 1942

Dearest Max—what a delightful leader in the Times Lit. Sup.! it made me glow all over, so warm, so discriminating the tribute.¹ You have tried & indeed succeeded in dodging the limelight—if from time to time it has caught you, it has come to you, not you to meet it. But why do I mention this unwelcome glare! perhaps because I am thinking of Shaw & Barrie & Lawrence, 3 remarkable figures of our time to whom much praise has come, & with due praise, these overbright rays. You, almost alone, won the admiration of the old while you were young, of the young in your later years—I think of Meredith, Swinburne, Hardy, Henry James & Gosse & now, all the young writers make an exception of Max in their general condemnation of their elders. They will press round you on Monday. But before this more public applause, how many letters of grateful admiration & affection will reach you!² And mind goes back to the little sitting room whose door I never could pass on the way upstairs to a certain blue papered study, without entering for a few minutes' talk to a very small, very bright old lady whose kindness to me was unending because I cared for the apple of her eye, her son. I can still see the pictures on the wall, & the photographs on the mantel shelf, & the little silver nick-nacks on the small tables; & Meckie (how spell his name?) is barking round my feet & Constance is bidding him be silent. Well, all the little old lady believed would happen has come to pass—of how many mothers & sons can this be said? & with such a helpmate at your side [as] she would have chosen. Do you remember how worried Herbert used to be over your caricatures? That I think one of the remarkable things of your career—no one more observant of the human weaknesses

164

& more pungent in displaying them, yet going through life without an enemy; for the same vision which saw the frailties has been the quickest to perceive the charm, the gifts, the merits of your contemporaries. I wish I could turn on the wireless on Monday to hear what others will be saying &, above all, to listen to your own voice (I know your modesty about your speaking) fairly bristling as Henry James would say, with quiet wisdom & reserves of wit. Apart from the terrors of a long railway journey, the occasion would be too emotional for me. Since I gather ladies are not to be present, Florence too will have to content herself with what you will tell her later. But I am forgetting, I too am a Maximilian! & maybe I shall be present at the next meeting. Dearest Max & Florence, all my love, de coeur. Ever yours Will

¹ See an editorial, 'Happy Returns!' *The Times Literary Supplement*, August 22, 1942, p. 415.

² Alan Dent (1905–    ), drama and film critic, broadcaster, and biographer, planned a party for Max: 'Max Beerbohm, as you know, will be 70 on the 24th August. With this in mind I have had the notion of convening Seven Men of taste (Lord Berners—James Bone—Ivor Brown—Philip Guedalla—Moray McLaren—Raymond Mortimer—Alan Thomas), and we have founded something which is, for ever and a day, to be known as THE MAXIMILIAN SOCIETY. To this you obviously belong. . . . We must therefore assemble, somehow and somewhere. We are to number seven-and-seventy in all, and have no ladies. The speakers are to be limited to Sir Max himself—with one brief announcer and one terse thanker.' Rothenstein accepted, and Dent replied: 'The "Seven Men" agreed—in conclave—that "The Maximilian Society" was a good inobvious title for our brotherhood . . . though I am rather inclined to agree with you that it [has] a Holy Roman Empire ring. However 'tis done—and Max himself approves.' (Dent to Rothenstein, May 20, 30, 1942. RP: HL.) The Society met in the basement of the Players Theatre, Albemarle Street. Desmond MacCarthy was Chairman. The Theatre's company staged a music-hall bill revival. The half-guineas were spent on a gift to Max of sixty-three bottles of wine (intended to be seventy bottles, but fine wines were scarce in wartime). Of absent friends Max mentioned only Rothenstein and Maurice Baring; Rothenstein's health was unequal to wartime rail travel from Far Oakridge. Augustus John sent a fulsome acceptance, to offset which, Dent sent Max a copy of Shaw's refusal, 'which seems to us almost as charming in its way. It affects to be from his secretary, and it runs: "In reply to your letter of the 28th April Mr. Bernard Shaw asks me to say that he suffered too much from the celebration of his own 70th birthday 16 years ago to make himself a party to a repetition of the same outrage at the expense of an old friend who never harmed him".' (Dent to Beerbohm, June 27, 1942. BP: MC.) The letter from Blanche Patch, Shaw's secretary, to Dent, is in the Burgunder Collection of the Cornell University Library.

❖123          Far Oakridge     September 21, 1942

Dearest Max—James Stephens rang up to tell us you were to speak "on

165

the air" at 10.5 last night, otherwise we should have put out the light &
our heads on our pillows as likely as not, in any case would not have
gathered from the plain "talk" that it was *your* talk. And your talk it
was, voice & matter, every accent familiar, the next best thing to being
with you but how far from the best! when the announcer intervened &
all was over.[1] Let us meet shut off from any announcer—somehow we
must manage—perhaps the friendly little hotel will be able to put us up
for a night or 2.[2] I wonder how many of your listeners could visualise
that cartoon of yours to which you referred—I had been looking at it but
a short while ago—what monsters! It will need heavier tanks & more
powerful cannon than we have yet produced to crush the advertisers; but
your hand grenade thrown among them was at least a portent.[3] I
remember Eno's—there was also an omnipresent "Harness's belt" & a
Macassar Oil temptation in the Press. I met "Bubbles" when we visited
the Q[ueen] Elizabeth at Spezia—not unlike his uncle, the PRA.[4] Our
love to Florence. Ever yours, dearest Max—Will

[1] See Beerbohm, 'Advertisements', in his *Mainly on the Air*, pp. 43–51.
[2] Abinger Hatch Hotel, at Abinger Common.
[3] On Max's 'Miniature design for colossal fresco is . . . International Advertising Convention (Wembley, July 1924), . . .', see *Catalogue*, p. 177
[4] Admiral Sir William James (1881–1973) was model for 'Bubbles' (1886), by his Pre-Raphaelite grandfather, Sir John Everett Millais. This portrait was recruited to advertise Pears soap; see *The Illustrated London News*, Christmas Supplement, December 31, 1887. Present owner: A. and F. Pears Ltd.
The President of the Royal Academy: Sir Edward Poynter.


✧124                   Far Oakridge     [November 18, 1942]

Dearest Max—do you remember telling me that you could go through
the Oxford term sans cap & gown? And that I swore that I would see
you wearing them? But no vision was vouchsafed me that the gown
would be scarlet & grey, or, what was still less to be possible, that my
inelegant person would be hidden in that same disguise. But how right
& proper that Oxford should so honour itself by offering you what you
early disdained—a degree very much above zero. I wonder whether,
seated far at the back, so as to be unobserved, a slender, heavily veiled
elderly lady was present, distinguished by a certain elegance, a Miss
Dobson, who, I know, owed much to you—she used to tell me, from her
very birth. I hope you walked through the streets accompanied by 2
stately beadles from Merton to the Old Divinity School, from whence
you were ushered into the Vice-Chancellorian presence. Now that you

are twice Doctored, I should live to know you be-Rectored—Glasgow, Edinburgh, Aberdeen?[1]

I am deep in the Boswellized Shaw—small wonder he refused all honours, for how could they approach those heaped on his head by the great man himself! Let the centuries' old warning of Shakespeare now go unheeded, the grave violated, the bones cast in the river conveniently close & when the time comes, as alas, it some day must, the ashes of GBS take their place. I think always of your letter to Henry Arthur [Jones], at the time of his violence & Shaw's really Christian refusal of riposte, your hope that he would never die. For he has always, & finally, played a gallant part through his long life.[2]

Later.

Here comes the Times wherein I see that the actual conferring of the D.Litt is to be later: the D[aily] T[elegraph] misinformed us, & this note of gratulation has misfired. It will serve to remind you of cold days at Oakridge which were none the less fruitful days for you. My love to you both, yours ever Will

[1] On November 17, 1942, Max was awarded an honorary D. Litt. degree at Oxford; it was conferred November 21. Rothenstein was similarly honoured on May 24, 1934, when he gave the Romanes Lecture at Oxford; see his *Form and Content in English Painting*. On Max's gown, see *MM* I, 152.

Albert Rutherston wrote: 'I had to miss Max's "Investiture" which took place last Saturday at short notice. I was very sorry indeed not to be there and do him honour, all the more especially so since I contrived to get the University to bestow his D. Litt.' (Albert Rutherston to Rothenstein, November 25, 1942. RP:HL.)

[2] The 'Boswellized Shaw' was Hesketh Pearson's, *Bernard Shaw: His Life and Personality*. Jones attacked Shaw during World War I, and for some time thereafter, for his criticisms of England's views and behaviour. Max tried unsuccessfully to reconcile the two playwrights. See ibid., pp. 329–331; Doris Arthur Jones, *Taking the Curtain Call*, pp. 270–291.

◇125          Far Oakridge     February 28, 1943

Dearest Max—we hear of you both from the good Miss Flora—no longer from the equally good Miss Diana, for the time laid up at her Cottage hospital—who tells us of her pilgrimages to Saint Max & Saint Florence—bright days each time for her, looked forward to & cherished.[1] We have to be content with hearing that you are both well & cheerful. Things are certainly hopeful, the latest news reassuring. But a black curse on Gandhi, playing the Eminence Grise—I have always distrusted him. But if he dies while incarcerated there will be risings which will

167

have to be put down—we can't expect the millions who regard him as a Saint & his word as law to understand our ideas of abstract justice & political decencies, & I wish a way out could have been found. But did you read G.B.S.'s wicked letter in yesterday's Times?[2] Much as I love him I should like him [to] be shut up in Blenheim or Arundel, with a cellar of the finest vintages of liver extract at his disposal. Contrariwise let all freedom to range at will be given to Churchill—but not to his cigar, of which one gets more than a little tired—a photograph of him sans that barber's pole sticking out from his face would not lessen our confidence in him. I can imagine an essay in "Yet Again" on the association of public figures with objects that, without this, would have no meaning—Churchill's cigar & Chamberlain's eyeglass, his brother's umbrella. I had forgotten "The Naming of Streets," a perfect piece— there is much to be said, by me at least, for "the pleasures of forgetfulness"![3] Which reminds me, did I ever know A. Machen, on whose behalf you & others are appealing?[4] I cannot remember reading any of his books. I have lately re-read Hogg's life of Shelley—what an uncomfortable world for any but the wealthy! There is an account of a useless journey to Dublin; amusing to read, which makes even our war period comfortable by comparison. In reading of the past, it is we who supply the gilding, not those who lived in it. Hogg's account of a coach journey, seated, without an overcoat, in drenching rain, wet to the skin, stopping at inns where neither food nor warmth are to be had, is on all fours with Fanny Kemble's experience of travel in America about the same time.[5] Which reminds me of your "Ichabod"—where *are* all those red-lined hat boxes of seemingly imperishable leather?[6] My love to St Florence, ever dear Max, yours—Will

[1] Diana Russell was in the Cranleigh (Surrey) Village Hospital, recovering from a broken hip.

[2] M. K. Gandhi (1869–1948) was jailed at Poona, August 7, 1942–May 6, 1944, for his part in the 'Quit India' movement. On February 10, 1943, he began a twenty-one-day hunger strike. Shaw allowed the Tagore Society in London to publish a letter in which he called Gandhi's arrest the Government's 'stupidest blunder' in India. Flora Russell commented: 'I am in great sympathy with Bernard Shaw over vegetable diet to include eggs and cheese, but has he made many converts by his angry language? Also about Sane Socialism to which we have to come? What has his influence been? I think he has wit, great Wit but absence of humour like most Irish. I am told by a friend that Mrs Shaw has no humour but evidently they are a happy couple and perhaps he would not have liked a wife who occasionally laughed at him.' (Flora Russell to Rothenstein, February 6, 1943. RP:HL.) See 'Mr. G. B. Shaw on Gandhi "Blunder",' *The Times*, February 27, 1943, p. 2. For Rothenstein on Gandhi, see *IE*, p. 339.

In 1939 Sam Kahn sent Max, Shaw's *William Morris as I Knew Him.* 'It was most kind of you to give me G. B. S. on Morris,' Max wrote. 'Very many thanks for the great pleasure I have just been having in reading it. Pleasure mingled with pain—such as anything of G. B. S.'s always gives me. I love his brilliance and his cogency. But the hardness and *too* great brilliance of the style affect me unpleasantly. I feel rather as tho' he were the squeaking of a slate-pencil on a slate! Besides, his sums, so intensely mathematical tho' he is, so often come out wrong. Morris wasn't so wonderful a creature as G.B.S. thinks him; and if he hadn't been a socialist he wouldn't have been thought wonderful at all by G.B.S., who hasn't a spark of poetry in him and has a very faulty visual sense. The book is therefore a mitigated joy—but certainly a joy; and all the more so because of your kind thought in letting me possess it.' (Beerbohm to Sam Kahn, January 23, 1939. Starr.)

At about this same time, Rothenstein wrote: 'We lunched with the Shaws last week; he vital as ever; but his talk is now gramophone records, each one slipped into the machine according to his subject. But one can't be expected to invent constantly at Shaw's age.' (Rothenstein to Florence Beerbohm, n. d. BP: MC.)

[3] See Beerbohm, 'The Naming of Streets', in his *Yet Again*, pp. 207–225.

[4] An appeal in behalf of Arthur Machen (1863–1947), novelist and first English translator of Casanova's memoirs.

[5] Thomas Jefferson Hogg went in 1813, at the Shelleys' request, to join them in Ireland, but missed them by one day. See Hogg et al., *The Life of Percy Bysshe Shelley*, I, 392–415. On the English actress Fanny Kemble and her life in America, see Frances Anne Kemble, *Journal of a Residence in America;* and *Journal of a Residence on a Georgian Plantation in 1838–1839.*

[6] See Beerbohm, 'Ichabod', *The Cornhill Magazine*, n. s. 9 (1900), 636–648; reprinted in his *Yet Again*, pp. 123–145.

Rothenstein to Max and Florence Beerbohm

◇126                              Far Oakridge    May 23, 1943

Dearest Max & Florence, Alice was very pleased to hear from you. She didn't stay at Oxford as there was nor room nor bed to be found. Her arm was bound up, to the safety of the fracture but to her discomfort, by a complicated contraption of plaster & bandages, to be removed when she goes to Oxford again in 10 days' time. She has naturally some pain & discomfort but I hope once the fracture has set this will cease & be forgotten. Meanwhile she comes down to sit in the verandah, & enjoys the garden, now resplendent with roses. The unceasing fertility of nature takes one always by surprise, especially, as with mankind, among the lower classes of plants, bindweed, dandelion, chickweed. I looked in vain in the Times for an account of your Clarke lecture; this will, however, be printed, like the Romanes lectures at Oxford—why you haven't yet given this last I don't understand.[1] Cambridge recently acquired a complete set of my lithographs—one made by my brother Charles,

169

which includes a drawing of Conder I had completely forgotten, made in Glebe Place.[2] I notice that Conder is coming into his own again— John tells me the Queen is a keen collector of his work.[3] I had a letter from one A. E. Gallatin, who proposes to make an iconography of your writings—I have a book of his on Whistler portraits & he owns, or did own, one of my drawings of Aubrey Beardsley, often reproduced, on a settee.[4] I hear, at a tangent, that all goes well with you both. I was in Town for a couple of days & thought, for one moment, I caught sight of you, Max, bending over some books at the club, an illusion, alas. Much love to you both—Will

[1] Rothenstein writes plainly, 'Clarke Lecture' but means Max's Rede Lecture, *Lytton Strachey*, given at Cambridge on May 20, 1943.

[2] In 1943 the Friends of the Fitzwilliam gave the Museum Charles Rutherston's set of 138 lithographs. It is not complete; it includes some variant versions and stations, and some additional pulls.

[3] On May 15, 1942, Queen Elizabeth the Queen Mother purchased from Christie's a Conder watercolour on silk, 'Revel' (1898).

[4] A. E. Gallatin (1881–1952), bibliographer, painter, and collector, appealed through *The Times Literary Supplement* (April 17, 1943, p. 187) for Beerbohm materials. See his *Sir Max Beerbohm: Bibliographical Notes*; and Gallatin and L. M. Oliver, *A Bibliography of the Works of Max Beerbohm*.

A Rothenstein–Gallatin correspondence had begun in 1902. 'In 1894,' Rothenstein had written, 'I made 2 drawings of [Beardsley on a settee] at his house in Cambridge Street [Pimlico], on brown paper, with a little pastel added. One of these drawings was bought by one of his publishers, Mr Leonard Smithers. The other is still in my possession. I should be very glad to sell it to you should you wish to have it. The price of it would be £12.' (Rothenstein to Gallatin [postmark, November 14, 1902]. A. E. Gallatin Papers: The New-York Historical Society.) He offered to send Gallatin a photograph of the drawing owned by Smithers, but, when he could not find one, wrote that the drawing 'turned up at Christie's some time ago . . .' (Rothenstein to Gallatin, March 23, 1903. A. E. Gallatin Papers: Houghton Library.) It 'turned up' again in 1972 at The Fine Art Society, London, in a Rothenstein Centenary exhibition, was purchased for the Robert H. Taylor Collection, and is reproduced here. For the drawing of 'Beardsley on a settee' that was purchased by Gallatin, see Rothenstein, *The Portrait Drawings of William Rothenstein*, plate 3; present owner unknown. For Gallatin on Whistler, see his *Portraits of Whistler: A Critical Study and an Iconography*.


⋄127                                          Far Oakridge       July 9, 1943

Dearest Max—there came to-day your Rede lecture, not from the author but from his printer, thinking of me in flattering connection with yourself, no doubt (see the Inverness Courier, Feb. 24, 1931) because I am "a character in Max Beerbohm's story 'Enoch Soames' "—not, I hope, for he is as yet but a Pretender to the Throne, as homage to the

Common Man. Not long since I re-read Matthew Arnold's "Cultuee & Anarchy" in which he already has a passing shudder at the mere notion that the Common Man might at some future time cast his shadow over the Brahmin's platter. He did not live to see your prophetic cartoons, nor did you yourself know how accurate your fore-seeing, I imagine, "of England's smooth & asphalt land," beribboned with flat-roofed concrete homes for heroes. After the purring of Desmond & his Sunday colleague other words will sound flat in your ears.[1] But in mine my own purring was not lessened by Desmond's—who else can give perfect praise without flattery! With so poor a memory as mine it was well that I had lately read through the "Eminent Victorians" again. Now I shall send for the other essays (not the Essex & Elizabeth) & go through them too. I spend the mornings only in the studio so have leisure for reading. James Stephens brought over Frank Harris's book on Shaw—a better one than I expected it to be; but how Shaw could allow himself to play into Harris's soiling hands as he did surprises me.

Alice sends love to you & Florence; she is beginning to use her arm a little & is slowly getting rid of aches & pains. I find life pleasanter than I anticipated, thrown as one is almost entirely on one's own resources, but time passing no less swiftly—it always seems to be the week-ends. All good wishes to you & Florence, dearest Max. Ever yours affectionately—Will

[1] On the *Inverness Courier*, see Letter 99, note 1. See Desmond MacCarthy, 'On Lytton Strachey', *The Sunday Times*, July 4, 1943, p. 3. The 'colleague' was J. C. Trewin (1908–    ) of *The Observer*; see his 'Max on the Dais', *The Observer* (London), July 4, 1943, p. 3.

◇128          [Acland Nursing Home, Oxford      late June 1944]
Dearest Max—how delightful to hear from you! I thought if I slipped away without a word of adieu exchanged that it would be out of the natural course of things. Now comes your letter & in spite of the place nat[ural] science has taken I may in the end [owe] more to drugs— morphia & oxygen—than to the poets of the last generation. Not so with the earlier ones, for I think that Wordsworth's, & Keats's songs, the not too long poems of Milton & Gray's Elegy & the Scholar Gypsy, just kept me going until my brain began to get fuddled & I slept in the arms of Morphia. Now they say words of promise. Such letters as yours bring a new hope.[1] Ever your loving Will

[1] Rothenstein had a serious heart attack in May 1944 and was not out of danger until July 14.

◇129                    Abinger Manor Cottage      [June 24, 1944]

My dearest Will

I do hope you are making really good progress—and are submitting amenably to all that the doctors demand of you. I know how you hate resting, and I understand the foible—though I have never, alas, shared it! I am glad you are in Oxford. It's just a few weeks more than fifty-one years ago since first we met there, at dinner with St. Cyres. And what a lucky meeting for me that was! How much you and your friendship have meant to me ever since! You have always inspired and helped me so much. I have always learned so much from you. But "learning" is a rather dreary word. I prefer to say that I have always delighted in you and loved you. Do get well again quite soon. Florence and I are, as always, here, at this (now quite old) address. Sydney [Schiff] hasn't been at all well; he caught a chill the other day, but is now convalescing. Edward Behrens has just arrived from America, and gives good technical military reasons for assurance that the Germans *cannot* hold out for more than three more months.[1] Usually I am not much impressed by such predictions. But I am inclined to believe in this one. You and I were very fortunate in being born so long ago—in having had our young days in beautiful days of peace and ease and civilisation— auspicious and nutritive days, days before the world was ruined by science and machinery and other things darling to the Devil.[2] I caught a glimpse of those days this morning, here. You remember the plots of grass with the white posts and black chains around them. The grass has been growing very long and high in these days. A labourer came to-day from Raike's farm in a small old cart drawn by a large old brown cart-horse, accompanied by a son aged 6. The father was very active with his scythe. So also was the son, with a sickle small enough not to be out of proportion to him. They have now returned to the farm, the father lead-ing the horse, and the son perched aloft on the hay (for some of the grass-plots had been shorn a week or so ago). Have you seen the photo-graphs in *The Times* and elsewhere of the "prefabricated" homes which will presently arise all over England? I suppose these homes will be congenial enough to generations flourishing in the altogether pre-fabricated world which lies ahead. Well, well, let the future take care of itself. Though really it need hardly trouble to do that. It's going to be taken such very good care *of*. Meanwhile you and I have the past to revel in. But I am repeating myself.

Dearest Will, all fond love from Florence and from

your loving Max

¹ Sir Edward Beddington-Behrens (1897–1968), Violet Schiff's nephew; businessman and financier.

² Reprise on a consistently Maxian theme: 'Alice will have told you that I "rang her up"—on that infernal machine, the telephone, which I cannot understand your or her tolerance for—and told her, through the gruntings and gratings and hideous darknesses of space, faintly, weakly, how sorry I was that next Friday I had a previous engagement . . .' (Beerbohm to Rothenstein [1908?]. RP:HL.)

Rothenstein to Max and Florence Beerbohm

◇130                 Far Oakridge      September 23, 1944

Dearest Max & Florence, we were dismayed to hear of the flying bomb landing near you, but heard you had suffered no damage save for broken windows. Now I hear from Miss Russell that you have been driven forth & that you, dear Florence, go saving precious objects from what I gather is a wreck. Miss R. wrote that you were both unperturbed throughout; but what a disagreeable adventure! We hear you are with friends near Abinger, & that the Schiffs too have suffered & have left.¹

I rejoice in your safety—you are seldom absent from my thoughts. Alice has been reading "7 Men" & "Zuleika" to me & always I marvel at your genius. I am but a poor creature, dear Max, dozing, reading & lethargic, but my affection for my friends is unaltered. Meanwhile the enviable Shaw pours out counsel for the future, unchanged up to the threshold of his nineties in his pessi-optimism. A great figure, nobly clowning.² I send you my affectionate wishes for ripe years, for in you dwells sanity, so much wanted to-day & to-morrow. Ever with all my love—³ Will

¹ On August 3, 1944, a flying bomb hit Abinger Common Church, drove parts of a gargoyle and other debris through the Cottage, did major damage to the Manor. The Schiffs went to Hove; the Beerbohms went to the Abinger Hatch Hotel, then to various friends, and finally to Flint Cottage, George Meredith's home at Box Hill, Surrey. 'Would that the idiotic bomb had continued its idiotic course further than the Church and on yonder to one of the many fields where it could have fallen so harmlessly!' Max wrote. 'But one is thankful that it didn't do much more mischief than it did. Thankful too that no further mischief of the doodling kind can cross the Channel. The approaching end of the black-out here is rather

173

cheering too. . . . What horrible years of history to have lived through! And yet, for Florence and me, how vast an amount of happiness there was in the dear Cottage!' (Beerbohm to Violet and Sydney Schiff, September 15, 1944. BP: MC.) After a visit to Abinger, Flora Russell wrote: 'At last I have seen the Abinger ruins—and realized the miracle of the Beerbohms' survival.' (Flora Russell to Rothenstein, October 7, 1944. RP: HL.)

2 Shaw, *Everybody's Political What's What.*

3 William Rothenstein died at Far Oakridge on February 14, 1945.

*Epilogue*

Beerbohm to Alice Rothenstein

Flint Cottage, Box Hill, Dorking        February 15 [1945]

Very dearest Alice

Our hearts are with you in your grief. And so will the hearts of every one that knows you and knew him. Our love to you and to Rachel and Betty, and to John and Billy, and to Albert. I wish we could come to Gloucestershire, but various things make this impossible. Our dear Will, it is grievously sad that he is gone, that we shall never again see him and hear him. He was the oldest of all my friends. He was, absent or present, a part of me. There was no man whose mind and heart impressed me so much as his. I learned so much from him when I was quite young, and I have gone on learning from him ever since. He was always extraordinarily kind to me—and indeed to how many other people! I suppose no man of his time was so prodigal of helpfulness, so inspiring to younger men and to men of his own age—and elder men too! Death is a horrible thing. I hate to think that Will's great heart and brain—that brain which never ceased for one instant to function so swiftly and potently—are at work no longer, well though they have earned their rest. His life was a surpassingly full one. And how great a part of that fulness was of you, his devoted and beloved Alice! I am glad that you have in your loss of him the solace of his dear children. And grandchildren too.

His name is a name that will not fade in any future years. Besides his paintings, his drawings, and his books, there will be his letters—a storehouse in which posterity will spend a great deal of time with great advantage and gratitude.

Dearest Alice, again all our love and thoughts.

Your affectionate old Max

PS. I suppose there will be a Memorial Service in London. And to that we shall certainly be able to go.

# William Rothenstein: An Address Delivered by Max Beerbohm at the Memorial Service Held at Saint Martin-in-the-Fields, Tuesday, March 6th 1945.[1]

Will Rothenstein lies in a grave in Gloucestershire, a grave on his well-beloved Cotswolds. But it is right that his memory should be honoured by us here in London, where the greater part of his amazingly full, brilliant and beneficent life was spent. To London he came as a student, in his 'teens, and to it, at the age of twenty-one, he returned from his studies in Paris, bringing with him, and diffusing among his coevals and his elders, many whiffs of the bracing air of that capital. His elders, I imagine, may have been rather alarmed by him; we others were merely impressed and delighted: he was so much more mature than we, and so constantly dynamic, radiating ideas in all directions, all the time. And, as I look back, I am confirmed in my early impression that all—or almost all—these ideas were good ones. Young though he was, he had already wisdom. Exuberantly gay, he was already serious—serious not only about his art but also about life. In later years this austerity took precedence of his high spirits, but it never ousted them. In congenial company he was ever a laugher as well as a teacher, and I have known no man who so dearly loved a joke against himself. Any such joke, even a not very good one, was sure to win him and enchant him.

In one of his three books of memoirs, he suggests that strenuous men may be divided into two categories: the givers and the takers: on the one hand, men whose incentive is their own emolument, their own prestige, and so on; on the other hand, those who love their work for its own sake, and seek no reward but such pleasure and profit as the world may derive from it. Will himself was assuredly a giver, a giver with both hands, in the grand manner. His devotion to the arts of painting and drawing, his unswerving resolve to do nothing else than his best, was matched by his eagerness to help forward the work of others. A desire to be helpful is not uncommon. But very rare indeed is such a power to help as Will had. Few of us possess such terrific energy as *he* had, as he retained even when, in recent years, his health was weakened. And fewer still have that unerring instinct for discovery of raw but real talent, and for the direction in which it should be developed. I daresay that among those who are able to be here today are some who were students in the Royal College of Art at the time when Will was Principal of it. They, I am sure, would bear witness to his illuminating power. I, in old times, had the pleasure of friendship, or close acquaintance, with many of Will's contemporaries in art, and with many of the then rising generation. There was not one of them that did not owe much to his generous appreciation and wise counsel.

He is gone, but his work remains. In many of the galleries of England and of other countries his paintings will speak for him. And to him inquisitive posterity will constantly be indebted for that life-long series of drawings in which he portrayed so faithfully and so penetratingly the faces and the inward characters of all the most interesting men of the decades in which he lived. By the same token, future writers about those decades will have much to enlighten them in those three rich books of memoirs. And there will be further enlightenment in any such volume or volumes of his letters as may be vouchsafed to us. His wit and his wisdom overflowed in the art of letter-writing.

His spirit will remain. But that fine brain of his, and that fine heart of his, have ceased from work. He is gone, and for me, among many, the world will never be quite the same again without him.

---

[1] William Rothenstein was buried beside the Oakridge Lynch Parish Church, where the burial service was read on February 17, 1945.

# Bibliography

## MANUSCRIPT COLLECTIONS CITED

Ashley Library. British Museum.
Beerbohm Papers. The Houghton Library, Harvard University.
Beerbohm Papers. Merton College, Oxford University.
The Beinecke Rare Book and Manuscript Library, Yale University.
Berg Collection. The New York Public Library.
Brotherton Collection. University of Leeds.
William Andrews Clark Memorial Library, University of California at Los Angeles.
Cornell University Library.
Gordon Craig Collection. Bibliothèque Nationale, Paris.
H. A. L. Fisher Papers. Bodleian Library, Oxford.
A. E. Gallatin Papers. The Houghton Library.
A. E. Gallatin Papers. The New-York Historical Society.
D. S. MacColl Papers. Glasgow University Library.
Gerhart Hauptmann Archives. Staatsbibliothek Preussischer Kulturbesitz, Berlin.
Northcliffe Papers. British Museum.
Grant Richards Papers. Library of the University of Illinois at Urbana-Champaign.
Rothenstein Papers. The Houghton Library.
G. B. Shaw Papers. British Museum.
The Collection of Robert H. Taylor. Princeton, New Jersey.

## PUBLISHED WORKS

WORKS BY MAX BEERBOHM

*Around Theatres.* London: Rupert Hart-Davis, 1953.
*Caricatures of Twenty-Five Gentlemen.* London: Leonard Smithers, 1896.
*Cartoons: 'The Second Childhood of John Bull'.* London: Stephen Swift [1911].
[et al.] 'Championing a Critic' (letter), *The Daily Mail* (London), August 13, 1897, p. 4.
' "The Christian", Some Comments on Mr. Hall Caine's New Novel', *The Daily Mail* (London), August 11, 1897, p. 4.

177

*A Christmas Garland woven by Max Beerbohm*. New York: E. P. Dutton, 1912.

*The Dreadful Dragon of Hay Hill*. London: William Heinemann, 1928.

'Ex Cathedra: Mrs. Meynell's Cowslip-wine', *To-Morrow* (London), 2 (1896), 160–166.

'Ex Cathedra III: Modern Statuary; Oxford a la Rothenstein', *To-Morrow*, 2 (1896), 259–263.

*Fifty Caricatures*. London: William Heinemann, 1913.

'A Gallery of Significant Pictures', *The Saturday Review* (London), 95 (1903), 483–485.

*The Happy Hypocrite: A Fairy Tale for Tired Men*. 3rd ed. New York: John Lane, The Bodley Head [1896].

[comp.] *Herbert Beerbohm Tree: Some Memories of Him and of His Art*. London: Hutchinson, 1920.

'Hold, Furious Scot!' (letter), *The Saturday Review* (London), 82 (1896), 395–396.

*Leaves From The Garland Woven By Max Beerbohm*. New York: privately printed [Max Harzof], 1926.

'A Letter to the Editor', *The Yellow Book* (London), 2 (1894), 281–284.

*Letters to Reggie Turner*. Rupert Hart-Davis, ed. London: Rupert Hart-Davis, 1964.

*Lytton Strachey*. Cambridge: Cambridge University Press. 1943.

*Mainly on the Air*, rev. ed. London: William Heinemann, 1957.

'Miss Marie Corelli and Mr. Max Beerbohm', *The Westminster Gazette* (London), September 18, 1896, p. 3.

*More Theatres, 1898–1903*. London: Rupert Hart-Davis, 1969.

*Observations*. London: William Heinemann, 1925.

'Our Lady of "Pars."' *The Saturday Review* (London), 82 (1896), 337.

*The Poets' Corner*. London: William Heinemann, 1904.

*Rossetti and His Circle*. London: William Heinemann, 1922.

*Seven Men*. London: William Heinemann, 1919.

'An Unhappy Poet', *The Saturday Review* (London), 82 (1896), 315–316.

*William Rothenstein: An Address Delivered by Max Beerbohm at the Memorial Service Held at Saint Martin-in-the-Fields, Tuesday, March 6, 1945*. London: privately printed at the Curwen Press [1945].

*The Works of Max Beerbohm*. London: William Heinemann, 1896.

*Yet Again*. London: William Heinemann, 1909.

*Zuleika Dobson: or an Oxford Love Story*. London: William Heinemann, 1911.

WORKS BY WILLIAM ROTHENSTEIN

'A Basis for the Appreciation of Works of Art: A Lecture Delivered Before the Cambridge University', *The Modern Review* (Calcutta), 13 (1913), 125–136.

*English Portraits.* London: Grant Richards, 1898.
*Form and Content in English Painting.* Oxford: The Clarendon Press, 1934.
*Goya.* The Artist's Library. London: Unicorn Press, 1900.
*Liber Juniorum: Six Lithographed Drawings.* London: Unicorn Press, 1899.
*Manchester Portraits: Twelve Lithographed Drawings. First Series.* Manchester:
    J. E. Cornish, 1900.
*Men and Memories: Recollections of William Rothenstein, 1872–1900.* London:
    Faber and Faber, 1931.
*Men and Memories: Recollections of William Rothenstein, 1900–1922.* London:
    Faber and Faber, 1932.
[et al.] *Men of the R.A.F.* London: Oxford University Press, 1942.
'Mr. Beerbohm's Drawings' (letter), *The Times Literary Supplement* (London),
    April 22, 1926, p. 303.
*Oxford Characters: Twenty-Four Lithographs.* London: John Lane, 1896.
*A Plea for a Wider Use of Artists and Craftsmen.* London: Constable [1917].
*The Portrait Drawings of William Rothenstein, 1889–1925.* John Rothenstein,
    comp. London: Chapman and Hall, 1926.
'Recollections. I—The Slade School', *Artwork* (London), 5 (1929), 77–88.
'Recollections. II—Paris', *Artwork*, 5 (1929), 170–184.
*Since Fifty: Men and Memories, 1922–1938.* London: Faber and Faber, 1939.
*Six Portraits of Sir Rabindranath Tagore.* London: Macmillan, 1915.
*Twelve Portraits.* London: Faber and Faber, 1929.
*Twenty-Four Portraits.* London: George Allen and Unwin, 1920.
*Twenty-Four Portraits. Second Series.* London: Chatto and Windus, 1923.
' "The Vikings" ' (letter), *The Saturday Review* (London), 95 (1903), 588.

OTHER WORKS

Archer, William, 'Fabian Lectures: The English Drama of the Last Twenty-
    Five Years' (summary), *Fabian News* (London), 11 (1901), 34.
Arliss, George. *Up the Years from Bloomsbury: An Autobiography.* New York:
    Blue Ribbon Books, 1927.
Baron, Wendy. *Sickert.* London: Phaidon, 1973.
Behrman, S. N. *Portrait of Max: An Intimate Portrait of Sir Max Beerbohm.*
    New York: Random House [1960].
Bennett, Arnold. *Clayhanger.* London: Methuen, 1910.
—*Hilda Lessways.* London: Methuen, 1911.
—*These Twain.* London: Methuen, 1915.
Binyon, Laurence. ' "Max"; and a Peep at the Academy', *The Saturday Review*
    (London), 103 (1907), 553–554.
Bland, J. O. P. and E. [T.] Backhouse, comps. *China under the Empress Dowager,
    Being the History of the Life and Times of Tsu Hsi, Compiled from State
    Papers and the Private Diary of the Comptroller of Her Household.* London:
    William Heinemann, 1910.

Blomfield, Sir Reginald. *Memoirs of an Architect.* London: Macmillan, 1932.

Brown, Oliver. *Exhibition: The Memoirs of Oliver Brown.* London: Evelyn, Adams and Mackay, 1968.

Cecil, David. *Max: A Biography.* Boston: Houghton Mifflin, 1965.

Charteris, Evan. *The Life and Letters of Sir Edmund Gosse.* New York: Harper, 1931.

Clutton-Brock, Arthur. *More Thoughts on the War.* 3rd ed. London: Methuen [1915].

—*Thoughts on the War.* 4th ed. London: Methuen [1914].

Corelli, Marie [pseud.]. See Mackay, Mary.

Craig, Edward. *Gordon Craig: The Story of His Life.* London: Victor Gollancz, 1968.

[Craig, Gordon, comp.] *A Living Theatre.* Florence: [Gordon Craig], 1913.

Dowdall, The Hon. Mrs [Mary]. *Manners and Tone of Good Society.* London: A. and C. Black, 1926.

Drinkwater, John. *Collected Poems.* 3 vols. London: Sidgwick and Jackson, 1923–1937.

Felstiner, John. *The Lies of Art: Max Beerbohm's Parody and Caricature.* New York: Alfred A. Knopf, 1972.

Fry, Roger. *Letters of Roger Fry.* Denys Sutton, ed. 2 vols. London: Chatto and Windus, 1972.

—'Plastic Design', *The Nation* (London), 9 (1911), 396.

Gallatin, A. E. and L. M. Oliver. *A Bibliography of the Works of Max Beerbohm.* Cambridge, Mass.: Harvard University Press, 1952.

—*Portraits of Whistler: A Critical Study and an Iconography.* New York: John Lane, 1918.

—*Sir Max Beerbohm: Bibliographical Notes.* Cambridge, Mass.: Harvard University Press, 1944.

Gill, Eric. *Letters of Eric Gill.* Walter Shewring, ed. New York: Devin-Adair, 1948.

de Goncourt, Edmond and Jules. *Edmond and Jules de Goncourt, with Letters and Leaves from Their Journals.* M. A. Belloc and M. Shedlock, comp. and trans. 2 vols. London: William Heinemann, 1895.

Hardy, Thomas. *Tess of the D'Urbervilles: A Pure Woman.* Mellstock Edition. 2 vols. London: Macmillan, 1919.

Harris, Frank. *Bernard Shaw: An Unauthorised Biography Based on Firsthand Information with a Postscript by Mr Shaw.* London: Victor Gollancz, 1931.

Hart-Davis, Rupert. *A Catalogue of the Caricatures of Max Beerbohm* Cambridge, Mass.: Harvard University Press, 1972.

Hogg, T. J. et al. *The Life of Percy Bysshe Shelley.* 2 vols. New York: E. P. Dutton, 1933.

Holroyd, Michael, *Lytton Strachey: A Critical Biography.* 2 vols. New York: Holt, Rinehart and Winston, 1967–68.

Homer. *The Odyssey of Homer, Newly Translated into English Prose*. T. E. Shaw [T. E. Lawrence], trans. New York: Oxford University Press, 1932.

[Horne, Herbert] 'The Precocious School of Humour', *The Saturday Review* (London), 82 (1896), 221.

Hudson, W. H. *A Little Boy Lost*. London: Duckworth, 1905.

Jackson, Holbrook. *The Eighteen Nineties: A Review of Art and Ideas at the Close of the Nineteenth Century*. London: Grant Richards, 1913.

Jones, Doris Arthur. *Taking the Curtain Call: The Life and Letters of Henry Arthur Jones*. New York: Macmillan, 1930.

Kemble, Frances Anne. *Journal of a Residence in America*. Paris: A. and W. Galignani, 1835.

—*Journal of a Residence on a Georgian Plantation in 1838–1839*. London: Longman, Green, Longman, Roberts, and Green, 1863.

Lago, Mary M., ed. *Imperfect Encounter: Letters of William Rothenstein and Rabindranath Tagore, 1911–1941*. Cambridge, Mass.: Harvard University Press, 1972.

Lavery, Sir John. *The Life of a Painter*. London: Cassell, 1940.

Lawrence, T. E. *The Letters of T. E. Lawrence*. David Garnett, ed. New York: Doubleday, Doran, 1939.

—*Seven Pillars of Wisdom: A Triumph*. London: Jonathan Cape [1935].

Lee, Sir Sidney. *King Edward VII: A Biography*. 2 vols. London: Macmillan, 1925–1927.

Le Gallienne, Richard. *Prose Fancies*. London: Elkin Mathews and John Lane, 1894.

Leveson-Gower, Sir George. *Years of Content, 1858–1886*. London: John Murray, 1940.

—*Years of Endeavour, 1886–1907*. London: John Murray, 1942.

Lewis, Wyndham. *The Apes of God*. London: The Arthur Press, 1930.

Low, David. *The Modern 'Rake's Progress'*. See West, Rebecca.

MacCarthy, Desmond. 'On Lytton Strachey', *The Sunday Times* (London), July 4, 1943, p. 3.

MacColl, D. S. *Confessions of a Keeper and Other Papers*. London: A. Maclehose, 1931.

—'Portraits and a Caricaturist', *The Saturday Review* (London), 92 (1901), 738–739.

—'The Society of Portrait Painters', *The Saturday Review*, 90 (1900), 678–679.

[Mackay, Mary] 'Miss Marie Corelli and "Sport"', *The Westminster Gazette* (London), September 17, 1896, p. 3.

Maeterlinck, Maurice. *The Plays of Maurice Maeterlinck. Second Series*. Richard Hovey, trans. New York: Duffield, 1908.

Matthews, William, comp. *British Diaries: An Annotated Bibliography of British Diaries Written between 1442 and 1942*. Berkeley: University of California Press, 1950.

May, J. Lewis. *John Lane and the Nineties*. London: John Lane, 1936.

Michel, Walter. *Wyndham Lewis: Paintings and Drawings*. Berkeley: University of California Press, 1971.

Monroe, Harriet. 'Rothenstein Counsels Perfection as Standard for Museums of Art', *The Chicago Sunday Tribune*, January 14, 1912, Part 2, p. 5.

Nelson, J. G. *The Early Nineties: A View from the Bodley Head*. Cambridge, Mass.: Harvard University Press, 1971.

Nicolson, Sir Harold, *Diaries and Letters, 1930–1939*. Nigel Nicolson, ed. London: Collins, [1966].

Oliphant, Laurence. *Piccadilly: A Fragment of Contemporary Biography*. Edinburgh: William Blackwood and Sons, 1870.

Pearson, Hesketh. *Beerbohm Tree: His Life and Laughter*. New York: Harper [1956].

—*Bernard Shaw: His Life and Personality*. London: Collins, 1942.

Pocock, Tom. *Chelsea Reach: The Brutal Friendship of Whistler and Walter Greaves*. London: Hodder and Stoughton, 1970.

Raleigh, Sir Walter. *The Letters of Sir Walter Raleigh, 1879–1922*. Lady Raleigh, ed. 2 vols. New York: Macmillan, 1926.

Richards, Grant. *Author Hunting by an Old Literary Sports Man: Memories of Years Spent Mainly in Publishing, 1897–1925*. New York: Coward-McCann, 1934.

—*Memories of a Misspent Youth, 1872–1896*. London: William Heinemann, 1933.

[Ross, Robert] 'Art and Artists', *The Morning Post* (London), March 23, 1909, p. 4.

Rothenstein, John. *Brave Day, Hideous Night: Autobiography, 1939–1965*. London: Hamish Hamilton, 1966.

—*British Artists and the War*. London: Peter Davies, 1931.

—*Modern English Painters: Sickert to Smith*. London: Eyre and Spottiswoode, 1952.

—*Summer's Lease: Autobiography, 1901–1938*. New York: Holt, Rinehart and Winston, 1965.

[—] 'The Venetian Glass Nephew' (review), *The Times Literary Supplement* (London), April 22, 1926, p. 300.

Rutherston, Albert, gen. ed. *Sir William Orpen*. Contemporary British Artists Series. London: Ernest Benn, 1923.

S[alt], H. S. 'On Mr. Bernard Shaw's 70th Birthday', *The Times* (London), July 26, 1926, p. 15.

Scott, Clement. 'Come Out of Your Hole, Rat!' *The Era* (London), October 3, 1896, p. 13.

—*Lays and Lyrics*. London: G. Routledge and Sons, 1888.

Shaw, G. B. *Cashel Byron's Profession*. London: Modern Press, 1886.

—*Cashel Byron's Profession*, rev. ed. London: Grant Richards, 1901.

—*Collected Letters, 1874–1897*. Dan H. Laurence, ed. London: Max Reinhardt [1965].

—*Collected Letters, 1898–1910*. Dan H. Laurence, ed. London.: Max Reinhardt [1972].

—*Everybody's Political What's What*. London: Constable, 1944.

—'G. B. S. Vivisected', *The Saturday Review* (London), 85 (1898), 657–658.

—'Mr. G. B. Shaw on Gandhi "Blunder" ' (letter), *The Times* (London), February 27, 1943, p. 2.

—'Valedictory', *The Saturday Review* (London), 85 (1898), 682–683.

—*William Morris as I Knew Him*. New York: Dodd Mead, 1936.

Sickert, Walter. *A Free House! Or the Artist as Craftsman: Being the Writings of Walter Richard Sickert*. Osbert Sitwell, ed. London: Macmillan, 1947.

Speaight, Robert. *William Rothenstein: The Portrait of an Artist in His Time*. London: Eyre and Spottiswoode, 1962.

S[pence], E. F. 'The Stage from the Stalls', *The Sketch* (London), 42 (1903), 198.

Stevenson, R. L. *The Works of R. L. Stevenson*. Sidney Colvin, ed. Edinburgh Edition. 28 vols. London: Chatto and Windus, 1894–1898.

Strachey, Lytton. *Elizabeth and Essex: A Tragic History*. London: Chatto and Windus, 1928.

—*Eminent Victorians*. London: Chatto and Windus, 1918.

Street, G. S. *The Autobiography of a Boy: Passages Selected by His Friend*. London: Elkin Mathews and John Lane, 1894.

Tagore, Rabindranath. *Personality: Lectures Delivered in America*. London: Macmillan, 1917.

Trewin, J. C. 'Max on the Dais', *The Observer* (London), July 4, 1943, p. 3.

Wedmore, Frederick. '*The Yellow Book*', *The Academy* (London), 45 (1894), 349.

West, Rebecca, and David Low. *The Modern 'Rake's Progress'*. London: Hutchinson, 1934.

Whistler, J. M. *The Gentle Art of Making Enemies*. London: William Heinemann, 1890.

Wilde, Oscar. *The Letters of Oscar Wilde*. Rupert Hart-Davis, ed. London: Rupert Hart-Davis, 1962.

— *The Picture of Dorian Gray*. London: Ward Lock, 1891.

— *Salome: A Tragedy in One Act*. [Lord Alfred Douglas, trans.] London: Elkin Mathews and John Lane, 1894.

— *Sixteen Letters from Oscar Wilde*. John Rothenstein, ed. London: Faber and Faber, 1930.

Wright, Peter. *Portraits and Criticisms*. London: E. Nash and Grayson, 1925.

Wylie, Elinor. *The Venetian Glass Nephew*. New York: George H. Doran, 1925.

Young, Filson. 'Mr. Max Beerbohm's Entertainment', *The Saturday Review* (London), 115 (1913), 450–451.
Zangwill, I[srael]. *Children of the Ghetto: Being Pictures of a Peculiar People*. Philadelphia: The Jewish Publication Society [1892].

# Index

Academic Committee (Royal Society of Literature), 95 n.1
Acland, Sir Henry, 4, 5, 17
Acland, Sarah, 17
Addinsell, Richard, 148 n.1
Adkins, Sarah, 55 n.1, 140
'Advertisements' (broadcast by Beerbohm), 165–166
Air Ministry, 158 n.1
Allen, Grant, 36 n.1
Alpine Club, 115
American Academy of Dramatic Art, 12
Apuleius, 28
Archer, William, 12, 45, 57
Arliss, George, 45 n.1
Arnold, Matthew, 171
*Around Theatres* (Beerbohm), 16n., 19, 28 n.4, 46 n.1, 63 n.2
Art Institute of Chicago, 89 n.2
*Artwork* (Review), 132
Arundell, Dennis, 154 n.1, 156–157 n.1
Athenaeum Club, 127, 130, 134, 141, 142, 143, 146, 150, 152
Ashmolean Museum, 146
*Arabian Nights*, 25, 82
Ashton, Winifred, 148
'At the Imperial Theatre' (Beerbohm), 47 n.3
Austin, Alfred, 34

Bagshawe, Alexandra (Dody) (Mrs George Bagshawe), 75–77, 138;
    letters: 75–77, 116 n.1, 131 n.3
Bagshawe, George, 79 n.29
Baldwin, Stanley, 132
Ballet Russe, 52 n.2
Bancroft, George, 7
Baring, Maurice, 146, 165 n.2
Barnato, Barnett Isaacs (Barney), 33
Baron, Wendy, 42–43 n.2
Barrett, Wilson, 32 n.2, 34–35
Barrie, James, 57, 131 n.3, 132, 164
'A Basis for the Appreciation of Works of Art' (a lecture by W. Rothenstein), 59 n.2
Bate, Francis, 152
Baylis, Lilian, 146 n.1
Beardsley, Aubrey, 17–18, 30 n.1, 39 n.1, 154 n.2, 170; drawings by, 15 n.11, 17–18
Beaverbrook, Lord, 131
Bedales School, 104 n.6
Beddington-Behrens, Edward, 173 n.1
Bedford, Duke of, 142

Beerbohm, Agnes (MB's elder sister), 106, 112
Beerbohm, Constance (MB's elder half-sister), 34, 106, 112, 164
Beerbohm, Elisabeth (MB's second wife), 150
Beerbohm, Eliza (MB's mother), 11, 53 n.1, 63 n.1, 96–97, 164;
    death of: 105, 106–107
Beerbohm, Florence (MB's wife), 11–14, 63–64, 71, 73, 74, 75, 76–77, 84, 87, 90, 91, 96, 106, 109, 111, 112 n.4, 113, 115 n.3, 116, 118, 120, 122, 123, 124, 126, 128, 129, 130, 131 n.3, 132, 134, 138, 139, 141, 144, 145, 147, 150, 151, 152, 156, 157, 158–159, 160, 161–162 n.5, 163, 165, 172, 173, 174
Beerbohm, Julius (MB's father), 5, 12
BEERBOHM, MAX:
    and America: 6, 12, 74–75, 91, 112, 158;
    as artist: 8, 51, 54–55, 57, 92, 93–94, 164–165;
    as broadcaster: 147, 158–159, 165–166;
    caricatures of: Academic Committee, 95 n.1; J. M. Barrie, 57; Wilson Barrett, 31, 33–34; Arnold Bennett, 92; Oscar Browning, 57; 'John Bull', 51 n.2; Lord Burnham, 83 n.3; Henry Chaplin, 35 n.1; Edward VII, 49, 116 n.1; 'English M.P.'s', 51 n.2; frescoes, 115 n.3, 166 n.3; Roger Fry, 92; W. E. Gladstone, 155 n.2; Frank Harris, 35 n.1; Richard Le Gallienne, 35 n.1; David Lloyd-George, 94; Claude Lowther, 16 n.21; John Masefield, 94; Reginald McKenna, 94; George Meredith, 35 n.1; George Moore, 35 n.1; Lord Northcliffe, 38 n.4; Lord Rosebery, 83 n.1; D. G. Rossetti, 115; Albert Rothenstein (later Rutherston), 93 n.3; William Rothenstein, 51 n.1, 54, 56 n.1; 93 n.3; 123 n.1; 124, 125 n.1, 131–132; Lord Rowton, 33 n.1; R. L. Stevenson, 83; Herbert Tree, 35 n.1; Israel Zangwill, 83 n.2;
    as dramatist: 38 n.2; 39–40, 43–45, 134, 147–148, 153–154, 155, 156;
    exhibitions of caricatures by: (1901) 45–46 n.1; (1907) 56 n.1; (1908) 57; (1911) 73, 83, 84 n.4, 86; (1913) 91, 92–93; (1915, cancelled) 104 n.2; (1923) 116; (1928) 128 n.1; (1945) 49–50 n.1;
    friendship with WR: 3, 24 n.4, 58–62, 77,

*contd*—Beerbohm, Max
93–94, 100, 123, 151, 160, 172, 174, 175–176;
honours awarded to: 137 n.1; 149–151, 166–167;
and Italy: 13–14, 63 n.3, 73–74, 77, 84, 85, 87–88, 107–108, 115, 141;
letters to: Alexandra Bagshawe, 115 n.3; Florence Beerbohm, 12–13, 62 n.1, 73–74, 117 n.1; Ernest Brown, 73; Douglas Cleverdon, 156–157 n.1; [Douglas Doty] 74–75; Edmund Gosse, 31 n.1, 95 n.1, 102 n.2; L. M. Kahn, 75; Sam Kahn, 148 n.1, 161–162 n.5; John Lane, 24–25 n.4; Robert Ross, 23 n.4, 26 n.1, 45–46 n.1; 88 n.1, 102 n.2; Alice Rothenstein, 49 n.2, 50, 51 n.1, 52 n.2, 53 n.1 (top), 61 n.3, 108 n.1, 112 n.5, 115–116, 127–128, 140 n.2, 158–159, 162–164, 174; John Rothenstein, 50; William Rothenstein, 17–25, 26–27, 29–31, 32–35, 36–40, 43, 45–46, 47–48, 49–50, 52–54, 61–62, 63–64, 65, 79 n.36, 84–85, 87–88, 90–91, 93–94, 97–102, 104, 106–109, 110–112, 115–116, 117–119, 121, 123, 126–128, 129–131, 133, 135–136, 137, 138 n.1, 138–139, 144 n.2, 149, 150–151, 153–155, 156–160, 162–164, 172–173, 173 n.2; Albert Rutherston, 51 n.1; Siegfried Sassoon, 142 n.2; Sydney and Violet Schiff, 151 n.1, 173–174 n.1; G. B. Shaw, 7; E. F. Spence, 8; Reginald Turner, 5, 11, 49–50 n.1; 63 n.3
marriage: 62–64, 73–74
personality of: 3–4, 11–13, 17–18, 21, 61, 67, 75–77, 95 n.1, 105, 123, 136, 124 n.1, 164–165
Rede Lecture by: 170–171;
seventieth birthday of: 164–165;
war service: 104;
as writer: 6–8, 59–60, 74–75, 77, 90, 95 n.1, 100
*Beerbohm Tree* (Pearson), 15 n.16
Behrens, Edward: *see* Beddington-Behrens
Belloc, Hilaire, 96
Bennett, Arnold, 92, 104 n.2, 138, 141
Bentinck, Lord Henry, 108 n.1
Berenson, Bernard, 86, 160
Berenson, Mary, 160
Beresford, Admiral Lord Charles, 36 n.1
Berners, Lord, 149, 165 n.2
*A Bibliography of the Works of Max Beerbohm* (Gallatin and Oliver), 170 n.4
Biddulph, Claud, 126
Biddulph, Margaret, 126
Binyon, Laurence, 39 n.1, 56 n.1
Blanchamp, Henry, 6
Blanche, Jacques-Émile, 52 n.2
Blomfield, Reginald, 146
Board of Education, 72, 118
Bodley Head, 3, 15 n.11
Bone, James, 165 n.2
*Brave Day, Hideous Night* (J. Rothenstein), 155 n.1, 158 n.1

Bridges, Robert, 146
*British Artists and the War* (J. Rothenstein), 142 n.3
British Broadcasting Corporation, 147 n.1, 153–154, 156 n.1, 158
*British Diaries* (Matthews, comp.), 137 n.1
British Museum, 34
British School (Rome), 119 n.3
Brontë Museum, 144
Brooke, S. A., 50 n.2
Brown, Ernest, 73
Brown, Frederick, 152
Brown, Ivor, 165 n.2
Brown, Oliver, 78 n.22, 100, 101
Browning, Oscar, 57
Browning, Robert, 160
'Bubbles': *see* James, Admiral Sir William
Burnham, Lord, 83 n.3
Bussy, Dorothy, 86
Bussy, Simon, 87 n.6
Byron, Lord, 163
Bywater, Ingram, 15 n.9

Caine, Hall, 38
Campbell, Stella (Mrs Patrick Campbell), 34, 39, 45, 134
Carfax Gallery, 52 n.2
*Caricatures of Twenty-Five Gentlemen* (Beerbohm), 29 n.1
Carlton House Terrace, 146
Carpenter, Mrs Mary, 157
Carson, E. C., 31
Carson, Murray, 37
*Cartoons: 'The Second Childhood of John Bull'* (Beerbohm), 51 n.2, 140 n.4
*Cashel Byron's Profession* (Shaw), 46 n.1
*A Catalogue of the Caricatures of Max Beerbohm* (Hart-Davis), 56 n.1, 57 n.2, 83 n.2, n.3, 115 n.3, 125 n.1, 166 n.3
*Cavalcade* (Coward), 142
Cecil, Lord David, 20 n.1
Chadbourne, Grace, 58–59 n.1
Chadbourne, Thomas, 58 n.1
Chamberlain, Austen, 122 n.1, 132, 168
Chamberlain, Joseph, 97
'Championing a Critic' (Beerbohm *et al.*), 38 n.5
Chaplin, Henry, 35 n.1
Chatto and Windus, 114
Chelsea Arts Club, 108 n.1
*Chelsea Reach* (Pocock), 108 n.1
Chevalier, Albert, 22
*China under the Empress Dowager* (Bland and Backhouse, comps.), 86
'The Christian' (Beerbohm), 38 n.5
*A Christmas Garland woven by Max Beerbohm*, 33 n.2, 91 n.3
Churchill, Winston, 99, 159, 168
Clarke, Edward, 31
Clausen, George, 152
Cleverdon, Douglas, 153, 155
Clinton-Baddeley, V. C., 155 n.3
Clutton-Brock, Arthur, 96
Colefax, Lady Sibyl and Sir Arthur, 76, 79 n.32, 100, 113

*Collected Letters, 1874–1897* (Shaw), 15 n.18
*Collected Letters, 1898–1910* (Shaw), 15 n.17, 16 n.19
*Collected Poems* (Drinkwater), 126 n.1
Collier, Constance, 11
Colvin, Lady Frances, 50, 83, 84
Colvin, Sir Sidney, 50
*Commercial Appeal* (Memphis), 161–162 n.5
Conder, Charles, 9, 124, 170
Conder, Stella, 125 n.3
Conens, Miss, 109
*Confessions of a Keeper* (MacColl), 142 n.5
Conover, Grace, 11, 38, 41, 45
Conrad, Joseph, 109
Contemporary Art Society, 160
'Conversation Caricatures of Yesterday' (Beerbohm), 83 n.3
Corelli, Marie (pseud.): *see* Mackay, Mary
Cornford, Frances, 56, 58
Cornford, Francis, 57 n.1 (top)
*Cornhill Magazine*, 100, 101, 102 n.2
Craig (Mrs Gordon): *see* Meo, Elena
Craig, Gordon (Teddie), 47 n.3, 48, 84, 86, 110–111, 112–113, 114–115, 124, 132, 141
Cranach, Lucas the Elder, 128
*Crime and Punishment* (Dostoievsky), 143
Cripps, Sir Stafford, 160
Crofter (unidentified), 31
Cummins, Brian, 156–157 n.1
'A Cursory Conspectus of G.B.S.' (Beerbohm), 46
Cust, Emmeline (Nina) (Mrs Harry Cust), 22, 147 n.3
Cust, Harry, 22, 147 n.3

'Dandies and Dandies' (Beerbohm), 1, 32 n.3
Dane, Clemence (pseud.): *see* Ashton, Winifred
Dante Alighieri, 81
Darwin, Frances: *see* Cornford, Frances
Darwin, Sir Francis, 56, 58
Debenham, Ernest, 97
'A December Rain-Scene' (Hardy), 116 n.3
'A Defence of Cosmetics' (Beerbohm), 26 n.1, 28 n.1, n.3
Degas, Edgar, 9
de la Mare, Richard, 129 n.1
Dent, Alan, 165 n.2; letters: to MB, 165 n.2; to WR, 165 n.2
Derby, Lord, 133
Desborough, Lady Ethel, 142
Devonshire, 9th Duke of, 31
*Diaries and Letters, 1930–1939* (Harold Nicolson), 161 n.1
Disraeli, Benjamin, 32
Doll and Richards Gallery (Boston), 89 n.2
*Don Juan* (burlesque), 21
Douglas, Lord Alfred (Bosie), 24
Dowdall, H. C., 61 n.2
Dowdall, Mary, 61 n.2, 124
Dowson, Ernest, 29 n.1, 102 n.2, 139
Doyle, Richard, 146, 161

Drachmann, Holger, 44 n.2
*The Dreadful Dragon of Hay Hill* (Beerbohm), 143
Drinkwater, John, 102 n.1, 109, 110, 125
Duckworth (publisher), 96, 98 n.2
Dürer, Albrecht, 128
Durga, 77

*The Early Nineties* (Nelson), 15 n.11, Eddington, A. S., 132
Edinburgh University, 137
*Edmond and Jules de Goncourt . . . Journals* (Belloc and Shedlock, comps.), 14 n.1
Edward VII, 116 n.1; as Prince of Wales, 43 n.3, 49
Edward VIII, as Prince of Wales, 162 n.7
Einstein, Albert, 132
'Elegy Written in a Country Churchyard' (Gray), 171
Eliot, T. S., 130
Elizabeth I, 28
Elizabeth, The Queen Mother, 170
Elliott and Fry (photographers), 20
Ellis, Robinson, 4, 25
*English Portraits* (W. Rothenstein), 36 n.1, 37 n.1, 38 n.1
'Enoch Soames' (story by Beerbohm), 3, 4, 74, 100, 101, 102 n.1, 137 n.1, 153–154, 155, 156, 170–171
Epstein, Jacob, 10, 68, 69, 70
*Everybody's Political What's What* (Shaw), 174 n.2
'Ex Cathedra' (Beerbohm), 35 n.3
'Ex Cathedra III' (Beerbohm), 28 n.1
*Exhibition* (Brown), 104 n.2
Exhibitions: (1896) 34–35; (1900) 42, 43 n.1; (1901) 45–46 n.1; (1903) 60–61 n.1; (1906) 53–54 n.1; (1909) 61 n.1; (1910) 67, 78 n.7; (1912) 71; (1913) 93; (1915) 98–99. *See also*: MB, WR, exhibitions.

Faber and Faber, 129 n.1, 132, 151
Fabian Society, 45
Fantin-Latour, Henri, 9
Far Oakridge, 71, 97, 98 n.1, 99, 102, 103 n.3, 104 n.7, 107, 109, 113, 120, 125, 140, 144, 147, 152, 163, 167
Felton, Felix, 155 n.3
*Fifty Caricatures* (Beerbohm), 83 n.3, 94 n.2, 95 n.1
Firminger, Walter, 31
Fisher, H. A. L., 72, 73, 109 n.3; letters to WR, 72
Fitzgerald, Betty: *see* Rothenstein, Mrs Michael
Fitzwilliam Museum, 170 n.2
*The Fly on the Wheel* (Beerbohm and Carson), 38 n.2
*Form and Content in English Painting* (W. Rothenstein), 167 n.1
*The Fortnightly Review*, 116
Fra Angelico, 85
Fraser, Claud Lovat, 110 n.3
*A Free House!* (Sickert), 42 n.2

Fry, Roger, 3, 8, 9, 67–71, 92; letters to WR, 70, 70–71
Furniss, Harry, 31
Furse, Charles, 37–38

Gallatin, A. E., 170
'A Gallery of Significant Pictures' (Beerbohm), 60–61 n.1
Galsworthy, John, 130
Gandhi, M. K., 167–168
Garvin, J. L., 84, 121
Gaskell, Mrs Elizabeth, 41
Gaskell, Julia and Marianne, 41
'G.B.S. Vivisected' (Shaw), 16 n.19
*The Gentle Art of Making Enemies* (Whistler), 41 n.3
George VI, 133, 142
Gill, Eric, 10, 68, 69, 70
Giotto, 54, 63, 94
Gladstone, W. E., 155 n.2
*Globe* (Milwaukee), 161–162 n.5
*The Golden Ass* (Apuleius), 25
Goncourt, Edmond de, 3
Goncourt, Jules de, 14 n.1
*Gordon Craig* (Craig), 85 n.2
Gosse, Edmund, 32 n.1, 41 n.3, 43, 53, 95 n.1, 101, 164; letters to MB, 102 n.1, n.2
Goupil Gallery, 127
Goya, Francisco de, 9, 35, 145 n.2
*Goya* (W. Rothenstein), 35 n.2
Graham, R. B. Cunninghame, 16 n.23, 36 n.1, 40
Granby, Lady, 22, 40
Granville-Barker, Harley, 116
Granville-Barker, Helen, 116
Graves, Robert, 88 n.2
Greaves, Walter, 107–108
Guedalla, Philip, 49–50 n.1, 142, 155, 165 n.2

'Habit' (Beerbohm), 63 n.2
Hadow, Sir Henry, 106 n.1
Haldane, Lord, 53
Hamilton, General Sir Ian, 101
Hammersley, Hugh, 48 n.1
Hammersley, Mary, 47, 48–49
*The Happy Hypocrite* (Beerbohm), 39–40, 40 n.1, 134, 140, 147–148
Hardy, Florence, 116, 134
Hardy, Thomas, 32 n.2, 116, 156, 164
'Harlequin: A Signboard' (Beerbohm), 37 n.3
Harmsworth, Alfred: *see* Northcliffe, Viscount
Harmsworth, Mary: *see* Northcliffe, Lady
Harris, Frank, 6, 7, 32, 35 n.1, 44 n.1, 45, 171
Hartrick, A. S., 26
Hauptmann, Benvenuto, 119 n.1, 139
Hauptmann, Gerhart, 118, 124, 125–126, 139, 150, 161 n.1; letters to WR, 125–126, 144 n.2
Hauptmann, Margarete, 126 n.3, 139
Hazlitt, William, 144 n.2

Heath, A. M., 121 n.4
Heinemann, William, 87, 88 n.1; 95 n.1
Henley, W. E., 24 n.4, 36, 43, 127
*Herbert Beerbohm Tree* (M. Beerbohm, comp.), 112 n.4
Herodotus, 28
Hesslein, Edgar, 52 n.1
Hesslein, Emily (WR's sister), 52 n.1
'Hilary Maltby' (Beerbohm), 104 n.7
'Hilary Maltby and Stephen Braxton' (Beerbohm), 104 n.7, 107, 162
'His Majesty's Theatre' (review), 148 n.1
Hodge, Harold, 45, 46
'Hold, Furious Scot!' (Beerbohm), 34 n.3
'Holly: Al*c* M*yn*ll' (Beerbohm), 33 n.2
Horne, Herbert, 31, 63
Housman, A. E., 143
Housman, Laurence, 39 n.1
House of Commons, 73, 125
Hudson, Stephen (pseud.): *see* Schiff, Sydney
Hudson, W. H., 99 n.1
Hugo, Victor, 138
Hunt, William Holman, 42

'Ichabod' (Beerbohm), 168
Iles Farm: *see* Far Oakridge
*Imperfect Encounter* (Lago), 16 n.24, 87 n.4, 112 n.6, 143 n.8
Impressionism, 9
India Society, 9–10
India House, 142
Indian art, artists, 9–10, 143 n.8
Indian High Commission, 143 n.8
*Inverness Courier*, 137 n.1
Irving, Henry, 117 n.1
Irving, H. B., 117 n.1
Israëls, Jozef, 49 n.4

Jackson, Holbrook, 102 n.2
Jacomb-Hood, G. P., 4, 5
James, Henry, 33, 164, 165
James, Admiral Sir William, 166 n.4
John, Augustus, 48 n.1, 58, 68, 69, 70, 101, 108 n.1, 140, 149 n.2, 165 n.2
*John Lane and the Nineties* (May), 15 n.11
Jones, Henry Arthur, 21 n.2, 47, 167
Joyce, William, 160
Julian's Academy, 3, 9
Jungmann, Elisabeth: *see* Beerbohm, Elisabeth

Kahn, Alexandra (Dody): *see* Bagshawe, Alexandra
Kahn, Florence: *see* Beerbohm, Florence
Kahn, Louis, 12
Kahn, L. M. (Mannie), 75, 89 n.1, 91, 138
Kahn, Morris, 87 n.8, 89 n.1, 91
Kahn, Nell, 75, 138
Kahn, Sam, 148 n.1
*Kama Sutra*, 25
Kemble, Frances Ann (Fanny), 168
Kennington, Eric, 149 n.2
Kerr, Frederick, 45 n.3

188

Kessler, Count Harry, 128
'Kilseen': see Conover, Grace
King Alfred's School, 104 n.6
Kingsley, Alice: see Rothenstein, Alice
Kipling, Rudyard, 82
Knewstub, Alice Mary: see Rothenstein, Alice
Knewstub, Grace: see Orpen, Grace
Knewstub, Walter, 16 n.26
Knoedler and Company, 99 n.1
Knowles, R. G., 22

Labouchere, Henry Du Pré, 34
Lady Cecilia: see Loftus, Cissie
'Laider, A. V.' (story by MB), 74
Lamb, Charles, 144 n.2
*Land and Water*, 96
Landseer, Sir Edwin, 16 n.35
Lane, Sir Hugh, 90
Lane, John, 3, 4, 5, 6, 15 n.11, 17, 18 n.2, 20, 33
Lane, Mrs. John, 124
Lavery, Sir John, 99 n.2
Lawrence, T. E., 149; letter to WR, 149 n.2
*Lays and Lyrics* (Scott), 34
*Leaves from the Garland woven by Max Beerbohm*, 33 n.2, 35 n.3
Lee, Sir Sidney, 116 n.1
Lee, Stirling, 53
Leeds City Art Gallery, 146 n.2
Le Gallienne, Richard, 4, 5, 15 n.12, 35 n.1
Legros, Alphonse, 9, 99
Leicester Galleries, 91, 92, 100 n.2, 116, 123
Leopold, King of the Belgians, 98 n.3
Lessore, Thérèse, 126 n.4
'A Letter to the Editor' (Beerbohm), 28 n.3
*Letters of Roger Fry*, 78 n.2, n.9
*Letters of Eric Gill*, 16 n.25
*Letters to Reggie Turner* (Beerbohm), 15 n.10, n.12, n.15, n.16, 26 n.3, 33 n.2, 44 n.2, 45 n.2, 63 n.3
*The Letters of Oscar Wilde*, 21 n.4, 37 n.2, 148 n.1
Leveson-Gower, Sir George, 161
Lewis, Wyndham, 152 n.2, 154, 155–156
*Liber Juniorum* (W. Rothenstein), 39, 115
*The Lies of Art* (Felstiner), 27 n.3, 148 n.1
*The Life of Percy Bysshe Shelley* (Hogg), 168
Literary Society, 152
*A Little Boy Lost* (Hudson), 99 n.1
'Little Tich': see Relph, Harry
*A Living Theatre* (Craig, comp.), 85 n.2
Lloyd, Marie, 22
Lloyd-George, David 94
Locarno Pact, 122 n.1, 133 n.2
Lodge, Sir Oliver, 143
Loftus, Cissie, 18, 19–22, 24
London County Council, 141
'London Revisited' (Beerbohm), 147
'Lord Haw-Haw': see Joyce, William
Low, David, 161; letter to WR, 162 n.7
Lowther, Claude, 16 n.21
*The London Mercury*, 77
Lubbock, Percy, 160
Lubbock, Sybil, 160

Lucian, 27
'Luck among Theatres' (Beerbohm), 47 n.2
*Lytton Strachey* (Beerbohm), 170 n.1
*Lytton Strachey* (Holroyd), 110 n.1

MacCarthy, Desmond, 69, 165 n.2, 171
MacColl, D. S., 45–46 n.1, 56 n.1, 97 n.3, 130, 131 n.1, 132, 134, 137, 138, 141, 152; letter to MB, 97 n.3
MacDonald, J. Ramsay, 130, 131, 132, 133, 135, 146
McEvoy, Ambrose, 68, 69, 70, 101
Macfie, W. S. and M. A., 22
Mackay, Mary, 35
McKenna, Reginald, 94
McLaren, Moray, 153, 165 n.2
MacLehose (printer), 155
Macmillan and Company, 98, 132
Maccabaeans, 49
Maeterlinck, Maurice, 85
Magniac, C. V., 50 n.2
Magniac, Hubert, 49 n.3, 50 n.2
*Mainly on the Air* (Beerbohm), 147 n.1, 159 n.1, 166 n.1
*The Manchester Guardian*, 91
*Manchester Portraits* (W. Rothenstein), 40–42, 97 n.2
Marshall, Alfred, 57 n.1
Mary, Queen, 133, 142, 155
Masefield, John, 94
*The Mask*, 132
Masaccio, 81
Masters, Miss, 104
Mathews, Elkin, 14 n.1
Maturin, Charles, 37 n.2
*Max: A Biography* (Cecil), 15 n.14, 16 n.29, 20 n.1, 104 n.2, 110 n.1
Maximilian Society, 165
Melchett, Lord, 132
*Memories of a Misspent Youth* (Richards), 14 n.3, 145 n.1
*Men and Memories, 1872–1900* (W. Rothenstein), 38 n.1, 41 n.1, 129 n.1, 135–136, 137 n.1, 138–139
*Men and Memories, 1900–1938* (W. Rothenstein), 78 n.2, 100–101 n.3, 106 n.1, 137, 141, 143–144 n.1
*Men of the R.A.F.* (W. Rothenstein), 162–163
Meo, Elena, 132
Meredith, George, 35 n.1, 156, 164, 173 n.1
Meynell, Alice, 33
Millais, Sir J. E., 166 n.4
Ministry of Information, 158 n.1
'Miss Marie Corelli and Mr. Max Beerbohm' (Beerbohm), 35 n.2
Mistress Mere: see Loftus, Cissie
*Modern English Painters* (J. Rothenstein), 94 n.3
Moira, Gerald, 111
Monet, Claude, 42
Monroe, Harriet, 89 n.2
Moore, George, 35 n.1, 51
*More Theatres, 1898–1903* (Beerbohm), 47 n.3

189

Morris, William, 126 n.4, 145 n.2, 168–169 n.2
Mortimer, Raymond, 165 n.2
Moser, Jacob, 56 n.1
'Mr. Beerbohm's Drawings' (W. Rothenstein), 125 n.1
'Mr. G. B. Shaw on Gandhi "Blunder"' (Shaw), 167–168
'Mr. Pinero's Literary Style' (Beerbohm), 28 n.4
Mudie, George, 23 n.1
Mulholland, J. B., 7
'Music Halls of My Youth' (Beerbohm), 159 n.1

'The Naming of Streets' (Beerbohm), 168
The National Observer, 24–25 n.4
New English Art Club, 5, 52 n.2, 59, 68, 70, 71, 128 n.2, 152;
see also Exhibitions
Nicholson, Ben, 87
Nicholson, Christopher, 88 n.2
Nicholson, Mabel, 87
Nicholson, Nancy, 87
Nicholson, Tony, 87
Nicholson, Sir William, 85, 87, 108 n.1
Nicolson, Harold, 161 n.1
Northcliffe, Lady, 37–38
Northcliffe, Viscount, 37–38; letter to MB, 38 n.4
Novello, Ivor, 148

Oakridge: see Far Oakridge
Observations (Beerbohm), 123 n.1
Odd Volumes, 24
Old Vic Theatre, 145
Oliphant, Laurence, 161, 163
Order of Merit, 130–131, 132, 133
Orpen, William, 59 n.2, 140
Orpen, Grace, 59 n.2
'Our Lady of "Pars."' (Beerbohm), 35 n.2
Oxford Characters (W. Rothenstein), 3–4, 14 n.4, 15 n.9, 23 n.5, 26 n.1, 28 n.1, 32 n.1
Oxford Preservation Trust, 148 n.1
Oxford School of Painting and Design, 110 n.3
Oxford Union, 6
Oxford University 3, 5, 117 n.1, 166

Palmer, John, 74
Paquin, 90
Parker, Eric, 24
Parker (of Iles Farm), 109
Parvati: see Durga
Patch, Blanche, 165 n.2
Pateman, Robert, 21
Payne, Edmund, 24
Pegram, Frederick, 57
Pennell, Joseph, 108 n.1
Personality (Tagore), 114 n.1
'The Pervasion of Rouge' (Beerbohm), 26 n.1
Phidias, 94
Phillips, Cecil, 78 n.22, 100

Phillips, Stephen, 39 n.1
Phillips, Wilfred, 78 n.22 100, 101
The Picture of Dorian Gray (Wilde), 148 n.1
Pirandello, Luigi, 139
Plarr, Victor, 102 n.2
'Plastic Design' (Fry), 84, n.4
Playfair, Nigel, 134
A Plea for a Wider Use of Artists and Craftsmen (W. Rothenstein), 72
The Poets' Corner (Beerbohm), 51
The Portrait Drawings of William Rothenstein, 15 n.12, 120 n.1, 125 n.1
Portrait of Max (Behrman), 37 n.3, 104 n.7
Post-Impressionism, 9, 67, 68, 71, 73, 78 n.7
Pound, Ezra, 160
Powell, Frederick York, 3
Poynter, Sir Edward, 113, 166 n.4
Pre-Raphaelite Brotherhood, 115
Prometheus Unbound (Shelley), 102 n.2
Proust, Marcel, 151 n.1, 157
Pryde, James, 88 n.2
Puvis de Chavannes, Pierre, 9

Queensberry, Marquis of, 24 n.1

Raleigh, Sir Walter, 124
Rau, Leo, 157, 158, 159
Reece, Harry, 39
Relph, Harry, 24 n.2
Rembrandt, 9, 16 n.23
Repington, Charles à Court, 104 n.2
Richards, Grant, 3, 35, 36, 38 n.1, 144
Richmond, George, 4
Ricketts, Charles, 9, 28 n.4, 41, 62 n.1, 140, 142
Robbins, Hugo, 22
Roberts, Arthur, 22
Roberts, Ellis, 138, 141, 144–145, 146 n.1, 149 n.3; letter to MB, 139 n.1
Roberts, Harriet, 141, 144–145, 146 n.1, 149 n.3, 151
Rodin, Auguste, 9
Rogers, Bruce, 149 n.2
Romeike (press service), 84
Roosevelt, F. D., 158
Rosebery, Lord, 83
Ross, Alexander, 42
Ross, Robert, 11, 42 n.1, 57, 59 n.2, 69; letter to WR, 11
Rossetti, D. G., 16 n.26, 42 n.1, 94
Rossetti and His Circle (Beerbohm), 115 n.2
Rothenstein, Albert: see Rutherston, Albert
Rothenstein, Alice (WR's wife), 10–11, 41, 45, 47, 51 n.1, 53 n.1, 54, 55, 59, 60, 62, 69, 71, 74, 85, 89, 91, 94, 97, 101, 103, 105, 107, 109, 111–112, 114, 118, 119, 126, 127, 134, 137, 138, 139, 140, 141, 146 n.1, 147, 156, 157, 160, 162, 169, 171, 173 n.2; letters to MB, 55 n.1, 108 n.1; to Moritz and Bertha Rothenstein, 10–11, 47 n.1; to WR, 53 n.1
Rothenstein, Bertha (WR's mother), 40
Rothenstein, Bertha Strettel (Betty) (WR's younger daughter), 54 n.1, 85, 105, 109, 118, 120, 125, 127, 147

190

Rothenstein, Charles: *see* Rutherston, Charles
Rothenstein, Elizabeth, 127 n.1, 145–146, 152
Rothenstein, John (WR's elder son), 45, 46 n.2, 54, 55 n.1, 85, 94, 97, 103, 105, 109, 114, 116–118, 119, 124, 127, 129 n.1, 141, 145–146, 153, 160, 161 n.2, 170
Rothenstein, Moritz (WR's father), 3, 5, 12, 40
Rothenstein, Rachel (WR's elder daughter), 54, 85, 109, 114, 118, 120, 122, 123, 124, 125, 127, 141, 147
ROTHENSTEIN, WILLIAM:
  and America: 71, 86, 87, 88–89, 91;
  as art administrator: 72–73, 109 n.3, 110-111, 113–114, 118–119, 175–176;
  as artist: 8–9, 67, 68–70, 92, 93–94, 128, 132, 134, 136;
  caricatures by: 29 n.1, 103, 104;
  as character in 'Enoch Soames': 137 n.1, 153–154, 170–171;
  death of: 174, 175–176;
  exhibitions of works by: (1911), 69–70, 71, 78 n.7, 84, 86, 89; (1912), 89; (1916), 99–100, 101; (1929), 128 n.2; (1932), 146;
  friendship with MB: 58–62, 77, 93–94, 95, 105;
  honours awarded to: 138 n.1, 167 n.1;
  and India: 9–10, 14, 67–68, 69, 74, 78 n.13, 81–82, 88;
  letters to: Florence Beerbohm, 122, 142 n.4, 169 n.2, 169–170, 173; Max Beerbohm, 25–26, 27–28, 31, 35–36, 40–43, 43–45, 46–47, 48–49, 50–51, 54–61, 62–63, 81–84, 85–87, 88–90, 92–93, 95–97, 102–104, 105–106, 108–109 n.2, 109–110, 112–115, 115 n.1, 116–117, 119–121, 122–123, 124–126, 128–129, 131–133, 134–135, 134 n.2, 136–137, 137–138, 139–148, 149–150, 151–152, 155–156, 156–157 n.1, 160–162, 164–172, 173–174; Mary Berenson, 48 n.2; Gordon Craig, 120 n.2, 144 n.2; John Drinkwater, 106 n.1; Roger Fry, 3, 8–9, 67–70; A. E. Gallatin, 170 n.4; Eric Gill, 10; Lord Northcliffe, 38 n.4; John Lane, 5; Wyndham Lewis, 152 n.2; Grant Richards, 3; Robert Ross, 78 n.7; Alice Rothenstein, 10, 71; Flora Russell, 164 n.2; Albert Rothenstein (later Rutherston), 71–72, 74, 158 n.1; G. B. Shaw, 126 n.2; Reginald Turner, 137 n.1; Margaret Woods, 4, 24 n.1, 28 n.3, 41 n.1, 59 n.2, 145 n2. 147 n.3, 158 n.1;
  as Official War Artist: 102, 104, 105–106, 159 n.1, 164 n.2;
  personality of: 3, 10–11, 19, 22–23, 58–62, 67, 86, 91, 121, 156, 160;
  paintings of: Max Beerbohm, 43 n.1; Edith Williams, 26 n.2; Synagogue paintings, 50–51, 56 n.1; Moritz and Bertha Rothenstein, 41 n.1; Alfred Marshall, 57 n.1; Ernest Debenham, 97; 'Little Boy Lost', 98–99; mural for House of Commons, 120; James Stephens, 160; Sir Charles Welby, 147; portrait drawings of: Sir Henry Acland, 4, 5, 17; Grant Allen, 36 n.1; Stanley Baldwin, 132; Aubrey Beardsley, 39 n.1, 170 n.4; Florence Beerbohm, 120; Max Beerbohm, 39 n.1, 101, 129–130, 132, 146; Laurence Binyon, 39 n.1; Robert Bridges, 146; Mrs. Patrick Campbell, 34; Gordon Craig, 114; John Drinkwater, 109, 110–111; A. S. Eddington, 132; Albert Einstein, 132; T. S. Eliot, 130; Robinson Ellis, 4, 15 n.9; Misses Gaskell, 41; Edmond de Goncourt, 3; Edmund Gosse, 101, 102 n.1; R. B. Cunninghame Graham, 36 n.1; Ian Hamilton, 101; Laurence Housman, 39 n.1; Indian drawings, 69, 71, 84; Augustus John, 101; Richard Le Gallienne, 4–5; Ramsay MacDonald, 132; Ambrose McEvoy, 101; Stephen Phillips, 39 n.1; A. W. Pinero, 35, 37; R.A.F. drawings, 157, 162–163; Viscount St. Cyres, 26 n.1; G. B. Shaw, 101, 130, 132; W. B. Yeats, 39 n.1;
Rothenstein, William Michael (Billy) (WR's younger son), 97, 102, 103 n.1, 104, 112, 114, 118, 127, 129, 141, 142 n.2, 147
Rothenstein, Mrs Michael, 147 n.2
Rothermere, Viscount, 131
Rothschild. Alfred de, 56 n.1
Rowat, Tom, 103
Rowley, Charles, 41 n.1; letters to WR, 41 n.1
Rowton, Lord, 31
Royal Academy, 93, 152 n.2
Royal Air Force, 158 n.1
Royal College of Art, 72–73, 109 n.3, 111–112, 119 n.2, 125, 176
Royal College of Music, 109
Royal Fine Art Commission, 142, 146
Royal Geographical Society, 115
Royal Society of Literature, 95 n.1
Runciman, J. F., 7
Ruskin, John, 16 n.26, 55
Ruskin School (Oxford), 134 n.2
Russell, Alys, 160
Russell, Bertrand, 143 n.6; 161–162 n.5
Russell, Diana, 161 n.1, 163, 167
Russell, Flora, 143 n.6, 160, 163, 173; letters to WR, 161 n.1, n.3, 168 n.2, 174 n.1
Rutherston, Albert (WR's younger brother), 43, 53 n.1, 54, 55–56, 61 n.2, 71, 86, 90, 100, 102, 108, 109 n.4, 110, 120, 126, 134, 140, 146; letters to WR, 51 n.1, 100–101 n.3, 167 n.1
Rutherston, Charles (WR's elder brother), 100–101 n.3, 169–170
Rutherston, Margery, 108, 146

Sadler's Wells Theatre, 146 n.1

191

St. Cyres, Viscount, 25, 93, 172
*Salome* (Wilde), 18
Sassoon, Siegfried, 142 n.2, 159 n.1; letter to WR, 159 n.1; letter to MB, 147 n.1
*The Saturday Review*, 6, 13, 15 n.18, 34, 35, 36, 46, 47, 48, 74; Christmas Supplement, 31 n.2
Savile Club, 140 n.2
'Savonarola Brown' (story) (Beerbohm), 107, 162
*Savonarola Brown* (drama) (Beerbohm), 134
Schiff, Sydney and Violet, 151 n.1, 154, 155–156, 157, 159, 161, 172, 173–174 n.1
Schwabe, Randolph, 134, 138 n.1
Scott, C. P., 131, 132, 133
Scott, Clement, 34
Scott, Lady Sybil: *see* Lubbock, Sybil
*Seven Men* (Beerbohm), 14 n.1, 79 n.28, 104 n.7, 108–109 n.2, 162, 173
de Sévigné, Mme, 150
Shannon, Charles, 9, 28 n.4, 41, 119 n.3, 140
Shaw, Charlotte (Mrs G. B. Shaw), 168 n.2
Shaw, G. B., 6–7, 39, 40, 46, 101, 130–131, 132, 164, 165 n.2, 167, 168, 171, 173; letters: to Blanchamp, 6–7; to WR, 48 n.2
Sheffield School of Art, 72
Sheffield University, 72
Siva, 77
Sickert, W. R., 9, 16 n.23, 37, 42, 52, 94, 108 n.1, 126, 145, 152, 154 n.2
Sidgwick, Arthur, 22
Simmonds, William, 110 n.1
Simon, Louis, 41 n.1
Simon, Louisa (WR's elder sister), 41 n.1; death of, 106–107
*Since Fifty* (W. Rothenstein), 145 n.3, 151, 154–157
Sitwell, Mrs. Frances: *see* Lady Colvin
*Six Portraits . . . Tagore* (W. Rothenstein), 96, 97–98, 132
*The Sketch*, 22
Slade School, 3
Slade Professorship (Oxford), 67
Smithers, Leonard, 29, 170 n.4
Society of Portrait Painters, 43 n.1
'Some Pen-Pricks at Prominent Persons' (Beerbohm), 83 n.1, 83–84 n.3
'The Sorrows of Millicent' (Beerbohm), 35 n.3
*Sowing the Wind* (S. Grundy), 23 n.4
Spitalfields Great Synagogue, 51 n.1
Squire, J. C., 146
Stead, W. T., 3
Steele, Robert, 47
Steer, P. W. 9, 15 n.12, 48 n.1, 70, 132, 140
Stephens, James, 160, 165–166, 171
Stevens, Alfred, 9
Stevenson, R. L., 50, 83
Strachey, Lytton, 87 n.6, 110 n.1, 141, 171 n.1; letters to MB, 142 n.4
Strang, William, 99
Strangeways and Sons, 7
Street, George, 4, 14 n.5, 90

Strong, Eugénie, 118–119; letters to WR, 119 n.3
*Struwwelpeter* (Hoffmann), 128
Suetonius, 25
*Summer's Lease* (J. Rothenstein), 127 n.1
Sutherland, Duchess of, 84
Swan, Annie S., 82–83 n.2
Swann, Flora Annie: *see* Swan, Annie S.
Swinburne, Algernon, 164
Symons, A. J. A., 125 n.3
Symons, Arthur, 29 n.1, 33, 102 n.2

Tagore, Rabindranath, 71, 78 n.13, 87 n.4, 93 n.3, 96, 98, 110, 112–113, 132
Tagore Society (London), 168 n.2
Tarleton, Richard, 37 n.3
Tate Gallery, 160, 161 n.3
*T. E. Lawrence by His Friends*, 149 n.1
Tennyson, Alfred Lord, 138
Terry, Ellen, 47 n.3
Theatre Royal (Huddersfield), 139 n.2
Thomas, Alan, 165 n.2
Titian (Tizian), 81
Tonks, Henry, 48 n.1, 49, 63, 70, 121, 134
Tree, Herbert, 6, 11, 16 n.30, 18 n.1, 21 n.2, 23 n.9, 34, 35 n.1, 38, 41, 47 n.2, 55, 91 n.2, 112 n.4, 150, 156, 164
Tree, Maud, 112, 148, 150
Trewin, J. C., 171 n.1
Trollope, Anthony, 77, 163
Turner, Reginald, 5, 6, 62 n.1, n.3
*Twelve Portraits* (W. Rothenstein), 129 n.2, 132
*Twenty-Four Portraits* (W. Rothenstein), 109, 110, 112–113
*Twenty-Four Portraits: Second Series* (W. Rothenstein), 115 n.1

'An Unhappy Poet' (Beerbohm), 34 n.3

Vandervelde, Emile, 98 n.3
Velázquez, Diego, 43 n.2
*The Venetian Glass Nephew* (Wylie), 124
Verlaine, Paul, 156
'The Vikings' (W. Rothenstein), 48
*The Vikings at Helgeland* (Ibsen), 47 n.3
Villino Chiaro, 75, 77, 89, 122, 124, 125–126, 138, 143 n.9, 151 n.1

Wareing, Alfred, 139 n.2, 144, 145, 146 n.1
Waterloo Bridge, 141, 142
Watson, William, 33
Waugh, Arthur, 120 n.1
Wedmore, Frederick, 48
Welby, Sir Charles, 147 n.3
Welby, Emmeline (Nina): *see* Cust, Emmeline
Welby-Gregory, Lady, 23 n.3
Wells, H. G., 130
Whibley, Charles, 24
'What Public Opinion Says' (Beerbohm et al.), 146 n.4
Whistler, J. M., 3, 9, 14 n.1, 27, 31, 40, 60, 108 n.1, 156, 170
'Whistler's Writing' (Beerbohm), 27 n.3

192

'Why I Ought Not to Have Become a Dramatic Critic' (Beerbohm), 16 n.19
Wilde, Oscar, 16 n.29, 18, 21, 26 n.2, 28, 29 n.1, 32 n.1, 36, 37 n.2, 38, 39 n.1, 44 n.1, 156
Wilde, William, 21
Wilder, Thornton, 161
Wilkinson's School, 112
Wilhelm, Crown Prince of Germany, 83 n.3
*William Morris As I Knew Him* (Shaw), 169 n.2
*William Rothenstein* (Speaight), 41 n.1, 78 n.19, 101 n.3, 102 n.1, 106 n.3
*William Rothenstein* (memorial address by Beerbohm), 175–176
Williams, A. F. B., 25, 26 n.2
Williams, Edith, 25
Winstons Cottage (Far Oakridge), 110 n.2, 162
Wolmark, Alfred, 51 n.1
Wood, Derwent, 111
Woods, Henry, 15 n.9

Woods, Margaret, 4, 15 n.9, 27; letter to WR, 15 n.9
'Words for Pictures' (Beerbohm), 37 n.3
*The Works of Max Beerbohm*, 26 n.1, 31–32 n.3, 32 n.1
Wratislaw, Theodore, 102 n.2
Wright, Peter, 155

Yeats, W. B., 39 n.1, 84, 85, 86, 101, 156
*The Yellow Book*, 18 n.2, 26 n.1 (foot), 28 n.3
*Yet Again* (Beerbohm), 27 n.3, 37 n.3, 169 n.3, n.6
Yorke, Alexander, 33
Young, Dalhousie, 26 n.2
Young, Filson, 79 n.27

Zangwill, Israel, 40, 41 n.2
Zola, Emile, 21
*Zuleika Dobson* (Beerbohm), 40, 73, 76, 86, 87, 89, 90, 91, 142, 166, 173